SEPARATE BUT EQUAL BRANCHES
Congress and the Presidency

Charles O. Jones

*University of Wisconsin–Madison
and the Brookings Institution*

Chatham House Publishers, Inc.
Chatham, New Jersey

SEPARATE BUT EQUAL BRANCHES
Congress and the Presidency

Chatham House Publishers, Inc.
Box One, Chatham, New Jersey 07928

Publisher: Edward Artinian
Editor: Christopher J. Kelaher
Production Supervisor: Katharine Miller
Cover Design: Lawrence Ratzkin
Composition: Bang, Motley, Olufsen
Printing and Binding: R.R. Donnelley & Sons Company

LIBRARY OF CONGRESS CATALOGING-IN-PUBLICATION DATA

Jones, Charles O.
  Separate but equal branches : Congress and the presidency / Charles O. Jones.
    p. cm.
  Includes bibliographical references (p.   ) and index.
  ISBN 1-56643-015-1
  1. Separation of powers—United States. 2. Presidents—United States. 3. United States. Congress. 4. United States—Politics and government—1945–1989. 5. United States—Politics and government—1989–   I. Title.
JK305.J66   1995
320.473—dc20
                                                        94-36362
                                                          CIP

Manufactured in the United States of America

Contents

To Joseph Mire and the memory of Anne M. Mire

Acknowledgments

I wish to acknowledge those colleagues who commented on one or more of the chapters included in this volume. Some were editors of volumes in which the papers were first published, others were panelists when a paper was presented at a conference, and a few were generous enough to have read my initial drafts for no other reason than that I asked them to do so. The list includes Eric L. Davis, Anthony King, John W. Kingdon, Thomas E. Mann, Norman J. Ornstein, Samuel C. Patterson, Nelson W. Polsby, Bert A. Rockman, Steven S. Smith, Randall Strahan, Stephen Wayne, Joseph White, and James Sterling Young.

I also want to identify the various sources that provided financial support for one or more of the papers included in this collection: The Brookings Institution, American Enterprise Institute, University of Wisconsin–Madison (Graduate School and the Hawkins Chair in Political Science), University of Pittsburgh (Falk Chair in Politics), University of Virginia (The Miller Center and the Gooch Chair in Government and Foreign Affairs), Gerald R. Ford Library, and John Simon Guggenheim Memorial Foundation.

Chatham House Publishers provided their usual superb editorial and publication assistance in the production of this book. Ed Artinian even selected the title. I am very grateful for his help and his friendship. Irene Glynn carefully edited the manuscript, offering a number of important suggestions for improving the readability of works written at different times. Roger and Grace Egan prepared the index.

The chapters in this book were originally published in the sources shown below. I am very grateful to each of the journals and publishers for permission to reprint the selections, as revised.

Chapter 1: Reprinted from Christopher J. Deering, ed., *Congressional Politics* (Chicago: Dorsey Press, 1989), chap. 16. (Permission granted by Wadsworth Publishing)

Chapter 2: Reprinted from proceedings of a conference on "Policy Administration Issues in the New Korea Program," Kyung Pook National University, Taegu, Korea, August 1993. (Permission granted by Professor Kyong Sam Moon)

Chapter 3: Reprinted from Anthony King, ed., *The New American Political System,* 2d version (Washington, D.C.: AEI Press, 1990), chap. 1. (Permission granted by American Enterprise Institute)

Chapter 4: Reprinted from *Governance: An International Journal of Policy and Administration* 4 (April 1991): 150–67. (Permission granted by Blackwell Publishers)

Chapter 5: Reprinted from James P. Pfiffner, ed., *The Managerial Presidency* (Pacific Grove, Calif.: Brooks/Cole Publishing, 1991), chap. 14. (Permission granted by Wadsworth Publishing)

Chapter 6: Reprinted from Thomas E. Mann and Norman J. Ornstein, eds., *The New Congress* (Washington, D.C.: American Enterprise Institute, 1981), chap. 7. (Permission granted by American Enterprise Institute)

Chapter 7: Reprinted from Anthony King, ed., *Both Ends of the Avenue: The Presidency, the Executive Branch, and Congress in the 1980s* (Washington, D.C.: American Enterprise Institute, 1983), chap. 4. (Permission granted by American Enterprise Institute)

Chapter 8: Reprinted from the *British Journal of Political Science* 15 (July 1985), 269–85. (Permission granted by Cambridge University Press)

Chapter 9: Reprinted from Charles O. Jones, ed., *The Reagan Legacy: Promise and Performance* (Chatham, N.J.: Chatham House, 1988), chap. 2. (Permission granted by Chatham House)

Chapter 10: Reprinted from Colin Campbell and Bert A. Rockman, eds., *The Bush Presidency: First Appraisals* (Chatham, N.J.: Chatham House, 1991), chap. 2. (Permission granted by Chatham House)

Chapter 11: Reprinted from *The Brookings Review,* Summer 1994, 42–45. (Permission granted by The Brookings Institution)

Introduction

The post–World War II period has witnessed remarkable developments in relations between the president and Congress. From 1901 to 1947, it was rare to have split-party arrangements between the White House and Capitol Hill. Each of three cases—the 62d Congress (1911–13), the 66th Congress (1919–21), and the 72d Congress (1931–33)—occurred in the last two years of an administration, presaging a party change in the White House. In the 62d and 72d Congresses, only the House of Representatives had a majority of the other party. Since 1947, there have been split-party arrangements a majority of the time—two years with a Democratic president and Republican Congress (1947–49), twenty years with a Republican president and a Democratic Congress (1955–61, 1969–77, 1987–93), and six years with a Republican president and Senate and a Democratic House (1981–87). Three Republican presidents—Richard Nixon in 1969, Ronald Reagan in 1981, and George Bush in 1989—entered office with the Democrats in a majority in one or both houses of Congress. And three Republican presidents—Dwight Eisenhower in 1957, Nixon in 1973, and Reagan in 1985—began their second terms under the same conditions.

Clearly, split-party government has become commonplace, and therefore it is incumbent on students of politics that they seek to understand how it works. Unfortunately, many observers prefer simply to decry the emergence of divided government as an aberration to be rectified, concentrating their attention on the palliatives. Meanwhile, American voters continue to split their tickets, sending mixed signals and doubling the checks and balances by separating the politics as well as the powers in Washington.

These developments in the post–World War II period have interested me greatly, and I have from time to time written articles and book chapters that seek to identify and analyze their importance for the national political system. I should state at the outset that I accept split-party government as legitimate in a system of separated and disconnected elections. It is also evident to me that there is substantial support among the American public for this option. Put otherwise, most people would sooner live with the consequences of divided government than sacrifice their right to split their vote among candidates as they see fit. Additionally, it strikes me that even if I were to suggest reforms, I would be well advised first to understand how the present system works and then how change occurs. Reform and change are not necessarily synonymous; in fact, there are countless examples of reforms that fail to produce the desired change, and others that result in unwanted change.

I have organized the chapters in this book into two parts: "The Separated System" and "Presidents Working with Congresses." The first part directs attention to broad questions regarding the nature of the separation between the executive and legislative branches. Various common perspectives are introduced, along with discussions of contemporary developments that should influence analysis of the modern national government. A diffusion of responsibility perspective is advanced that accommodates the split-party arrangements that are now so common. Clear, focused accountability is unlikely in a separated government, whatever its partisan form. It is definitely sacrificed when the two parties compete for shares of power—as happens when a Republican is in the White House and the Democrats have a majority in one or both houses of Congress (the most common split-party result). The chapters in this first part also seek to downgrade the emphasis on the president as representing the whole government. Ours is not a presidential system, as is commonly thought. By design, it has been from the start a separated system, with three coequal branches sharing, and sometimes competing for, power.[1] In accepting this formulation, one is encouraged to account for the relationships among the branches, with presidential-congressional interactions being the most important for short-term, continuous policymaking. The entries in part I describe and discuss that process.

Part II treats specific developments in presidential-congressional relations in recent decades and analyzes the experience and styles of presidents (focusing primarily on Johnson, Nixon, Ford, Carter, Reagan, and Bush with speculations about Clinton). Some chapters make explicit comparisons. The effect of the entire part is to provide evidence for the proposition that presidents are not created equal in terms of either the resources they have available to them or their personal capacities for making the most of those resources. Also apparent in these chapters is the emergence of a different, if not exactly new, U.S. Congress. One of the most interesting and challenging developments in the latter half of the twentieth century is the growth of policy analytical capability on Capitol Hill.

The two houses of Congress have sought to prepare themselves to participate in policy activities previously thought to be primarily the province of the executive branch (e.g., problem definition, agenda setting, program implementation and evaluation). Moreover, they have justified a greater role in policy areas once judged beyond their competence, such as national security, foreign policy, and international economic policy.

Taken as a whole, these chapters offer a portrait of institutional adaptation to political change. The United States has formed a different, if not wholly new, political system. It has demonstrated a capacity to enact laws and perform governing functions in a cross-partisan manner. For their part, American voters have regularly encouraged each political party by awarding it part of the elected government, but they have seldom sanctioned strong partisan management of their affairs. Gridlock is often declared to be the result of split-party arrangements, but, as David R. Mayhew has shown, major laws continue to pass.[2] These laws may not be the best ever, but that is different from saying that the system cannot act at all.

The chapters have been edited for this volume to eliminate redundancy; to alter tense, since some chapters were written during an administration now past; and occasionally to provide updated material.

NOTES

1. Richard E. Neustadt's reformulation of the separation of powers is "separated institutions sharing powers." See his *Presidential Power and the Modern Presidents* (New York: Free Press, 1990), 29.
2. David R. Mayhew, *Divided We Govern: Party Control, Lawmaking, and Investigations, 1946–1990* (New Haven: Yale University Press, 1991), chap. 4.

Part I

The Separated System

I

The Constitutional Balance

Of all the powers with which the people have invested the Government, that of legislation is undoubtedly the chief ... the Legislature is the only power which can create other powers.... The members of the House of Representatives are the special delegates and agents of the people in this high trust. They, and they alone, proceed immediately from the suffrage of the people. They, and they alone, can touch the mainspring of the public prosperity. They are elected to be the guardians of the public rights and liberties.

This well-stated and forceful theory of legislative primacy is to be found in a report on raising the compensation of members of Congress, dated 18 December 1816.[1] Note that the rationale for congressional dominance is twofold: the significance of the lawmaking function itself and the legitimacy of legislators as having electoral connections to the people. The theory of legislative primacy was even more elegantly outlined by Representative John C. Calhoun from South Carolina in the ensuing debate over the congressional pay bill. Calhoun was determined to show that members of Congress deserved better pay. Indeed, he argued that compensation was "intimately connected with the very essence of our liberty." Surely their pay ought to be commensurate with the duties and the station of their position. Here is what Calhoun had to say on 17 January 1817:

This House [of Representatives] is the foundation of the fabric of our liberty.... If ... understood correctly the structure of our Government, the prevailing principle is not so much a balance of power as a *well-connected chain of responsibility*. That responsibility commenced here, and this House is the centre of its operation. The members are elected for two years only; and at the end of that period are responsible to their constituents for the faithful discharge

3

of their public duties. Besides, the very structure of the House is admirably calculated to unite interest and duty. The members of Congress have in their individual capacity no power or prerogative. These attach to the entire body assembled here.... We then as individuals are ... not less amenable to the laws which we enact, than the humblest citizen. Such is the responsibility, such the structure, such the sure foundation of our liberty.

This, then is the essence of our liberty; *Congress is responsible to the people immediately, and the other branches of Government are responsible to it.*[2]

Nowhere do we find a more articulate expression of the institutional linkage within the separation of powers. Nor is one likely to find clearer argument on the important point that separated powers, or institutions, are not necessarily equal and independent. Calhoun's position should be modified to account for the popular election of the Senate and the president. But it remains a forceful theory of democratic accountability.

This chapter examines the role of Congress in the constitutional system. It identifies the constitutional, political, and policy contexts within which the three branches competitively coexist and change. It is organized to consider the original constitutional design, the emergence of countertheories of institutional balance, various periods of congressional and presidential dominance, Congress and the courts, and the ever-present reform mood to alter whatever balance happens to exist at any one time. Final comments direct attention to the policy context within which the issues of balance and competition among institutions have practical significance for the ongoing political system.

The central thesis of this chapter is very close to that of Calhoun: Congress is the centerpiece of democracy. The democratic connections are of three types: senators individually representing states, House members representing districts, and the institution collectively representing the nation. Institutional legitimacy is conferred by these three forms of agency, and therefore Congress is justified in overseeing and checking the other branches. Of course, the greatest challenge is to control the executive, since a growing government naturally enhances the power of that branch. Much of the history of the modern Congress is a study of efforts to preserve a constitutional balance that maintains representational ties to the people through an effective legislature.

In what has become my favorite definition of the term, E. E.

Schattschneider claims that "democracy is a competitive political system in which competing leaders and organizations define the alternatives of public policy in such a way that the public can participate in the decision-making process."[3] Surely for national-level policy matters, Congress is the principal institution for accomplishing Schattschneider's functions. Presidents come and go, bureaucracies and courts stay but hardly promote participation in their decision making. Congress structures itself to be competitive within policy issues and in so doing encourages public participation. As Calhoun argues, then, Congress is base camp; it is the first and most important institutional link in the chain of responsibility.

The Original Design

The Congress under our first constitution, the Articles of Confederation, was the dominant institution, but it was part of a weak national government. The states entered into what was called "a firm league of friendship." Congressional delegates were annually appointed "in such manner as the legislature of each state shall direct." They could be recalled, they could serve no more than three years out of six, and though the number of delegates from states varied from two to seven, each state had only one vote "in determining questions." "A Committee of the States" was appointed by Congress "to sit in the recess of Congress"—thus serving one function of an executive. One member of the Committee of the States served as president, but for no more than "one year in any term of three years." Other committees, too, could be appointed by Congress "for managing the general affairs of the United States."

Since Congress appointed this weak, interim executive, government under the Articles of Confederation was not characterized by separation of powers. At the least, the legislature and executive must be independently elected for the political system to qualify as separationist. And though we think of the separation of powers as a central feature of our government today, the fact is that it was not a part of either of the two major plans considered in Philadelphia. The Virginia Plan served as a basis for the deliberations and provided that the "National Executive" and the "National Judiciary" both were "to be chosen by the National Legislature." One can hardly label any such plan "separationist." The New Jersey Plan (offered as an alternative to the Virginia Plan) likewise provided that "the United States in Congress be authorized to elect a federal Executive." Had either plan been adopted, we presumably would have developed exactly the parliamentary system so admired by many modern-day reformers. That is, the majority party in Congress would have selected its leadership to serve in the executive—as a president or prime minister and a cabinet.

The mode of selection of the executive was debated at length during the convention. Election of the president by Congress "was in fact adopted three times, and was incorporated into the penultimate draft."[4] Many of the delegates feared legislative dominance of the executive branch, however, and supported some form of popular election. Even James Madison, who had been instrumental in preparing the Virginia Plan, came to support the separationist plan of independent elections for the two branches. As William H. Riker points out, one concern among the separationists was that parliamentary cabals might form in Congress that would lead to "intrigue." "By 'intrigue' the Framers probably meant no more than maneuvering to form cabinets in fragmented parliamentary systems."[5]

At the very last moment, the delegates approved a rather strange electoral process—one with no precedent and one that has been heavily criticized since. Viewed in the context of the debate in Philadelphia, however, the plan satisfied many fears that had been expressed. Riker summarizes the advantages of this new, Electoral College system as follows:

> The committee [on postponed matters] tailored a plan to satisfy all those who might oppose legislative election. For distant states, electors were to meet in the states, thereby saving a trip to the capital. For those in favor of popular election, electors were to be chosen in the manner prescribed by state legislatures, which allowed for popular election. For the separationists, the college avoided the legislature entirely, if any candidate got a majority. For the small state interest, there were two provisions: First, each state was to have as many electors as representatives and senators, which gave the small states an edge [due to the equality of representation in the Senate]. Second, if no candidate had a majority of electoral votes, the [House, with each state having just one vote] ... was to choose from the five highest.[6]

Here was a classic compromise. Every worry was addressed and legislative institutions were involved without actually controlling the outcome (except in unusual circumstances). However odd it may appear today, the provision for electing the president was at the time the result of old-fashioned bargaining.

One might well argue that the resolution of this debate was in the direction of a weakened legislature. I urge a somewhat different interpretation. Above all, the delegates were determined to prevent tyranny. They were, however, anxious to establish a viable government. Creating a government is no simple task for those who believe in the corruptibility of power and its bad effects. Republicanism, in the form of a representative legislature, is a natural remedy. But legislatures too can tyrannize, and so they must be checked. Here is how the argument was stated in *The Federalist*:

- □ In republican government, the legislative authority necessarily predominates. (*No. 51*)
- □ [The legislature's] constitutional powers being at once more extensive, and less susceptible of precise limits, it can, with the greater facility, mask, under complicated and indirect measures, the encroachments which it makes on the coordinate departments. (*No. 48*)
- □ We have seen that the tendency of republican governments is to an aggrandizement of the legislative at the expense of the other departments. (*No. 49*)[7]

Legislative primacy was accepted as inevitable, yet absolute power in a legislature could lead to tyranny. Indeed, the encroachment might well be masked by the representative nature of the institution. Possible excesses were therefore to be guarded against. This view is not contrary to that of Calhoun's stated above. Rather, it establishes the rationale for a chain of responsibility and for "still further precautions" (*No. 51*) to prevent the chain from becoming a whip.

It is also interesting to contemplate whether having approved legislative selection of the executive would have in fact led to even greater congressional power. Based on the parliamentary experience in Great Britain, it seems an unlikely outcome. Indeed, Congress today compares favorably with parliaments around the world in terms of its independent authority. The means devised for selecting presidents also preserved the separateness of the legislative branch and in so doing permitted Congress to make its own adaptations to changing circumstances—including those favoring an imperial presidency. It would have been difficult for Congress as a parliament to withstand growth of executive power in the twentieth century. Separation permitted the members to justify resistance as reflecting their individual and collective mandates from the people.

The Unresolved Debate

A debate so fundamental as that involving the relative power of the executive and the legislature is unlikely ever to be resolved. Indeed, the growth of national government functions may be expected to intensify the debate. One can identify at least four perspectives of the balance of power: legislative primacy, presidential primacy, cooperative mixed government, and adversarial mixed government.

The perspective of *legislative primacy* has already been described as dominant at the Constitutional Convention; Calhoun's statement exemplifies the rationale of those who cling to this outlook. Does it exist today among members of Congress? Unquestionably it does. A day hardly passes on Capitol Hill without a member of Congress expressing the theory of legislative primacy. Members do not doubt the important role played by the president, but they are stubbornly protective of their prerogatives. Indeed, not even his own party members will support the president if it is judged that he has exceeded his authority and thwarted the will of Congress. Thus, for example, the Budget and Impoundment Control Act of 1974, which was, in large part, a response to what was judged to be President Nixon's excesses in the exercise of budget authority, passed both houses by huge margins. In another example, Congress overwhelmingly overrode President Reagan's veto of a clean water bill in early 1987; a large majority of his own party voted against him in both chambers. Reagan had used the "pocket veto" to defeat the bill in 1986 after the bill had passed with no dissenting votes in either house. Speaker Jim Wright, of Texas, suggested that the issue was less a dispute between Republicans and Democrats than between Congress and the White House.[8]

Whereas the legislative primacy perspective has had advocates throughout our history, the *presidential primacy* perspective is of more recent vintage. Woodrow Wilson's book *Congressional Government* contains a classic statement regarding the rationale for presidential power. Having spotted what he judged to be exactly the encroachments that worried the Founding Fathers, Wilson concluded that it was time for a change:

> [The presidency] has fallen from its first estate of dignity because its power has waned; and its power has waned because the power of Congress has become predominant....
>
> Congress is (to adopt Mr. Bagehot's description of Parliament) "nothing less than a big meeting of more or less idle people." In proportion as you give it power it will inquire into everything,

settle everything, meddle in everything.... Accordingly it has entered more and more into the details of administration, until it has virtually taken into its own hands all the substantial powers of government.[9]

Wilson judged that presidential dignity and power had to be reestablished. Among other things, he worried about accountability with a predominant Congress. *"Somebody must be trusted,* in order that when things go wrong it may be quite plain who should be punished."[10] That somebody, in his judgment, should be the president, since he was a single individual, elected by the nation.

It is not certain that Wilson would be pleased with developments subsequent to his presidency. On the one hand, presidential responsibilities have grown enormously; on the other hand, it is doubtful that trust has increased that much. Wars and sizable increases in the role of the federal government in the domestic sphere have resulted in a greater reliance on the executive branch. Media attention, too, has naturally tended to focus on the White House. Thomas Cronin speaks of the "prime-time presidency" and the "television-magnified presidency." Unquestionably, this attention enhances the role of the chief executive, and yet the authority of the office is still rather limited. The president may thus be held accountable for actions that he may not fully control. And as Cronin observes, "Television has helped to make [presidents] more important but less popular."[11]

The greatest increment in presidential power undoubtedly occurred during Franklin D. Roosevelt's administration, when the combination of domestic policy breakthroughs and wartime responsibilities contributed to executive-centered government. Post–World War II presidents have had to meet grand expectations. According to Richard Neustadt, "A president may retain liberty, in Woodrow Wilson's phrase, 'to be as big a man as he can.' But nowadays he cannot be as small as he might be." With the growth of government, Neustadt observes, "Everybody now expects the man inside the White House to do something about everything."[12]

Yet this designated primacy of the executive branch is accompanied by the same suspicions expressed at the Constitutional Convention. Thus the realization that all presidents were powerful—even those less likely to be entrepreneurial—led scholars and others to examine critically the constitutional balance of power. In 1965, James MacGregor Burns published *Presidential Government,* in counterpoint to Woodrow Wilson's *Congressional Government,* written decades earlier.[13] Then, in 1973, Arthur M. Schlesinger, Jr., published *The Imperial Presidency*. Schlesinger found the presidency to be "resurgent" in World War II, "ascendant" in the Korean war, and "rampant" in the Vietnam war. He found Richard Nixon's presidency to be a particular threat to the system—a "revolutionary presidency."[14] The Watergate scandal had a profound effect on those advocating presidential primacy. Unquestionably the status of the office was badly damaged by that incident and by the first resignation of a president in history. Still, as Neustadt correctly observes, it is difficult nowadays to manage the government with a "small" chief executive.

Equality of the branches is central to the third and fourth perspectives. They differ in the style or manner of relationship that is advocated. I label these *mixed government* perspectives. The notion of balanced strength rather than primacy for one institution clearly has advocates—at least among members of Congress if not among presidents. In fact, for many members the reform efforts during the 1970s were directed toward coequality, not congressional primacy. Former Texas Democratic Representative Barbara Jordan argued that the "revitalization of Congress need not result in a weak presidency." And as James Sundquist points out, a Democratic representative from Indiana, Lee Hamilton, even doubted that Congress could or should achieve coequality. Sundquist quotes Hamilton as stating:

> The effort of the Congress to reassert itself should not be misunderstood to mean that the Congress can truly become an equal branch of government. It is simply too difficult for 535 strongminded aggressive persons "to get it all together" on all the issues on the nation's agenda.... No one advocates a weakened presidency ... a shackled presidency would not be wise. Our system requires a strong presidency, but a strong president *under* the Constitution.[15]

In considering mixed or balanced government, a useful distinction can be made between a *cooperative* and an *adversarial* style. Cooperative mixed government depends on harmony between the branches, which normally can be achieved only if the same party is in control of both. We never expect full cooperation, of course, but there are instances when the president and Congress have worked effectively together. Furthermore, there are definite advocates of cooperative mixed government. These tend to be the so-called *party responsibility* advocates who promote changes that will encourage unified government through the political parties. The classic statement in favor of this position was that prepared by the Committee on Political Parties of the American Political Science Association. Quoting from their report:

> The president could gain much when party leaders in and out of Congress are working together with him closely in matters concerning the party program. As party head, the president could then expect more widespread and more consistent support from the congressional leaders of his party. These, in turn, would present a more united front. As a result, on issues where the party as a party could be expected to have a program, the program of the party, of the party leaders in each house of Congress, and of the president would be the same program, not four different programs.[16]

For this outcome to be realized, political parties would have to be greatly strengthened—they would somehow have to overcome all the roadblocks built into the system by the Founders. Otherwise, realizing cooperative mixed government will continue to be circumstantial—that is, merely a consequence of a particular set of electoral conditions or of a special relationship between a president and congressional leaders (note its infrequency in table 1.1).

TABLE 1.1

VARIATIONS IN THE CONSTITUTIONAL BALANCE OF POWER
(TWENTIETH CENTURY)

Variations	*Periods when dominant*
1. Congressional primacy	1903–11 (the Cannon era); 1921–33 (weak president era)
2. Presidential primacy	1933–45 (Roosevelt); 1964–66 (Johnson)
3. Mixed government–cooperative	1913–17 (Wilson); 1945–47 (Truman); 1953–55 (Eisenhower); 1981–83 (Reagan)
4. Mixed government–adversarial	1919–21 (Wilson); 1947–53 (Truman); 1955–61 (Eisenhower); 1961–63 (Kennedy); 1967–69 (Johnson); 1969–77 (Nixon-Ford); 1977–81 (Carter); 1983–89 (Reagan)

SOURCE: Compiled by the author.

Adversarial mixed government has occurred more frequently and, indeed, one might even conclude that it has come to be the dominant mode of presidential-congressional relations in the post–World War II era. In this view, the two branches are coequal and highly competitive. Most often the adversarial posture is a consequence of divided government, where one party controls the White House and the other party has a majority in one or both houses of Congress. Note, in table 1.2, how exceptional that condition was during the first forty-six years of this century. In only one Congress—the second Congress following Woodrow Wilson's reelection—were both houses under the control of the other party. Divided control has occurred a majority of the time since the war and, remarkably, 77 percent of the time in the past twenty-six years.

TABLE 1.2
DIVIDED GOVERNMENT IN THE TWENTIETH CENTURY

	Form		
Time period	President and Congress (no. of years)	President and House (no. of years)	As a percentage of the total period
1901–47	2	4	13%
1947–95	22	6	58
(1969–95)	(14)	(6)	(77)

SOURCE: Compiled by the author.

The argument for adversarial mixed government is simply that good policy is the result of competition between the institutions. Although I know of few advocates of such a position, the American voters are responsible for frequently producing such outcomes in recent decades. Many Americans appear to support the idea of this further check on government, even doing James Madison one better by adding partisan divisions to the Madison design for separation. In 1980 the voters went to the extent of providing split partisan control of the House and Senate—an outcome then repeated in 1982 and 1984.

It should be noted that split-party control does not necessarily result in an adversarial relationship. During his first Congress (1981–82), President Reagan can be said to have had cooperative mixed government despite the fact that the Democrats were a majority in the House. Republican congressional leaders cooperated with him in enacting his program, and sufficient Democrats as well were willing to vote with the president. Furthermore, same-party control of Congress and the White House does not ensure cooperation. President Carter experienced tense relationships with the Democratic Party leaders in Congress. The special circumstances of his election (taking office in the post-Watergate mood) encouraged him to separate himself from his own party.

The four perspectives on the constitutional balance of power between the president and Congress have been discussed (1) as a set of *preferences* by students and other observers of our national political system, and (2) as a set of *characteristics* of particular eras in the twentieth century. Table 1.1 gives examples of the periods when each perspective has been dominant, although no perspective can be said to be "pure." Also, there may be variations in which perspective or set of characteristics is dominant even within one administration. Nevertheless, table 1.1 illustrates the variations in institutional balance in this century.

Congress and the Courts

The largest portion of this discussion has focused on the constitutional balance between the president and Congress because policy relationships between the two branches are continuous, whereas the issue of balance between Congress and the federal courts is less immediate and more episodic. William Keefe and Morris Ogul observed that "legislative-judicial relations in the United States are ordinarily marked by harmony and mutual indifference."[17] The courts unquestionably decide important policy matters, and the power of the Supreme Court to judge the constitutionality of congressional acts was settled early in our history, in *Marbury* v. *Madison* (1803). But the process of policymaking by the Court is less direct than in the case of either the president or the Congress. Typically, the Court's influence comes either as a consequence of objections to policy solutions by the other branches or because of the failure of those branches to act on an important issue. To be sure, conflicts do arise between the Congress and the Courts, but they do not actively compete in the ongoing national policy process because their agendas differ in kind and by source.

As in relationships with the president, the potential for imbalance is two-directional—the Court over Congress and vice versa.

Two types of interaction characterize both: that which is more institutional or procedural in nature and that which is more substantive in nature. In regard to the first type, the Court occasionally makes judgments about congressional elections and the authority of Congress in relationship to the executive. Important recent examples include

- □ *Wesberry* v. *Sanders* (1964)—a decision stating that Art. I, sec. 2 of the Constitution is to be read as requiring that congressional districts must be as equal in population as possible.
- □ *Immigration and Naturalization Service* v. *Chadha* (1983)—a decision that invalidated the so-called *legislative veto*, an increasingly common practice by which Congress (or one of its organizational entities) reserved the right to disapprove of executive actions.

Of course, any such institutional or procedural actions by the Court have important substantive policy implications. Such decisions are directed to the broader constitutional issue of congressional structure and authority and less to the range of substantive policy matters that might be affected.

In regard to the second type of interaction—Court rejection of a substantive policy solution by Congress—the actual issue involved may be relatively minor. Also, the Court is often reluctant to use constitutional grounds in substituting its judgment for that of Congress (in fact, the actual number of congressional acts held unconstitutional is quite small—approximately 130). The range of issues that the Court may choose to act on is quite considerable, given the authority of Congress itself to act on so many policy issues. The following are examples illustrating different substantive policy issues:

- □ *United States* v. *Romano* (1965)—invalidated a provision of the Internal Revenue Service that presence at an unregistered still (unless otherwise explained to the jury) was sufficient for conviction.
- □ *Frontiero* v. *Richardson* (1973)—held that statutory differentiation between male and female spouses of members of the armed forces for certain dependents' benefits violated equal protection, as guaranteed by the Fifth Amendment.
- □ *Jimenez* v. *Weinberger* (1974)—held that statutory differentiation among illegitimate dependents for disability insurance

benefits under the Social Security Act violated equal protection, as guaranteed by the Fifth Amendment.

☐ *National League of Cities* v. *Usery* (1976)—held that sections of the Fair Labor Standards Act extending wage and hour coverage to state and local government employees are invalid as beyond congressional authority under the commerce clause of the Constitution.

As these illustrations suggest, the Court's decisions do not necessarily pose a major threat to congressional power. Still, there have been periods, as with the development of Roosevelt's New Deal program, when Court actions were interpreted as interfering with the national policy process and both the president and Congress threatened actions to limit the Court's role.

Congress is by no means helpless in the face of Court decisions. And, indeed, it has constitutional authority regarding the structure and makeup of the federal courts. Article III is brief. In fact, as one observer noted, "the convention . . . only crayoned in the outlines. It is left to Congress to fill up and colour the canvas."[18] Congress can create inferior courts, determine the number of judges, and regulate the appellate jurisdiction of the Supreme Court. Appointments to the federal courts must be made "by and with the advice and consent of the Senate." The Judiciary Act of 1789, one of the first acts by the new Congress, set forth the basic structure of the federal court system. Many acts have been passed subsequently. And, of course, congressional influence in appointments has been important in shaping the courts. Few Supreme Court nominees have been rejected (only four in this century), but the hearings on appointments may be influential in projecting congressional expectations.

Congressional reaction to Court decisions regarding its authority or its policy decisions may take several forms. Congress may seek to accomplish its goal by enacting new legislation that avoids the constitutional issue raised by the Court. Or an effort may be launched to change the constitution through amendment. Several unsuccessful attempts to do so have been made in recent years in reaction to Court decisions on topics including the rights of criminal suspects, abortion, school prayer, redistricting in the states, and school busing, suggesting that the Court definitely has power on policy issues. One successful effort was in response to a Court decision in *Oregon* v. *Mitchell* (1970). The Court held that a provision of the Voting Rights Act of 1970 setting the minimum voting age at eighteen could not be applied to state and local elections. Congress responded by passing a constitutional amendment, which was then quickly ratified by the requisite number of states (now the Twenty-Sixth Amendment).

There are always a few issues that lead to conflict between the Supreme Court and members of Congress. Walter Murphy observes a pattern associated with these differences. First is the decision on a controversial issue of public policy. Next is "severe criticism of the Court coupled with threats of remedial and/or retaliatory legislative action." And the third step "has usually been a judicial retreat."[19] Even at its most serious, however (as with conflicts between Congress and the Warren Court), the competition pales in comparison to that between Congress and the executive. Thus, in regard to the Warren Court, Murphy concludes that "the crisis . . . passed without serious injury to the prestige or power of either institution."[20] The same cannot be said about the Watergate crisis and other conflicts during the Nixon administration.

Members of Congress will complain bitterly about a particular Court decision, even to the point of expressing concern about constitutional imbalance. Further, they will frequently criticize the Court "because it doesn't cost anything."[21] But they worry daily about the growth of presidential power and act frequently to curb it. The difference in congressional attitudes is traceable to the nature of the power struggle within each branch. As David O'Brien observed, "On major issues of public policy, Congress is likely to prevail or, at least, temper the impact of the Court's rulings."[22] The same cannot always be said in the matter of competition with the president.

Reform and the Balance of Power

As Roger Davidson, David Kovenock, and Michael O'Leary taught us more than twenty years ago, the "pathways to reform" are heavily influenced by the preferences of the reformers.[23] Thus, for example, those preferring a strong executive will propose changes that increase the president's authority and protect his prerogatives from congressional encroachment. Those favoring congressional preeminence will suggest greater resources for the legislative branch and restrictions on the exercise of presidential power. It is useful for purposes of this essay to review congressional reforms because of what they reveal about the balance of power between the branches. Particularly relevant are the many reforms enacted during the 1970s. At no other time in its history did Congress make such important changes. And as compared to other reform eras, many of these changes were designed to reestablish congressional preeminence in national policy-making.

There have been four major reform eras in this century. The first occurred in 1910–11 in response to the significant growth in the power of the Speaker of the House and specifically to the exercise of that power by Joseph Cannon. The issue at the time was less the balance of power between Congress and the other branches, however, and more the concentration of power in the hands of one man. The reforms enacted at that time decentralized authority to the committees and to political party units.

The second set of reforms (1945–46) was stimulated by a perceived imbalance in the roles played by the president and Congress. Presidential power increased markedly during World War II. In part, this development was to be expected given the need for centralized leadership. It was also the case, however, that Congress was poorly organized.[24] Burdened with too many committees and cumbersome procedures, it was ill equipped to participate actively and constructively in the war effort. A first priority following the war was to modernize the Congress. The Legislative Reorganization Act of 1946 sought to accomplish that goal: committees were abolished, staffing increased, new budget procedures introduced, and oversight capability enhanced.

The third important reform occurred in 1961 with the enlargement of the House Rules Committee. This reform can also be classified as having been stimulated by a perceived imbalance between the two branches. In this case the president, John F. Kennedy, expressed concern that his program might be stalled by the powerful Rules Committee. The twelve-member committee was then controlled by an "unholy alliance" among Chairman Howard W. Smith, a Virginian, the next ranking Democrat, William Colmer from Mississippi, and the four Republicans. The president won and the committee was increased by two Democrats (to ten) and one Republican (to five)—a change that gave liberals a slim 8–7 working majority.[25] Here was an opening salvo in the battle against arbitrary committee chairs, a battle fought out in the 1970s for the benefit, not of presidents, but of junior members.

The fourth and most dramatic period of reform started in hearings before the Joint Committee on the Organization of Congress in 1965 and ended in 1979. Before it was over, reform proposals had emanated from three joint committees, two major party groups in the House (plus several minor ones), three House committees or commissions, and two Senate committees or commissions.

TABLE 1.3
THE REFORMS OF THE 1970S: SEEKING
TO RESTORE THE BALANCE

Response to threats	Specific reforms enacted
1. Curbing presidential power	War Powers Act (1973); Budget and Impoundment Control Act (1974)
2. Curbing the power of committee chairs	More power for members (1970, 1976, 1977); seniority system modified (1970, 1971, 1973, 1975, 1977); subcommittee bill of rights (1973); greater role for Speaker and Democratic Steering and Policy Committee (1973, 1974)
3. Strengthening political parties	Reestablish Democratic Steering and Policy Committee (1973); increase in Speaker's powers (1973, 1974, 1975, 1977); Steering and Policy Committee nominates committees (1975); minority party rights (1970, 1975)
4. Increasing congressional capabilities	Staff increases (1973, 1975, 1977); enhancement of CRS and GAO (1970); creation of OTA (1972) and CBO (1974); computer services (1971); Budget and Impoundment Control Act (1974)
5. Reorganizing and improving procedures	Committee reorganizations (1974, 1975, 1977); committee appointments (throughout 1970s); electronic voting in House (1972); procedural modifications (throughout 1970s)
6. Reducing criticism from outside	Campaign regulation (1972, 1974); adoption of ethics codes (1977); opening committee deliberations (1973, 1975, 1977); televising the House (1978)

SOURCES: Compiled from information in Charles O. Jones, *The United States Congress: People, Place, and Policy* (Homewood, Ill.: Dorsey Press, 1982), 429; and Leroy N. Rieselbach, *Congressional Reform* (Washington, D.C.: CQ Press, 1986), 155–58.

The reforms enacted were responses to perceived threats to institutional authority and prestige from the following sources: (1) an aggressive president (Richard Nixon); (2) the arbitrary exercise of power by committee chairs; (3) weakened political parties and leadership; (4) limited policy analytical capabilities (particularly in competition with the executive); (5) cumbersome procedures; and (6) public and press criticism of the institution.

Little was left untouched by the reform advocates. Actions were taken to curb presidential power, disperse committee leadership, enhance party leadership, provide greater policy analytical support, and improve congressional standing with the public. Unquestionably these changes were motivated by the perspectives of legislative primacy and mixed or balanced government. Fearing loss of prerogatives due as much to congressional inadequacies as to presidential aggrandizement, members supported actions to reconnect the "chain of responsibility" and to equip themselves to meet the associated challenges.

Table 1.3 (page 18) categorizes reforms of the 1970s as responses to the threats cited above. One has to be impressed with the scope of the reforms, as well as their audaciousness (as with the War Powers Act and the Budget and Impoundment Control Act). It is still too early to judge the full effects of these changes, but we can confidently assert that they have not led to "congressional government." A balance, however, has been restored: one that encourages Congress to restrain the executive, not substitute for it.

Speaking to a conference in 1975 on the role of Congress, Democratic Senator Edmund S. Muskie from Maine warned against efforts to make Congress the whole government. In so doing, he also defined congressional responsibilities.

> Let me say this about Congress, incidentally. A Congress is not a President. A Congress, thank God, cannot be a President. A Congress should be nothing more, nothing less, than what it is: a reflection of the will of our people and the problems that disturb them and the actions they want taken. The Congress ought to improve its ability to serve that function, and the Congress ought not to try to become a President.[26]

Conclusion: The Constitutional Balance in Perspective

In an article on "The Legislator as Educator," former Arkansas Senator J. William Fulbright offered this wise counsel:

> Our proper objective is neither a dominant presidency nor an aggressive Congress but, within the strict limits of what the Constitution mandates, a shifting of the emphasis according to the needs of the time and the requirements of public policy.[27]

Often the debate regarding the balance of power among the branches is abstract and based on generalizations about the motives and exercise of power. Reforms are typically structural, organizational, or procedural in nature and assume changes in policy outcomes that are not at all guaranteed by the new structure.

Policy issues, meanwhile, continue to be fed into a system of separated institutions with variable constitutional prerogatives and policymaking capacities. In other words, competitive coexistence among the branches occurs within the continuing policy agenda of a working government. As Sundquist documents, "The balance between president and Congress [has] gone through nearly two centuries of ups and downs." He observes that "in the third century the seesaw would continue."[28] Personal quest for power surely plays a role in this competition, but it cannot explain the full extent of the shifts (nor should it under the terms of the original constitutional design); more important are the policy demands and how they change over time. The policy context also helps to explain the unanticipated consequences of reforms, for whatever the structural alteration may be, one can expect adjustments among those who want government to act on policy problems. Seldom are these adjustments predictable in advance (nor do most reformers even take them fully into account).

What, then, are we to say in conclusion about Congress and the constitutional balance of power? Most notably, that the issue is primarily rhetorical—associated with varying perspectives of the relative status, prestige, and power of the three branches. Saying that the issue is rhetorical is not to downplay its importance. It is, rather, to point out that the ongoing debate brackets the roles of and relationships among the branches, providing a rough measure of where we are and announcing the worries of those who spot excesses in the exercise of power. Much of the debate over the setting of boundaries will take place in Congress. That is as it should be, given the representational responsibilities of that body. It is in this sense that Calhoun's chain of responsibility theory has contemporary application. Congress must continue to be the primary forum for the debate on the balance of power. Should it abdicate that function, then the constitutional balance truly would have shifted and democracy would be threatened. "A Congress," as Senator Muskie said, "should not be a President." But in reflecting "the will of our people" it must monitor trends in the exercise of political power.

NOTES

1. Quoted in Charles S. Hyneman and George W. Carey, eds., *A Second Federalist* (New York: Appleton-Century-Crofts, 1967), 148–49.
2. Quoted in ibid., 150–51; emphasis added.
3. E. E. Schattschneider, *The Semisovereign People* (New York: Holt, Rinehart and Winston, 1960), 141.
4. William H. Riker, "The Heresthetics of Constitution-Making: The Presidency in 1787, with Comments on Determinism and Rational Choice," *American Political Science Review* 78 (March 1984): 3.
5. Ibid., 7.
6. Ibid., 13.
7. James Madison, *The Federalist,* Nos. 51, 48, and 49 (New York: Mentor, 1961), 322, 310, 315–16.
8. Joseph A. Davis, "House Rejects Reagan's Offer; Passes Clean Water Bill Again," *Congressional Quarterly Weekly Report,* 10 January 1987, 91.
9. Woodrow Wilson, *Congressional Government* (Boston: Houghton Mifflin, 1885), 43–45.
10. Ibid., 283.
11. Thomas E. Cronin, *The State of the Presidency,* 2d ed. (Boston: Little, Brown, 1980), 97.
12. Richard E. Neustadt, *Presidential Power* (New York: Wiley, 1960), 5–6.
13. James MacGregor Burns, *Presidential Government* (Boston: Houghton Mifflin, 1965).
14. Arthur Schlesinger, Jr., *The Imperial Presidency* (Boston: Houghton Mifflin, 1973), chaps. 5–8.
15. Both quoted in James L. Sundquist, *The Decline and Resurgence of Congress* (Washington, D.C.: Brookings Institution, 1981), 460; emphasis added.
16. E. E. Schattschneider et al., "Toward a More Responsible Two-Party System," *American Political Science Review* 44 (September 1950), supplement, 89.
17. William J. Keefe and Morris S. Ogul, *The American Legislative Process: Congress and the States,* 6th ed. (Englewood Cliffs, N.J.: Prentice Hall, 1985), 377.
18. As quoted in Congressional Quarterly's *Guide to the U.S. Supreme Court* (Washington, D.C.: CQ, Inc., 1979), 6.

19. Walter F. Murphy, *Congress and the Court* (Chicago: University of Chicago Press, 1962), 247.
20. Ibid., 268.
21. David M. O'Brien, *Storm Center: The Supreme Court in American Politics* (New York: Norton, 1986), 309.
22. Ibid., 316.
23. Roger H. Davidson, David M. Kovenock, and Michael K. O'Leary, *Congress in Crisis: Politics and Congressional Reform* (Belmont, Calif.: Wadsworth, 1966), chap. 2.
24. For details, see Roland Young, *Congressional Politics in the Second World War* (New York: Columbia University Press, 1956).
25. For details, see Douglas Price, "Race, Religion, and the Rules Committee," in *The Uses of Power: 7 Cases in American Politics,* ed. Alan Westin (New York: Harcourt Brace Jovanovich, 1962).
26. Edmund S. Muskie, "Dinner Speech," in *The Role of Congress II* (New York: Time, Inc., 1975). (Editorial project by the editors of Time, Inc.; not paginated.)
27. As quoted in Sundquist, *Decline and Resurgence of Congress,* 461.
28. Ibid.

2

Presidential Government and the Separation of Powers

The standard classification of democratic political systems directs attention to the relationship between the executive and the legislature. "The two principal alternative models are parliamentary and presidential government."[1] It is often further asserted that "the American political system is . . . the model and prototype of presidential government."[2] That there are differences within each prototype—parliamentary and presidential—is acknowledged, and numerous scholars have explored these differences.[3] Of special interest to students of American national politics, particularly those who concentrate on the Congress, is the seeming devotion to the label "presidential government" as ideally descriptive of what happens in Washington, D.C. Those using the term as an alternative model for comparing systems typically stress its association with the separation-of-powers concept, a practice I examine below. Those using the model of presidential government as a basis for reform typically endeavor to integrate or concentrate power in the White House, a disposition I discuss throughout.

I have organized the discussion as follows: (1) the curiosity of acknowledging the separation-of-powers principle, yet continuing to refer to the American system as "presidential government"; (2) the problems said to arise from presidential government, problems that derive primarily from a set of preferences as to how it should work; (3) the specification of the separation-of-powers system as a model of national decision making; and (4) the role of the presidency in the separated system, noting in particular the variations in partisan and institutional interaction on policy issues.

Presidential and Parliamentary Governments

In his comparison of the characteristics of parliamentary and presidential governments, Douglas V. Verney observes that "presidential government is often associated with the theory of the separation of powers."[4] G. Bingham Powell, too, identifies the separation of powers as "a second [basic] aspect of the presidential system."[5] And, indeed, there are few more distinctive features of the American national government than that of the separation of powers. Unquestionably that separation distinguishes the American system from the standard parliamentary system. But the separated elections that are basic to the independence (or interdependence) of the branches do not produce an all-powerful executive. It is as logical by reason of disconnected elections to label the American system "congressional government," as, in fact, some have done in the past.[6]

In his analysis of the traits of presidential government, Verney asks: "Where ... does supreme power lie in the event of a serious controversy?" The Congress cannot force the resignation of the president (except by impeachment), and the president cannot dissolve Congress. "The short answer is that it is intended in presidential government that the different branches shall check and balance one another and that none shall predominate."[7] He then postulates:

> Yet in a very real sense it is the assembly [Congress] which is ultimately supreme. The president may have considerable authority allocated to him in the constitution but he may be powerless unless the assembly grants him the necessary appropriations. If he acts unconstitutionally the assembly may impeach him. In the event of a serious conflict even the judiciary must bow to the will of the assembly because this body has the right to amend the constitution.[8]

And still the United States is given as an example of "presidential government."

In their review of the role of institutions in democracies, R. Kent Weaver and Bert Rockman essentially accept that a "presidential system" is a "separation-of-powers" or a "checks-and-balances" system. It is their purpose to compare the working of American political institutions with those of several parliamentary systems. Therefore they are naturally led to an analysis of the separated branches in their attempt to explain the comparative policymaking capabilities of presidential and parliamentary governments. They all but drop the term "presidential" in favor of "separation of powers" in characterizing American government in their concluding chapter. And, in fact, they employ the term "presidentialist" primarily to characterize the contentions made by those supporting the American system of an executive elected independently of the legislature.[9]

Most reformers seek to strengthen the executive branch. Reforms designed to perfect the workings of a separated system of balanced institutions are seldom proposed, since many, if not most, reformers do not accept the principle on which the American government is based—often judging it to be ill suited to contemporary policymaking.[10] Yet improving the effectiveness of American national government requires an understanding of the diverse and complex relationships between two independently selected policymaking institutions: the presidency and Congress. It even demands attention to divided government (i.e., to the many legitimate combinations of split-party control between the presidency, House of Representatives, and Senate) so as to make it more effective.[11]

Treating the Problems of Presidential Government

The problems of presidential government are freely discussed by scholars of comparative politics and those anxious to change the American system. Juan J. Linz speaks of "The Perils of Presidentialism," an essay in which he concludes that parliamentarism "is more conducive to stable democracy."[12] Linz is particularly troubled by the rigidity of designated terms of office and the "winner-take-all" feature of presidentialism: "Winners and losers are sharply defined for the entire period of the presidential mandate."[13] It should be noted that Linz is concerned mostly about presidentialism in Latin America. He makes an exception for the United States: "the world's most stable democracy . . . has a presidential constitution."[14]

Arend Lijphart provides a most useful summary of the advantages and disadvantages of presidentialism—drawing from several treatments of the subject. The advantages are executive stability created by the fixed term in office, greater democracy as a result of popular election rather than selection by the majority party (or a coalition), and more limited government as associated with the separation of powers (once again, identified as a major feature of presidentialism). The disadvantages are of particular interest here, however, since they are the basis for rationalizing change or rejection in favor of parliamentarism. The first of these disadvantages is familiar to Americans as an issue in the 1992 presidential election: "The problem of executive-legislative conflict, which may turn into 'deadlock' and 'paralysis,' is the inevitable result of the co-existence of the two independent organs that presidential government creates and that may be in disagreement."[15] As Lijphart notes, this fault has been recognized as a potential hazard by many of those writing about presidential government, including the earliest proponents of the separation-of-powers doctrine.

The other disadvantages noted by Lijphart are those of special concern to Linz: "temporal rigidity" caused by the fixed term of office (which must be weighed against the advantage of stability—see above) and the winner-take-all feature. I deal first with these second and third disadvantages, then turn to the matter of deadlock between the branches. Linz believes that the president's fixed term in office "breaks the political process into discontinuous, rigidly demarcated periods, leaving no room for the continuous readjustments that events may demand."[16] Perhaps he is correct in reference to a presidentialist system (i.e., a government in which there is a fusion of authority in the office of an elected president). In a separated system, however, there are ample opportunities for adjustment to events. An independently elected representative legislature is bound to create structures designed to monitor events. Congressional committees serve exactly that function. It is also true in the United States that the midterm and special election results are read carefully for their potential policy implications. Congressional terms, too, are fixed, but they occur frequently enough to reflect change.[17] There is, of course, no guarantee that a capacity to adjust to events will, perforce, produce correct policies, regardless of the governmental structure. Careful monitoring of intractable problems does not, in itself, lead to solutions.

The disadvantages cited for the "winner-take-all" or "zero-sum" result of presidentialism simply are not characteristic of American separationism. In fact, the designers of the Constitution were notably concerned about such an outcome and therefore provided an extraordinarily elaborate combination of competing legitimacies for the president, senators, and representatives. It is exactly the failure of the American system to provide a zero-sum result that so frustrates many reformers. Consider the 1992 election, when unified party government returned to Washington. President Clinton won a sizable majority of the Electoral College vote but only 43 percent of the popular vote. Though their presidential candidate lost badly, congressional Republicans made gains. Thus the judgment that voters were endorsing unified government had to be modified by the contrary results of their decisions. Then consider the split-party results of the 1956, 1968, 1972, 1980, 1984, and 1988 elections; in no one of these elections (six of the twelve in the post–World War II period) could it conceivably be said that the winner took all. It was, in fact, difficult to identify a definitive winner. Elections in a separationist system can produce huge victories for the president's party, but in this century there are few such instances, most notably in 1920, 1932, 1936, 1964, and 1980.

In elaborating on the disadvantage of "winner-take-all," Lijphart points out that "the concentration of power in the president's hands gives him or her very little incentive to form coalitions or other power-sharing arrangements or to take part in give-and-take negotiations with the opposition that may be needed to deal with divisive problems."[18] Again, this lack of incentive may well be characteristic of presidentialism as an ideal type of government, but it is an unlikely outcome for a separationist system of competing legitimacies. For how else will the president achieve his programmatic goals but by attempting to form coalitions in Congress and working with the opposition party under conditions of split-party control? Ironically, whereas separation of powers is identified as a characteristic of presidentialism, its attributes are ignored by those specifying the disadvantages of that form of government. It is unimaginable that the elected executive in a separationist government could long ignore a legislature of equal constitutional status, even if his or her political party had a majority there.

The disadvantage of deadlock for presidentialism, as defined by comparative politics scholars, is, to say the least, confusing. On the one hand, the winner takes all and is impervious to events. On the other hand, the government is paralyzed because of the "co-existence of the two independent organs that presidential government creates."[19] Powell explains that "the major characteristic of the presidential system is the selection of a *strong* chief executive for a fixed term, usually in a direct election."[20] Yet this "strong" executive finds that "the division of executive and legislative authority often makes it difficult to create and implement coherent, positive programs to deal with national problems."[21]

Two points are relevant to the issue of deadlock. First is simply to reiterate that those defining presidentialism typically confuse it with separationism when it comes to discussing the United States. Presidentialism should be reserved to describe those systems with the strong executives that Powell expects to find, most likely identified with one-party states. Further, *separationism should be recognized for what it is: an identifiable form of government distinct from presidentialism or parliamentarism.*[22]

Second, the deadlock presumed to exist between a president and a legislature in a separationist system should, at the least, be demonstrated to exist. In the case of the United States, David R. Mayhew has shown that the system can produce major legislation, even under the most strained partisan relationships. The highest production of major legislation for an eight-year period since World War II occurred during the Nixon-Ford presidencies—surely identified by most analysts as an era of high partisan conflict and institutional rivalry. Yet a total of seventy-four major laws were enacted during that time, exceeding the sixty-six major laws enacted during the Kennedy-Johnson years.[23] Not even during the "lame-duck" period of the last two years of the Reagan administration could it be said that there was deadlock.[24] The point is that a separated system offers various opportunities for negotiation between the president and Congress and between the political parties (variations for each are discussed below). There is no reason to assume that deadlock will result or that action by one institution to negate the policy intent of the other is necessarily bad.

The Separationist Perspective

In the United States the presidentialist perspective tends to be associated with the party responsibility model of government. The classic formulation of this model was presented in the American Political Science Association report *Toward a More Responsible Two-Party System.* In this view, it is the task of the political party, with the president as its leader, to overcome the separation of powers. James L. Sundquist has provided a recent review of how it was that the party responsibility model presumably worked in the past:

> The political party was the institution that unified the separated branches of the government and brought coherence to the policy-making process. And because the president was the leader of his party, he was the chief policymaker of the entire government, presiding directly over the executive branch and indirectly working through and with his party's congressional leadership over the legislative branch as well.[25]

For the present, ignore the fact that past presidents varied greatly in the extent to which they followed this pattern; for example, Theodore Roosevelt, Woodrow Wilson, Franklin D. Roosevelt, and Lyndon Johnson accepted a strong leadership role, whereas William Howard Taft, Calvin Coolidge, Dwight D. Eisenhower, and Jimmy Carter did not. Instead, concentrate on the fact that the Constitution, as originally designed and as amended, creates conditions under which different types of governments can legitimately exist. Given the three major elected institutions—House of Representatives, Senate, and the presidency—there are eight possible combinations of party control. Either party can win all three, just the White House and the House of Representatives, just the White House and the Senate, or the White House only. All eight combinations have been experienced since the founding of the modern two-party system.[26] Five of the eight combinations have occurred since the end of World War II, with split-party combinations being the most frequent (twenty-eight years, 1947–93).[27]

The separationist perspective differs in important ways from the presidency-centered party responsibility perspective. In this view, responsibility is seldom fused, it is more often diffused—between the parties and between the institutions. Representation is rarely unified in the presidency; it is typically mixed and multidirectional, with limited correlation between congressional and presidential elections. The role of the president in the separated system varies substantially, depending on his strategic position and political resources. As Richard E. Neustadt has argued, however, a president's advantages are to be used in working with and persuading Congress and others with political power that what he wants is consistent with their own responsibilities and interests, not in commanding them to follow.[28]

The separationist perspective does not exclude the possibility of a presidency-centered responsible party government. Instead, it places it on a continuum of institutional participation and control —from presidential preponderance and influence to congressional preponderance and influence. Above all, the separationist perspective recognizes the dynamics of politics. Far from being insensitive to change, a separated system provides access through complex representational structures for monitoring public response. That is not to say that a separated system is prepared to respond quickly to new demands by producing new policy. The initial reaction may be to thwart present plans or policies, seemingly resulting in stalemate. It is precisely that potential outcome that encourages reformers to make change, typically designed to increase the power of the president.[29]

Institutional and Partisan Policy Interaction
in the Separated System

There are several positive consequences from viewing the American system as separationist. Instead of being preoccupied with why the government is not working properly, one is encouraged to explore the variations in strategies and conditions that explain the politics of a separationist policy process. Rather than expect political party to overcome the constitutional division of the executive and legislative branches, one may anticipate that party will function within its presidential or congressional context to facilitate the functions of each institution. The results will not always be a compatible performance by the same party in these different policy settings. Nor would one suppose that having the same party win the White House and majorities in both houses of Congress would necessarily result in anything approaching parliamentarism.

Put otherwise, a separationist perspective advances the expectation that mixed representation will produce diverse approaches to policy issues, as was intended by the framers of the Constitution. Since, by definition and design, no one is in charge of the whole system, it follows that any one major policy decision will be the consequence of negotiation among those with the legitimate right to participate (as a result of their representative status). Assorted patterns of partisan interaction may be expected, even when there is unified government.

If it happens that the same party controls each branch, there is then a strong basis for communication on public policy issues, with the president in a position to lead through persuasion.[30] There is no magic formula by which the separated system is transformed into a parliamentary government of responsible parties by an election, however. Negotiation must still take place, majority-party leaders can never ensure loyalty of all members on all policy issues, and all majority-party representatives and several majority-party senators are always just two years from an election even at the point of having achieved unified government.

The variation in partisan interaction can also be displayed as a continuum—from partisanship to bipartisanship, with differences in the numbers of those defecting marking the points along the continuum. Four patterns are distinguishable:[31]

> *Partisan.* Those instances in the policy process when the majority party is sufficiently unified that it is not necessary to

compromise so as to attract support from the other party (though the president will typically have to strike bargains within his own party to retain support).

Cross-partisan. There are at least three forms: (1) those instances in unified government when defections are certain and therefore support from the requisite number of opposition party members is required; (2) divided-government cases, when the president's party must gain support from the other party if he has an active legislative program; and (3) those instances when a larger majority may be desirable to demonstrate broad support, thus typically requiring crossover votes from the other party.

Bipartisan. Those instances in either unified or divided government when a major national issue (e.g., the European Recovery Program) transcends party differences and there is active involvement by both party leaders early in the policy process.

Co-partisan. Those instances in divided government when leaders of both political parties have strong advantages and policy interests. Both then prepare and press for alternatives to the point of compromise. Co-partisanship often leads to sufficient cross-partisan support for passage of legislation, which may occur at any stage of the lawmaking process.[32]

A separated system invites a complex and highly articulated lawmaking process. An independent and coequal legislature will develop elaborate internal processes for representation and decision making and will be protective of the prerogatives that such procedures are designed to fulfill. The House of Representatives and the Senate have the most complex organization and rules of any legislature in the world. Since many members of both chambers have made a career of legislative service, they tend to shield the institution from aggrandizing agents, as well as each chamber from the other. Put simply, the independence resulting from separated elections encourages an enunciation of procedures that have the effect of preserving constitutional status.

Presidents, therefore, must continuously design strategies for building majority coalitions in two assemblies. If their party has a majority in each, then they have the advantage of a strong base, but no guarantee that support will be automatic. If the other party has a majority in one or both houses, then, obviously, the straightforward partisan option is not available unless they are seeking an issue more than a policy (i.e., unless there is a strategic advantage to be gained by a defeat or by sustaining a veto).

Many studies of partisan interaction use roll-call votes on the floor as the database. Important as this stage is in lawmaking, prior actions are also vital—notably in subcommittees, committees, scheduling, floor debate, and amendments not subject to roll-call votes. In a study of twenty-eight major laws in the post–World War II period, all patterns of partisan interaction were evident at the various stages of the lawmaking.[33] Three examples will suffice to demonstrate the range, one each from cases of presidential preponderance, congressional preponderance, and institutional balance.

Presidential preponderance. Reagan: The Economic Recovery Tax Act (1981). House of Representatives (Democratic majority): Committee action was partisan; floor action was cross-partisan (many southern Democrats defecting to support the Reagan program), as was the vote on final passage. Senate (Republican majority): Committee action was cross-partisan, as was floor action and final passage (though support from Democrats was not needed on the final vote).

Congressional preponderance. Truman: Labor-Management Relations Act (Taft-Hartley, 1947). House of Representatives (Republican majority): Committee action was co-partisan, leading to a cross-partisan agreement; floor action was cross-partisan, as was final passage. Senate (Republican majority): Committee action was co-partisan, leading to a cross-partisan agreement; floor action was cross-partisan, as was final passage. Truman vetoed the bill, and it was overridden in a cross-partisan vote in each house, since Democratic votes were required to override.

Institutional balance. Ford: Energy Act (1975). House of Representatives (Democratic majority): Committee action was co-partisan with a partisan final result; floor action was cross-partisan, as was final passage (though Republican votes were not needed in two of the final votes). Senate: Committee and floor action, as well as votes on final passage were mixed because the legislation was divided into several bills, each with its own characteristic partisan pattern.

What a detailed examination of specific legislation shows is that partisan interaction varies through the process of any one chamber in a bicameral legislature, between the two chambers, between the final result in each chamber and the conference (if there is one), between the two chambers in acting on a conference report, and among policy issues during a presidential term. It is characteristic of the two-party separated system that partisanship provides a basis and need for a stunning array of majority-building strategies.

Exporting the Separated System

Seldom in history have there been more political systems in transition at the same time. Scores of nations are experimenting with new governmental forms, with many seeking to emulate what is understood to be the presidential system. There are several lessons from the review and analysis provided by this chapter:

1. Don't look to the United States as a model presidential system; even its advocates acknowledge that it does not exist and are, accordingly, constantly proposing reforms.
2. The separated system is not well understood primarily because most analysts prefer a presidency-centered responsible party system and are therefore not moved to accept a separationist perspective seen by them to be flawed.
3. Policymaking in a separated system is commonly characterized by multiple participation, mixed representation, variable institutional and partisan interaction, and diffused responsibility.
4. No state should adopt a separated system that cannot tolerate a substantial degree of ambiguity and uncertainty in policymaking and implementation, where decisions are typically made as a series of approximations.
5. It may well be possible to establish a separated system over time in stages, with each phase designed to test the capacity of officials and the public to accept as legitimate the representation and participation of interests other than their own.

To make public policy while avoiding the concentration of power cannot be made to seem simple. And there are substantial costs to the legitimation of counterforces that must be weighed as states define and refine political, institutional, and policy purposes. The first step toward those ends may well be protecting the right to criticize, even ridicule—but not to thwart—the ideas people have about governing themselves.

NOTES

1. Arend Lijphart, "Introduction," in *Parliamentary versus Presidential Government,* ed. Arend Lijphart (New York: Oxford University Press, 1992), 1. See also R. Kent Weaver and Bert A. Rockman, eds., *Do Institutions Matter? Government Capabilities in the United States and Abroad* (Washington, D.C.: Brookings Institution, 1993), esp. 1–41.

2. Douglas V. Verney, "Parliamentary Government and Presidential Government," in Lijphart, *Parliamentary versus Presidential Government,* 40.

3. See, for example, Weaver and Rockman, *Do Institutions Matter?* 1–41, 445–61, and passim; and the work of Lijphart, Verney, Juan Linz, Seymour Martin Lipset, G. Bingham Powell, and Fred W. Riggs, among others.

4. Verney, "Parliamentary Government," 38. This excerpt is taken from *The Analysis of Political Systems* (London: Routledge and Kegan Paul, 1979), chap. 3.

5. G. Bingham Powell, Jr., *Contemporary Democracies: Participation, Stability, and Violence* (Cambridge: Harvard University Press, 1982), 218.

6. Woodrow Wilson, *Congressional Government* (Boston: Houghton Mifflin, 1885).

7. Verney, "Parliamentary Government," 44–45.

8. Ibid., 45.

9. See in particular, Weaver and Rockman, *Do Institutions Matter?* 445–61.

10. For an example of how these reformers view the constitutional arrangements, see James L. Sundquist, *Constitutional Reform and Effective Government,* rev. ed. (Washington, D.C.: Brookings Institution, 1992), esp. chap. 1.

11. The thought of trying to improve divided government is heresy to many political reformers in the United States because it is precisely split-party control that is judged to be a deficiency, even a perversion, of proper governing. See, for example, James L. Sundquist, "Needed: A Political Theory for the New Era of Coalition Government in the United States," *Political Science Quarterly* 103 (Winter 1988–89): 613–35.

12. Juan J. Linz, "The Perils of Presidentialism," an edited version of the original article reprinted in Lijphart, *Parliamentary versus Presi-*

dential Government, 118–27. The article appeared in the *Journal of Democracy* 1 (Winter 1990): 51–69.

13. Ibid., 124.

14. Ibid., 126. Linz's discussion illustrates the problem of including the United States as a presidential government. Having been informed by his comparativist colleagues that it is the "prototype," he then must make references to it as such, yet finds it consistently exceptional.

15. Arend Lijphart, "Introduction," in Lijphart, *Parliamentary versus Presidential Government,* 15.

16. Linz, in Lijphart, *Parliamentary versus Presidential Government,* 120.

17. Though the high rate of incumbent return in recent decades, primarily in the House of Representatives, has resulted in strong criticism of legislators as not sufficiently responsive to change. A term-limitation movement gained momentum in 1990–92 that was successful in imposing limits in several states. For details, see Gerald Benjamin and Michael J. Malbin, eds., *Limiting Legislative Terms* (Washington, D.C.: CQ Press, 1992).

18. Lijphart, *Parliamentary versus Presidential Government,* 19.

19. Ibid., 15.

20. Powell, *Contemporary Democracies,* 218; emphasis added.

21. Ibid.

22. I reiterate the need for comparative scholars to define the characteristics of presidentialism, to drop the United States as its prototype, and to include separationism among their categories. The full range of democratic systems should then be presidentialism, separationism, and parliamentarism, with subcategories for each accounting from the number of political parties—one, two, many.

23. David R. Mayhew, *Divided We Govern: Party Control, Lawmaking, and Investigations, 1946–1990* (New Haven: Yale University Press, 1991), 118.

24. On the other hand, President Bush and the 102d Democratic Congress found it very difficult to reach agreement on major issues—more because of the weakness of each than the strength. Each side lost the incentive and status to negotiate meaningfully.

25. Sundquist, *Constitutional Reform,* 624.

26. Though it should be noted that the combination of a Republican president and House of Representatives occurred in 1880 when the Senate was evenly split between Democrats and Republicans, with two independents.

27. As Morris Fiorina, among others, has pointed out, divided government is not unique to the United States. "Most of the world's governments are *not* unified like the idealized British parliamentary sys-

tem." Instead, they are coalition governments due to the failure of any one political party to win a majority of seats in parliament. The locus of compromise in the process of making law may differ but the requirement for cross-party negotiation nonetheless is present in both systems. Morris Fiorina, *Divided Government* (New York: Macmillan, 1992), 112 and chap. 7. See also Michael Laver and Kenneth A. Shepsle, "Divided Government: America Is Not 'Exceptional,'" *Governance* 4 (1991): 250–69.

28. Richard E. Neustadt, *Presidential Power: The Politics of Leadership* (New York: Wiley, 1960).

29. For a review of various reforms, see Sundquist, *Constitutional Reform,* chaps. 5–8.

30. As Richard E. Neustadt taught us some time ago, presidents will vary in the number and strength of their advantages in persuading others of their policy preferences—even under circumstances of unified party control. Neustadt, *Presidential Power,* chap. 3.

31. These patterns are treated and illustrated in detail in Charles O. Jones, *The Presidency in a Separated System* (Washington, D.C.: Brookings Institution, 1994), chaps. 1, 6, 7.

32. Co-partisanship may also be evident in a nominally unified government, that is, one in which the president's party has a narrow margin in one or both houses of Congress and there are predictable defections so that the minority party is encouraged to form coalitions in support of its alternatives.

33. See Jones, *Presidency in a Separated System,* chap. 7.

3

The Presidency in Contemporary Politics

In his classic work *Presidential Power,* Richard E. Neustadt observed that "the constitutional convention of 1787 is supposed to have created a government of 'separated powers.' It did nothing of the sort. Rather, it created separated institutions sharing powers."[1] This formulation encourages Neustadt to define presidential power as the power of persuasion.

> When one man shares authority with another, but does not gain or lose his job upon the other's whim, his willingness to act upon the urging of the other turns on whether he conceives the action right for him. The essence of a president's persuasive task is to convince such men that what the White House wants of them is what they ought to do for their sake and on their authority.[2]

Presidents have advantages in persuading their fellow shareholders in authority to support their attempts to apply power to social, economic, and political issues. But so do their shareholders—a fact that both creates the bargaining situation and sets its conditions.

In looking ahead to the 1960s, Neustadt expressed doubt that Congress would consistently support the president—any president. In fact, he predicted, "If ballot-splitting should continue through the Sixties it will soon be 'un-American' for president and Congress to belong to the same party."[3] He foresaw a "fighting time." "Bargaining 'within the family' has a rather different quality than bargaining with members of the rival clan."[4]

As it happened, ballot splitting did continue to characterize voting in the 1960s, but the Democrats were successful in controlling both branches for the first eight years of the decade. For two of the eight years (1964–65) the presidential and congressional Democratic parties seemed as one. That situation was not to last, however. The election that was to terminate the Republican Party (1964) failed to do so. President Lyndon B. Johnson ran afoul of Congress on his Vietnam war policies, and he chose not to seek reelection in 1968. Since that time, Republicans have won the White House five times.

Meanwhile, congressional Democrats continue to do well. They have won 60 percent of the House seats since 1968 and have been in the majority in each of the thirteen Congresses (twice by a two-thirds margin). Although their fortunes in the Senate have not been as impressive, they have won 55 percent of the seats in this period. On three occasions, however, they were in the minority (1981–87).

Given these unusual circumstances, it is a fair restatement of Neustadt's sage observation to say that we have a government of separated institutions competing for shared powers. The separation of powers interpreted as institutions sharing authority finds a president performing legislative-like functions (Neustadt cites the veto) and Congress performing administrative-like functions (Neustadt cites the dispensing of authority and funds). The separation of powers interpreted as a competition for authority in addition finds each institution protecting and promoting itself through a broad interpretation of its constitutional and political status, even usurping the other's power when the opportunity presents itself. Impoundments, budgeting one-upmanship, the legislative veto, congressional foreign policymaking, all come to mind, along with covert intelligence operations, as evidence for worrisome mistrust between the branches.

Presidential power as persuasion is altered somewhat under the circumstances of political separation, as are a president's advantages. He may prefer more indirect methods of getting congressional support—for example, persuading the public through use of the media or impressing foreign leaders through foreign policy initiatives. He may not wish to persuade Congress at all on certain domestic issues, preferring that it not act or concluding that there is a strategic advantage in its taking the initiative. One thinks of congressional Democrats declaring Ronald Reagan's several budgets "dead on (or before) arrival." Given the problems of producing a satisfactory budget in a period of staggering deficits, one can only imagine the president sighing in relief as his political opponents accepted a responsibility they could not fulfill. What is best politically may not be at all the same for a separated president as for a sharing president.

The Founders may not have created a government of separated powers, as Neustadt contends, but they set conditions under which competitive power centers could emerge. They separated the elections, thereby making it possible to have eight combinations of party control—White House, House of Representatives, and Senate—once the two-party system developed (table 3.1). Presumably James Madison would be satisfied—perhaps he even knew it would turn out this way.

TABLE 3.1
COMBINATIONS OF PARTY CONTROL

Combination	Republican control	Democratic control
1	All three	None
2	Presidency	House, Senate
3	Presidency, House	Senate
4	Presidency, Senate	House
5	House	Presidency, Senate
6	Senate	Presidency, House
7	House, Senate	Presidency
8	None	All three

We have experienced five of the eight combinations (1, 2, 4, 7, 8) since World War II. Occasional split-party control—as occurred before World War II—is unlikely to reshape national politics, since it is exceptional. A prolonged period of partisan division, however, commands our attention. Beginning in 1968 we observe a separation of politics in which the Republicans have successfully laid claim to the White House, the Democrats to Capitol Hill. Most observers consider this condition bad. "It's a poor way for democracy to do business," is how the eminent columnist David S. Broder puts it. Split government encourages each branch "to usurp the other's power."[5] Broder was commenting on an article by James L. Sundquist in which he argued that this new condition of split-party control is "an accident of the electoral system." The result is a disjuncture between theory and practice—between the unity of party government and the practice of what Sundquist calls "coalition government" (the split-party condition).[6]

Sundquist quite rightly asks for some attention to this development, first to acknowledge its existence, possibly to correct it with constitutional reforms, or perhaps to offer "an alternative theory that tells us how that kind of government can be made to work."[7] I join Sundquist in his call. I proceed, however, from the assumption that the condition is not accidental. Instead, it is an option that is and has been available to voters in our political system—one exercised frequently in recent decades. Large numbers of voters appear to make a conscious decision to separate the president from the rest of the system. We need to explore the nature of that separation to consider the usefulness of the standard expectations of presidential performance during the contemporary period of separated institutions competing for power. We need to understand how presidents accommodate to their separation if we are to respond to Sundquist's challenge for an alternative theory. Actually we may find that theory incorporated in the original thinking that inspired our system.

The Presidency as Separated

What has been separated from what in this truncated system of ours? Seemingly it is the presidency that has been detached by the voters from Democratic party preeminence elsewhere in American politics. When asked, more Americans continue to identify themselves with the Democratic Party than with the Republican Party. Few facts of American politics have been more consistent in recent decades. Those voters professing independence of the two parties have at times matched the number identifying with the Democratic Party, making both parties minorities among the voters. But the Republicans remain the smaller of the minorities.

Democratic Party preeminence also shows up in the states. George Bush's impressive victory in the 1988 presidential race had no perceptible effect on state legislatures, where the Democrats held majorities in both houses in twenty-eight states and the Republicans in just eight, with split control of the two houses in thirteen states (Nebraska's single-house legislature is nonpartisan). Majorities in the state legislatures meant control of the crucial redistricting process following the 1990 census and reapportionment. The national Republican Party worked hard to increase the number of state legislators and made some progress during the early Reagan years. But it had to live with Democratic dominance of congressional districting in the majority of states after the 1990 census.

Democrats do less well in dominating gubernatorial races. It seems that the Republicans can find attractive candidates and garner crossover votes from Democrats. Even so, there have been many more Democratic than Republican governors during the past twenty years. After the 1988 election there were twenty-eight Democratic and twenty-two Republican governors. Governors have been an important source of presidential candidates for Democrats.[8]

What have the voters done? The Democrats seem to have been successful in state and local elections in holding their own party identifiers and attracting independent voters. Yet in presidential elections many Democratic Party identifiers and huge numbers of independents vote Republican. Here is the record of Republican candidates' advantage among party defectors and independents in the four elections from 1976 to 1988 (proportions of total voters in parentheses):

☐ 1976: 20 percent Democratic defectors (37 percent); 11 percent Republican defectors (22 percent); 52 percent of independents voted Republican (41 percent).

☐ 1980: 27 percent Democratic defectors to Reagan, 6 percent to Anderson (43 percent); 11 percent Republican defectors to Carter, 4 percent to Anderson (28 percent); 56 percent of independents voted Republican (23 percent).

☐ 1984: 26 percent Democratic defectors (38 percent); 7 percent Republican defectors (35 percent); 64 percent of independents voted Republican (26 percent).

☐ 1988: 17 percent Democratic defectors (37 percent); 8 percent Republican defectors (35 percent); 57 percent of independents voted Republican (26 percent).[9]

Note that even in the 1976 election, the Democrats' first victory since 1964, the Republican candidate, Gerald Ford, attracted a significant number of Democrats and a majority of independents.[10] And the bonus for Republicans is greater than the difference between the percentages of defectors, since the proportion of Democratic voters was larger in each of the elections.

Sizable numbers of voters are splitting toward Republican presidential candidates, away from their partisan preferences or, in the case of independents, their other voting preferences. Two conclusions seem reasonable: that the presidency has been separated from the rest of American politics, and that this separation is a result of the preferences of American voters (a combination of stalwart Republicans, a majority of independents, and a significant number of Democratic defectors). Meanwhile, the turnout of eligible voters continues to decline (with the exception of a slight uptick in 1984), thereby calling into question the legitimacy of presidential and, even more, congressional winners.

What does it all mean? How is the separated presidency to be managed? What are the effects of a separated presidency on the political system? These are the questions to be treated in this chapter.

Reading the Returns — What the Elections Have Meant

According to the party responsibility model of separated institutions sharing powers, the last "pure" election was that of 1964. Incumbent President Johnson won overwhelmingly in both the popular and the electoral vote count, and congressional Democrats won huge margins—295 House seats (68 percent of the total, the largest margin since 1936) and 68 Senate seats (the largest margin since 1938). The postelection interpreters (as distinct from the longer-term survey analysts) were able to spot a definite mandate, and the 89th Congress produced a policy record second only to that of the early Congresses of Franklin D. Roosevelt.

What seemed like the beginning of another Roosevelt era for the Democrats ended in less than four years. Johnson could do no wrong in 1965; seemingly he could do nothing right soon thereafter. He declined to seek reelection, arguing that he could serve better by removing himself from politics, an unusual position for a Texas Democrat. The 1968 Democratic convention was one of the most contentious in history—both inside and outside the hall. The Democrats became a party in name only—unable to collect themselves as a unit for nominating a winning ticket. Southern Democrats in 1968 were even given the opportunity to vote for a third-party candidate, George C. Wallace (who won five Deep South states). A review of each presidential election from 1968 through 1988 reveals the mixed messages conveyed by the voters and therefore encourages an analysis of governing strategies by presidents.

THE 1968 ELECTION

Richard Nixon won by the narrowest of margins (43.4 percent of the popular vote, 26.4 percent of the voting-age population), and a Democratic Congress was returned. The turnout was 60.9 percent. The return rates were, for the House, 91 percent of all members, 96.8 percent of those seeking reelection; for the Senate, 86 percent of all members, 71.4 percent of those seeking reelection.

The message in 1968 was that the Republicans could eke out a victory when the majority party was seriously divided. But a Republican president had to be cautious in his dealings with Democratic majorities in Congress. Although 1968 was a harbinger, it did not confuse the analysts at the time. Nor did it mislead the president. Nixon won because the Democrats were divided. Even then, Hubert Humphrey nearly won in the closing days of the election. There was no strong message from the voters to separate the presidency from the rest of the system. The instructions to Nixon were reasonably clear—govern within the limits of mixed electoral results.

THE 1972 ELECTION

Nixon won by a huge margin (60.7 percent of the popular vote, 33.5 percent of the voting-age population), but again a Democratic Congress was returned. The turnout was 55.2 percent. The return rates were, for the House, 83.9 percent of all members, 93.6 percent of those seeking reelection; for the Senate, 87 percent of all members, 74.1 percent of those seeking reelection.

Between 1968 and 1972 the Democrats reformed their nominating process in a manner that accentuated and amplified the party's diversity on issues and provided outside avenues to its nomination. As a result, their platform slipped out of the mainstream, and their ticket of George McGovern and Sargent Shriver lacked credibility among the voters. The candidate of the majority party in the nation won seventeen electoral votes and 37.5 percent of the popular vote. Congressional Democrats, however, retained majorities in both houses, with a net loss of just twelve House seats and a net gain of two Senate seats. Nixon's victory was by the greatest popular vote margin in history and the second greatest electoral vote total. But the Democrats organized Congress. Separation had begun in earnest. Nixon could be excused for believing he had won a strong mandate to govern. He acted on his interpretation, seeking to establish an independent presidency. Yet his actions in foreign, domestic, and budgetary policy invited talk of impeachment even before the revelations of the Watergate hearings. My interest here is in the problem he faced, not the solution he contrived. After his victory, Nixon, like his successors, had to calculate how to govern in the politics of a new era. In Sundquist's terms he sought to develop his theory to meet the political practices of a seriously split government.

We will never know how Nixon's approach would have worked through a full term. The Watergate scandal destroyed his presidency, presumably providing the majority party with an opportunity to regain control of the whole government. Congressional Democrats were the first to profit from the voters' negative reactions to the scandal, realizing a net gain of forty-three House seats and three Senate seats in the 1974 midterm elections. Once again they had comfortable margins in each chamber (67 percent in the House, 61 percent in the Senate).

THE 1976 ELECTION

Carter won by a very narrow margin (50.1 percent of the popular vote, 26.8 percent of the voting-age population). The turnout was 53.5 percent. The return rates were, for the House, 84.6 percent of all members, 95.8 percent of those seeking reelection; for the Senate, 83 percent of all members, 64 percent of those seeking reelection.

In 1976 two factors contributed to the likelihood of the Democrats' nominating an outsider: (1) further democratizing (or so it was believed) changes in their nominating process and (2) the post-Watergate anti-Washington mood among voters. Going too far out of town risked the selection of a candidate unfamiliar with Congress and the national Democratic Party. Selecting from among old Washington hands (such as Henry Jackson, Edward Kennedy, or Walter Mondale) risked losing the advantage of the post-Watergate public mood; but, as it happened, any calculation of risk taking by party leaders was irrelevant. Carter, of Plains, Georgia, well understood the situation and worked the nominating system to his advantage. He did it in part by separating himself from his party, including those like Jackson and Kennedy who would return as majority-party leaders in Congress.

The results in 1976 were hardly a triumphal return to the White House for the Democrats. Carter won with narrow margins of both the popular and the electoral vote counts against an opponent who was the first appointed vice-president and who trailed Carter by thirty points in the polls after the Democratic convention. Meanwhile, congressional Democrats did not appear to suffer from the political distance imposed on them by their presidential candidate. They retained the huge margins they had gained in 1974. Further, Carter's separated campaign left them nearly as independent as though a Republican had won. Carter ran ahead of just twenty-two successful House Democrats and one successful Senate Democrat.

Thus 1976 offers a variation of the separation hypothesis: a Democrat in the White House convinced that he has a mission separate from that of his party and sizable Democratic majorities in Congress confident of public support for their legislative approach. Meanwhile, there is evidence in the election for voters' support of separation: (1) the probability of a Republican victory if Watergate had not occurred, (2) Ford's near victory (a switch of fewer than 10,000 votes in Hawaii and Ohio would have given him a majority of electoral votes), and (3) the independence of Carter (as well as his closeness to Ford on many domestic issues).

Accepting the separation-of-politics hypothesis should lead one to predict serious problems when the separation is expressed within one party—that is, with the president interpreting his election as an instruction to maintain a distance from his party in Congress. Among other effects, a member of the president's own party may be encouraged to challenge the president's renomination on the basis of an argument for party responsibility. That is precisely what occurred in 1979, when Senator Kennedy of Massachusetts announced his intention to seek the Democratic presidential nomination. Carter won renomination, but at great political cost. Kennedy's challenge was important in itself, owing to his national prominence, but it also amplified the problems the president faced internationally and in the domestic economy. And it confirmed the separation of the Carter years.

THE 1980 ELECTION

Reagan won by a decisive margin (50.7 percent of the popular vote, 26.7 percent of the voting-age population), and the Republicans made significant gains in Congress. The turnout was 52.6 percent. The return rates were, for the House, 83 percent of all members, 90.7 percent of those seeking reelection; for the Senate, 82 percent of all members, 55.2 percent of those seeking reelection.

With Watergate all but forgotten and the Democratic Party once again displaying serious divisions, Reagan won a massive victory in 1980. A sitting majority-party president won just six states and the District of Columbia (9 percent of the electoral vote). In 1976 Carter won thirteen of fifteen southern and border states; in 1980 he won two. But something more happened in 1980. The rejection of Carter was strong enough to harm the congressional Democrats too. Although many sought to separate themselves from Carter in the campaign, the Republicans had a net gain of twelve Senate seats (returning a majority for the first time since 1952) and a net gain of thirty-three House seats (the greatest increase for Republicans in a presidential election since 1920).

These results are as close to the party responsibility model of separated institutions sharing power as are ever likely to occur for a minority party (1952 being another recent case). Unless such a sizable victory by the minority party's candidate is followed by realignment (and elections analysts did speculate about that possibility), interinstitutional unity is unlikely to last very long. In this case the congressional elections of 1982 restored a strong majority to the

House Democrats, nearly wiping out the losses suffered in 1980. But substantial policy achievements had been realized. Indeed, the agenda was significantly altered as a result of tax cuts, increases in defense spending, and cuts in the rate of growth of many domestic programs and in the so-called social welfare safety net. This combination produced huge deficits, thereby depriving the Democrats of their traditional ability to support an increased government role in resolving social and economic problems. In fact, as Aaron Wildavsky observed:

> At one stroke the Democratic Party denied its traditional ... recourse to create employment; it also obligated itself to keep the revenues it can raise from new taxes to reduce the deficit. ... Even if he had lost the [1984] election, Ronald Reagan would have won the battle over future domestic policy.[11]

But, of course, he did not lose the 1984 election.

THE 1984 ELECTION

Reagan won by an overwhelming margin (58.8 percent of the popular vote, 31.2 percent of the voting-age population), but essentially the same Congress was returned. The turnout was 53.1 percent. The return rates were, for the House, 90.1 percent of all members, 95.4 percent of those seeking reelection; for the Senate, 93 percent of all members, 89.6 percent of those seeking reelection.

The 1984 election was a classic "approval" election—much like those of 1956 and 1972. In each case, the voters returned the whole government to an extraordinary degree, as shown in table 3.2. The three Republican presidents won overwhelmingly in the Electoral College and in the popular vote; yet the Democrats did relatively well in both houses of Congress, gaining slightly in the House once (1956) and in the Senate twice (1972 and 1984). These second-term victories for Republicans (the Democrats have had none since 1944 when Roosevelt won his *second* second term) were essentially personal triumphs and therefore not interpretable as providing a mandate. Separation was confirmed by the voters in each case, and Republican presidents were in the position of having to calculate how to govern under the circumstances. Reagan did not attempt the Nixon formula. He settled for protecting the domestic agenda advantage he had gained in the first two years of his first term and concentrating on foreign policy issues.

THE 1988 ELECTION

Bush won by a decent margin (53.4 percent of the popular vote, 26.8 percent of the voting-age population) but again with the same Congress. The turnout was 50.1 percent (the lowest in sixty-four years). The return rates were, for the House, 92.4 percent of all members, 98.5 percent of those seeking reelection; for the Senate, 90 percent of all members, 85.2 percent of those seeking reelection.

The previous approval elections (1956 and 1972) were followed by razor-thin Democratic victories. In fact, the Kennedy and Carter victories are alike in regional support (a combination of southern, northeastern, and industrial midwestern states) and the separateness of the presidential and congressional returns (Kennedy ran ahead of just twenty-two successful House Democrats, like Carter, and ahead of none of the successful Senate Democrats; Carter ran ahead of one). Both Kennedy and Carter could be expected to have difficulty leading their party in Congress.

Still, better one of "ours" than one of "theirs," and Democrats had historical reasons for optimism about recapturing the White House in 1988, probably, if it were to happen, by the same narrow margin. They even offered a regionally balanced ticket that would presumably repeat the 1960 and 1976 victories (a presidential candidate from the Northeast and a vice-presidential candidate from the Southwest). But there was no domestic policy advantage like the recession of the late Dwight Eisenhower years or political or institutional advantage like the Watergate scandal of the Nixon administration. In fact, there were few obvious reasons for changing the government at all. Therefore, 1988 looked very much like other approval elections, as table 3.2 shows. Without a significant intervening event, voters were satisfied once more to confirm their support for the separated presidency. They were possibly even apprehensive about a change.

Bush, therefore, like his predecessors Eisenhower, Nixon, and Reagan, had to determine what it all meant for governing. But there was a difference. He was not being reelected. His was the first election since Herbert Hoover's in 1928 in which the party succeeded itself when an incumbent left office, and he was the first sitting vice-president to be elected since Martin Van Buren in 1836. Here was a new condition in contemporary American politics, a vice-president from a successful administration faced with having to distinguish himself from his predecessor and seeking at the same time to manage the political and institutional separation enforced by the voters. Moreover, it was said that his forty-state victory lacked a policy

TABLE 3.2
APPROVAL ELECTIONS, 1956–88

	1956	*1972*	*1984*	*1988*
President				
Electoral vote (%)	86	97	98	79
Popular vote (%)	57	61	59	54
House				
Incumbents returned (%)	95	94	95	99
Net gains/losses[a]	–2	+12	+14	–3
Senate				
Incumbents returned (%)	86	74	90	85
Net gains/losses[a]	0	–2	–2	–1

a. For the president's party.

mandate. Yet presumably he was expected to take control of the government.

THE 1992 ELECTION

Clinton won in one of the most interesting, if confusing, elections in this century. He won in a three-way race with 43 percent of the vote, defeating the incumbent, George Bush, who garnered just 38 percent of the vote (Independent candidate Ross Perot received the remaining 19 percent). Turnout was up slightly. And the Democrats retained their majorities in the House and Senate, though by a reduced margin in the House. The return rates were, for the House, 74.7 percent of all members; 88.3 percent of those seeking reelection; for the Senate, 77 percent of all members, 82.1 percent of those seeking reelection.

Thus, in spite of a return of so-called unified government, there was substantial split-ticket voting. In fact, Clinton received a lower percentage of the vote than Michael Dukakis did in losing in 1988. The election was about "change," but seemingly the principal change that voters wanted was to remove George Bush from the White House and to defeat or force the retirement of large numbers of representatives and senators. Unquestionably, the Democrats shared a common fate following the election, since the pressure was on to make government work more effectively. But it was not in the least certain that they could accomplish that effectiveness.

Mixed and ambiguous messages abound in any recounting of

how we have elected our government in recent times. Presidents win with the support of one-fourth to one-third of the voting-age population. Meanwhile, by constitutional design in the Senate (only one-third up for reelection each time) and by electoral preference in the House, over 80 percent of the Congress is typically returned (counting both those retiring and those defeated as members not returning). In the House the return rates of incumbents seeking reelection varied little during this period—90.7 to 98.5 percent. In the Senate the return rates among incumbents seeking reelection varied more widely from one election to the next, ranging from 55.2 to 89.6 percent. Note that on four occasions during this period (1968, 1976, 1980, and 1988) the House returned a higher percentage of its full membership than the Senate, even though two-thirds of the senators were not up for reelection.

There is another way of looking at the mixed electoral messages that complicate how separated presidents approach the problem of governing. Since the total electoral vote is based on the total number of representatives and senators, it is interesting to compare the electoral count for presidents and for Congress (the latter as measured by the combined party split in the two chambers). Table 3.3 shows the results of this comparison from 1968 to 1992. Even with the forty-nine-state sweeps of Nixon and Reagan in 1972 and 1984, the congressional count still remained very much the same, in favor of the Democrats. Separation is even observed for Carter on this basis,

TABLE 3.3
PRESIDENT'S ELECTORAL VOTE COMPARED WITH
CONGRESSIONAL PARTY SPLIT, 1968–88
(PERCENT)

Election	Presidential electoral vote [a]	Congressional party split [b]
1968	56.2 R	56.2 D
1972	97.2 R	55.7 D
1976	55.0 D	66.0 D
1980	91.4 R	54.0 D
1984	98.1 R	56.1 D
1988	79.6 R	58.9 D
1992	68.8 D	58.7 D

a. Excludes the three electoral votes for the District of Columbia.
b. The combined totals of House and Senate Democrats.

since congressional Democrats retained a two-thirds margin although their party's president received the second lowest electoral vote percentage for any winning candidate in this century. Note also that Bush faced a higher percentage of Democrats in Congress than any of his immediate Republican predecessors, indeed higher than any minority-party president in this century (that is, at the time of his election).

In summary, recent American politics as conditioned by election results encourages an analysis on the basis of revised models—those that stress separation and competition. Though not exactly meeting Sundquist's challenge, such an analysis clearly draws from similar observations about political and institutional developments. Superficially this new politics appears to demand variable accommodative or independent behavior by presidents. More about the variation later. For now it is enough to acknowledge the changes and accept that they call for revised thought about how national politics and policymaking are and should be working. Toward that end it is worthwhile to review the effects of congressional reform and the collateral changes that have taken place in the president's control of the governmental agenda. Both reveal alterations in the political and policy landscape that help sharpen our understanding of the challenges facing the separated president.

Congressional Adjustment—Presuming to Govern from Capitol Hill

If Republican presidents have the problem of judging what it means to win without their party, so do congressional Democrats have to calculate what role to play when they are reconfirmed without the advantages of winning the White House. It is no coincidence that Congress began seriously to reform itself during the 1970s. The quintessential Republican was elected in 1968 and reelected overwhelmingly in 1972. Nixon was no national hero like Eisenhower or man of the Hill like Ford. Nixon had served as a campaign "hit man" for Republicans. He was unloved—though variably respected—on Capitol Hill, among the press, and within the bureaucracy. He was said to be paranoid. Perhaps so. But even paranoids have enemies.

Thus Nixon's elections were politically foreboding for Democrats. Given their continuing strength on Capitol Hill, it seems in retrospect that reform was predictable, since a Nixon presidency confirmed fears of institutional imperialism within the White House.

Those fears naturally encouraged careful review of congressional organization and practices so as to strengthen the legislature as a political and policy base. That is not to say that Nixon in the White House was the only cause of reform, but he was an important contextual stimulus.

There were at least ten reform commissions in Congress during the 1965–79 period, both partisan and bipartisan. Reforms were aimed at the committees, staff resources, presidential power, the budget process, party leadership, administrative capacities, ethics, campaign finance, and the rules. These reforms and other political developments in the decade of the 1970s contributed to the following important changes:

☐ In congressional attitude—members were more assertive in policymaking, expanding individual interests in policy and assuming more institutional initiatives, notably in foreign policy.

☐ In personnel—committee chairmen were removed, subcommittee chairmanships were distributed more widely among members, and new party leaders were elected.

☐ In policy capabilities—members of Congress provided themselves with significantly more staff and created special units to provide independent policy analysis (the Congressional Budget Office, the Office of Technology Assessment, and an expanded Congressional Research Service).

☐ In lawmaking—a new budget process that called for new kinds of laws was created, and committee and conference deliberations were opened to the public.

It is unquestionably true, as Samuel C. Patterson has written, that "if Henry Clay were alive today, and he were to serve again in the House and Senate ... he would find much that was very familiar."[12] Legislatures do have a common look. It is less certain that Clay would understand either the complex policy issues facing Congress or what his role was to be in a legislature in which sophisticated policy analysis was widely available to the members to back up political judgments.

Even more to the point, perhaps, is the likelihood that prereform modern presidents such as Johnson, Kennedy, Eisenhower, Truman, and Roosevelt would wonder what on earth was happening. It is not that past Congresses simply rolled over in the face of presidential initiatives. Instead, Congress has prepared itself to participate broadly in the national policy process, often offering alternatives or intervening in other ways at all stages of that process (from problem definition and agenda setting through program evaluation). In other words, Congress has moved in the direction of functioning as an entire government, alongside, or in competition with, the executive. And it all happened rather suddenly. Here is what Senator Mondale (D-Minn.) had to say in 1972 about the policy independence of Congress on important issues:

> I have been in many debates, for example, on the Education Committee, that dealt with complicated formulas and distributions. And I have found that whenever I am on the side of the Administration, I am surfeited with computer print-outs and data that comes within seconds, whenever I need it to prove how right I am. But if I am opposed to the Administration, computer print-outs always come late, prove the opposite point or [are] always on some other topic. So I think one of the rules is that he who controls the computers controls the Congress, and I believe that there is utterly no reason why the Congress does not develop its own computer capability, its own technicians, its own pool of information. I would hope that we do so.[13]

At that same time I argued that Congress had the computer capability, roughly, of the First National Bank of Kadoka, South Dakota. That is no longer true. Senator Mondale's hope was realized. Within the decade Congress was able to provide itself with independent computer-based policy analysis to challenge that from downtown.

How is the president to respond to these developments? That is the central question. "The executive Power shall be vested in a President of the United States of America" (Article II, sec. 1 of the Constitution). Although Article II is rather spare in specifying the details of authority, many of its provisions strongly imply policy and administrative leadership.

> The President shall be Commander in Chief....
> He shall have Power, by and with the Advice and Consent of the Senate, to make Treaties, provided two thirds of the Senators present concur; and by and with the Advice and Consent of the Senate, shall appoint Ambassadors, other public Ministers and consuls, judges of the supreme Court, and all other Officers of the United States. (sec. 2)

He shall from time to time give to the Congress Information on the State of the Union, and recommend to their Consideration such Measures as he shall judge necessary and expedient; he may, under extraordinary Occasions, convene both Houses, or either of them . . .; he shall take Care that the Laws be faithfully executed. (sec. 3)

A president who wins office by any margin has a right to assume the constitutional prerogatives commanding the military, creating a government, setting an agenda, convening the legislature, and executing the laws. What, then, is he to think of a Congress that prepares itself politically and structurally to encroach on the executive's authority? He will naturally react strategically, devising techniques for retaining his prerogatives. Given no guidance by the Constitution for dealing with their special situation, separated presidents, too, will try to govern by making the most of their position. We may expect their responses to vary, depending on their personal style, the issues at hand, and their political support.

Agenda Control and the Separated President

Scholars have maintained that the president determines the agenda of government. This common assertion follows from the many constitutional prerogatives just cited and seems suited to the policy and political conditions of a government that is growing. At least from Woodrow Wilson forward, we seem to have measured successful presidents by whether they aggressively pursued an expansive agenda. The failures were those presidents who were too passive. Government simply did not work right if the president did not provide a large agenda. Note, for example, the early assessments of Bush. The postelection judgments were that he lacked a mandate despite having won forty states. Yet the hundred-day review of his presidency criticized him for failing to provide an agenda. Presidents are supposed to drive the system, even when electoral analysis questions their right to do so. They are expected to overcome the weaknesses of their separation.

On reflection, such declarations as those regarding Bush's first months in office are based on two conditions that have changed dramatically: (1) a government with a limited, if expanding, domestic agenda; and (2) a president serving with a Congress in which his party has a majority. When our national government finally caught up to the rest of the world in the scope of its domestic programs and when voters came to support split-party control, the old agenda-setting generalizations became less apt. Here is some of what happened:

- Government expanded dramatically during the 1930s and the 1960s. Not even consolidative presidents like Eisenhower could roll back the New Deal, and the Great Society led to a federal budget with a life of its own. Much of the agenda came to be self-generating, deriving from programs already on the books. The budget did not reach $100 billion until 1962. Then it took just nine years to reach $200 billion, four to reach $300 billion, three to reach $400 billion, two to reach $500 billion, and another eight to reach $1 trillion. Ironically, during much of this period of escalation, the country was served by presidents devoted to budget cutting. Nixon, Ford, Carter, and Reagan served when budget outlays grew from just under $200 billion to over $1 trillion. At the least these numbers suggest that a sizable agenda is already and permanently in place. Therefore, reason dictates that the president's role is properly understood in the context of continuing commitments, which constrain the number and kinds of new policy initiatives that he can take.

- The mixed electoral signals discussed earlier likewise have significant implications for agenda setting. Of the elections since 1968, only that in 1980 could be said to bear a strong agenda-setting message, and even that message was more garbled than we initially thought (that is, we were told later that many voters were rejecting Carter, not endorsing Reagan's program). The other elections separated the two ends of the avenue in policy terms, providing little support for dependence of one branch on the other. Presidents were able to initiate legislation, to be sure. But increasingly their proposals were competitive with those from Capitol Hill—and responses from both were constrained by an agenda already in place.

- Many of the reforms cited earlier ensured a more aggressive role for Congress in agenda setting. House committee staff nearly tripled and Senate committee staff nearly doubled during the 1970s. Personal staffs increased by 50 percent in each chamber during the same period. Party committee and congressional support agency staff also underwent major increases. Some 25,000 to 30,000 people now go to work on Capitol Hill and in state and district offices around the nation. They are, for the most part, bright, able, and ambitious people seeking credentials for advancement in the U.S. government's company town. They are unlikely to sit around waiting for a president to tell them what to do. Instead, they constitute an inchoate policymaking machine. It is true enough that staff or individual members can seldom go all the way in the policy process without presidential support. But on many issues in recent years congressional initiative has been crucial—for example, trade, taxes, environmental issues, drugs—and presidents have had to respond.

Is the president then a captive of these developments? Can he never break out to effect significant change? Under most circumstances separated presidents are indeed captives. Our understanding of their role is enhanced if we acknowledge that fact. Yet the Roosevelt, Johnson, and Reagan administrations will forever be marked as having had profound effects on the agenda. Each administration transformed the work of government, with the subsequent effect of creating new issues. The expansive agendas of Roosevelt and Johnson led to a consolidative agenda. That is, quantum increases in government programs were followed by efforts to make them work A contractive agenda was created by Reagan's sizable tax cuts in 1981. Virtually for the first time in modern history, Washington policymakers sought to keep government from growing or actually to reduce it. Still failing substantially to reduce deficits, they were then faced with a fiscal agenda that concentrated on increasing revenues without paying the political price for such actions. This led to all manner of policy contortions—"revenue enhancement" being one of the more honest forms—but failure at this writing to reduce the deficit ensures that elected policymakers will continue to be managed by the existing agenda.

This brief review points to the weakness of the separated president for performing a vital function in the national policy process—that of agenda setting. Extraordinary political conditions are required to permit him to perform his expected functions of problem definition and priority setting. Congress has become his competitor—albeit a clumsy one—in these agenda-related activities. Yet the public and media expectations are that the president is still in charge.

Conclusion

Separated presidents face the challenge of governing under the contrary political conditions set by the American voters, the competitive institutional conditions created by a reformed Congress, and the policy conditions resulting from the huge post–Great Society self-generating agenda. At the least these changes should encourage us to question previous tests of presidential performance. Thus, for example, it seems inappropriate to judge a separated presidency by the amount of legislation enacted or by policy breakthroughs. Mixed electoral messages force the president to move cautiously or to suffer the consequences of a Nixon or a Carter.

Nor is it appropriate to judge one president's performance by that of the latest occupant of the office, by some earlier "model" president, or by his first year in office. Thus, for example, it is a questionable exercise to evaluate Bush by Reagan's first months in office, Carter's record by Johnson's, or Reagan's last year by his first. More justifiable is an evaluation based on an analysis of the political, institutional, and policy conditions facing a president, combined with consideration of his personal qualities. To what extent did the president maintain support and legitimacy in accommodating those conditions? Judgments about the policy success of separated presidents should be made in this context. That is not bad advice for evaluating any president. But it is particularly appropriate for a president as quarterback of a team over half of which is not on his side of the scrimmage line.

Recent thought about the presidency is consistent with the perspective offered here, even if it is not developed in exactly the same way. Terry Moe concludes that the variations identified here occur "within a long-term historical process whose general path and underlying logic are the fundamental components of institutional development." He finds that politicization and centralization have grown "because of the nature of our institutions and the role and location of presidents within them."[14] Presumably election results are important in determining the role and setting the location for presidents. I propose that the concept of the "separated presidency" captures much of the institutional development to which Moe refers.

Scholars appear to agree with Fred I. Greenstein that dilemmas for presidents are created by "high expectations of performance and the low capacity of presidents to live up to those expectations" and with Nelson W. Polsby that "Congress and the president are like two gears, each whirling at its own rate of speed."[15] Moe expects that "the gap between expectations and capacity will continue to characterize the presidency."[16] Theodore J. Lowi, describing a pathology of presidential government, believes that "the expectations of the masses have grown faster than the capacity of presidential government to meet them."[17]

These views set an agenda for political scholars—one that encourages analysis of the special challenge facing a president separated from, yet expected to lead, the rest of the political system. Within the broader development that Moe speaks of and that Sundquist and others worry about, the variation in approaches is a worthy subject of study. It begins, however, with the recognition of the changes that have occurred and directs attention to the variability in conditions for each new occupant of the office.

Wildavsky sees all of this as "an antileadership system" in which "presidents are tempted into action only to discover that whatever they do is not what they were somehow supposed to have done."[18] What that suggests is that presidents must be ever attentive to the constraints as well as the perquisites of power. Defining who you are and where you are is a starting point in the presentation of self. Doing so is an especially sensitive endeavor for the separated president, since there is an unusually small margin of error. Presumably, presidential attentiveness to position as a source of power would satisfy Madison as one of the "auxiliary precautions" that experience teaches are necessary if government is to control itself.

NOTES

1. Richard E. Neustadt, *Presidential Power: The Politics of Leadership* (New York: Wiley, 1960), 33.
2. Ibid., 34.
3. Ibid., 187.
4. Ibid.
5. David S. Broder, "Split Tickets Hurt Process of Democracy," *Wisconsin State Journal,* 10 April 1989, 7A.
6. James L. Sundquist, "Needed: A Political Theory for the New Era of Coalition Government in the United States," *Political Science Quarterly* 103 (Winter 1988–89): 613–35.
7. Ibid., 632.
8. For a summary of political party success, see Paul Allen Beck, "Incomplete Realignment: The Reagan Legacy for Parties and Elections," in *The Reagan Legacy: Promise and Performance,* ed. Charles O. Jones (Chatham, N.J.: Chatham House, 1988), chap. 5.
9. Data from CBS/*New York Times* exit polls as reported in *Public Opinion,* January/February 1989, 24–25.
10. The 1992 Democratic win was in a three-way race, with Clinton garnering a minority of the vote (43 percent).

11. Aaron Wildavsky, "President Reagan as a Political Strategist," in Jones, *The Reagan Legacy,* 290.
12. Samuel C. Patterson, "The Semi-Sovereign Congress," in *The New American Political System,* ed. Anthony King (Washington, D.C.: American Enterprise Institute, 1978), 132.
13. Comments made in a panel discussion entitled "The Role of Congress," sponsored by Time, Inc., in Chicago, 5 December 1972.
14. Terry M. Moe, "The Politicized Presidency," in *The New Directions in American Politics,* ed. John E. Chubb and Paul E. Peterson (Washington, D.C.: Brookings Institution, 1985), 269.
15. Fred I. Greenstein, "Change and Continuity in the Modern Presidency," in King, *The New American Political System,* 83; and Nelson W. Polsby, *Congress and the Presidency,* 4th ed. (Englewood Cliffs, N.J.: Prentice Hall, 1986), 209.
16. Moe, "The Politicized Presidency," 270.
17. Theodore J. Lowi, *The Personal President: Power Invested, Promise Unfulfilled* (Ithaca, N.Y.: Cornell University Press, 1985), xii.
18. Wildavsky, "Reagan as Strategist," 304.

4

The Diffusion of Responsibility: An Alternative Perspective

Political party analysts, both academic and journalistic, cling to a responsible party model in describing and analyzing national politics in the United States. James L. Sundquist outlines his own devotion to the dominant model by explaining that "the parties ... live to win elections in order to advance their philosophies and programs."[1] Devotees of the model seek to join what the Founding Fathers separated. Parties compete electorally on the basis of "their philosophies and programs." The winner is awarded a mandate to govern—to fulfill the policy promises of the campaign. Presidents propose programs; his majorities in Congress react, modify, then enact these programs. A two-year electoral test of policy support is taken by his congressional party. And a four-year test is taken by both branches.

I join Sundquist in asking that greater attention be paid to the realities of post–World War II politics. Divided government has been common, and such a condition, according to Sundquist "invalidates the entire theory of party government and presidential leadership":

> Competition is the very essence of democratic politics. It gives democracy its meaning and its vitality. The parties are the instruments of that competition. They are and should be organized for combat, not for collaboration and compromise. They live to win elections in order to advance their philosophies and programs. Therefore, each party strives and must strive to defeat the opposing party. But in a divided government, this healthy competition is translated into an unhealthy, debilitating conflict between the institutions of government themselves.[2]

Sundquist leaves little room for an alternative perspective: good is good and bad is bad. Yet he asks political scientists to acknowledge the new era of divided government and then to choose up sides. Either we must reaffirm our devotion to the old model and support changes that will restore unity through responsible parties or we must "provide a new body of theory" for the post-1955 model of what he labels "coalition government."

We (Sundquist and I) have been attending to many of the same developments. And, as it happens, some of what I have been thinking about forms a response to his call. In this chapter, I propose a *diffusion of responsibility* perspective as an alternative to that of the responsible party advocates. The perspective derives from a mixed representation result that is entirely consistent with our constitutional structure. The "new body of theory" that Sundquist seeks is available in a similar source. It is embedded in many of the deliberations in Philadelphia, and it is expressed most coherently in *The Federalist*. I also hope to show that the diffused responsibility or mixed representation perspective is useful in explaining contemporary American politics and policymaking.

Responsible Agenda Politics and the 1988 Election

Not even eight years of dramatically divided government was sufficient to modify the party responsibility expectations of the 1988 election. The evidence for this point is substantial. First was the view that Reagan was special, even extraordinary. The public appeared to like him personally beyond all political reason, if not fully approving of his policies. He was the "Teflon" president to whom nothing bad would stick, thus perverting the very essence of responsibility. Once he left, presumably the Democrats would recapture the White House and normal politics would return.

Second, just as interesting and relevant was the astonishment regarding the productivity of the 100th Congress. How could it be that a lame-duck Republican president and a Democratic Congress were able to deal with such major issues as trade, medical care, drugs, and welfare reform, to name but a few? Sundquist observes: "If the president sends a proposal to Capitol Hill or takes a foreign policy stand, the opposition-controlled House or houses of Congress—unless they are overwhelmed by the president's popularity and standing in the country—simply *must* reject it."[3] To endorse the president's ideas would be to accept his leadership, thus enhancing his party for the next election.

This perfectly rational view, given its premises, does not account for a president in his second term (one who cannot seek reelection). Nor does it allow for a congressional majority party that may not be primarily motivated to elect the next president. Thus, for example, congressional Democrats may be moved to survive, having been separated from the presidential nominating process or politically damaged by participating in it. Meanwhile, voters may be content to reward a president but not his party in Congress, perhaps in the belief, misguided or not, that divided political arrangements coincide with favorable policy outcomes.

Third, there was the criticism of the 1988 presidential campaign for failing to clarify the issues. Elections in the party responsibility model are about "philosophies and programs." But commentators could not detect clear and significant differences between the candidates in 1988. They were charged with avoiding issues.

Fourth was the immediate postelection announcement that the newly elected president had no mandate for his forty-state win. "Americans voted yesterday for a man—but not a message."[4] One postelection cartoon showed movers carrying a large trophy marked "mandate" out of the White House. As George Bush looked on, an aide explained: "That goes back with the Reagans, George." It was a common view derived in part from the return of a Democratic Congress and from Bush's presumed failure to meet the unspecified standards for issue clarity.

Soon after the declaration that he lacked a mandate, the new president was criticized for failing to produce a sufficiently elaborate and commanding agenda and program. Apparently one can draw from any stage of the party responsibility model in commenting on national politics. Failure to meet the standard of a previous stage does not negate the use of the model for subsequent evaluation. At no point, it seems, are the premises declared to be invalid as not applying to present conditions. In Bush's case, as leader of the system, he was expected to move aggressively in proposing new programs and forming his government in spite of the fact that he had no mandate to do so.

Finally, and predictably, the discussion about the midterm election focused on it as a test of national political party success—the Bush record for the Republicans, congressional leadership for the Democrats. The substantial evidence that most congressional elections are decided on state and local issues and/or voter endorsements of incumbents is often more decried than factored into the analysis.

The Model Election: Agenda Congruity
and Its Aftermath

I have selected the 1988 election to illustrate the dominance of the party responsibility thinking as a basis for political commentary and evaluation. I have not biased the analysis with that choice. The 1988 election had many special characteristics. The practice of critiquing it from the perspective of the party responsibility model is not one, however. The 1984 election was very different in other ways from that in 1988 but it, too, was criticized for lacking many of the qualities required for a proper party responsibility outcome.

Have there been "good" elections by the standards of the model? First, it is helpful to identify what those standards are. The best elections should meet most of the following conditions or tests:

1. Publicly visible issues being debated by the candidates during the campaign
2. Clear differences between the candidates on the issues, preferably deriving from ideology
3. A landslide victory for one of the candidates, thus demonstrating public support for one set of positions
4. A party win accompanying the victory for the president, notably an increase in the presidential party's share of congressional seats
5. A greater than expected win for the victorious party, preferably at both ends of Pennsylvania Avenue (thus amplifying the party responsibility result)
6. A postelection declaration of support from the congressional leaders of the president's party

These are demanding tests given our system of separated elections and variable voting turnout. Consider the fact that since 1968 the White House and both houses of Congress have been under the control of the same party for just one four-year period: 1977–81. And in that instance, the president believed he won by separating himself from his party—not in the least recommended by the party responsibility advocates.

What are the best elections in recent decades? The most obvious candidates are the 1932, 1964, and 1980 elections. While one might always argue about the extent of ideologically based conflict in any one of our elections, still these three elections offer more than most. No one appeared to doubt afterward that the Democrats were to be held responsible following the 1932 and 1964 elections. The situation was less clear after the 1980 election because the Democrats retained their majority in the House and added to their numbers in 1982. Still it was Reagan's revolution, so-called, and presumably the recession of 1982 was his and no one else's. Had it carried through to 1984, Reagan would have been held responsible.

Note that attention here has not been directed to voter intentions. Evidence for the conscious installation of party responsibility by voters is not plentiful even when the pundits are encouraged to call it that way (for example, in 1932, 1964, 1980). It is not by any means certain that voting for an alternative candidate (Roosevelt or Reagan) as a means of rejecting an incumbent president (Hoover or Carter) can be interpreted as favoring the ideological position of the challenger. Nor is it clear that a positive vote for a candidate carries with it the endorsement of all of his policy views: "As Chairman Mao might have said, 'Many issues, one vote.'"[5]

Even more problematic is the judgment that newly elected members of Congress from the president's party are elected on the basis of a unified set of policy instructions by the American voters. That is not to say members of Congress ignore election returns for whatever policy messages they might contain. But as Robert S. Erikson and Gerald C. Wright point out: "public opinion rarely takes abrupt liberal or conservative turns," even in those elections that produce dramatic political change (as in 1964 and 1980).[6]

What, then, have the voters done in such elections? They have created a seemingly rational basis for *declaring* a mandate. And mandates are basic to the workings of the party responsibility model. In those rare elections when candidates appear to differ substantially, and one party wins big all around, there is the appearance of *agenda congruity*—that is, seemingly loud and congruent policy messages emanating from the presidential and congressional elections. Those messages encourage those who supply the short-term interpretations, for example, the media analysts, Washington pundits, and elected officials themselves, to give an election its meaning. Later evidence from survey and aggregate data analysis typically casts doubt on the clarity of these policy messages. But often by then the declaration will have had its effect. The president and Congress will have acted on their mandate, meeting their own expectations and those of other short-term interpreters.

There are definite policy effects of "declared mandate" elections. Indeed, the 73d (1933–34), 89th (1965–66), and 97th (1981–82) Congresses are among the most productive in history—certainly among those with the greatest impact. In fact, it can be argued persuasively that such presidential administrations alter the agenda of government whether or not that was the intention of the voters. Subsequent policy action is oriented to the accomplishments of these Congresses. It is interesting to speculate about system responsibility during a period in which elected officials act on the basis of a declared mandate that may not, in fact, reflect the true policy intentions of the voters. Such cases are of special interest when the result is the creation of a self-generating agenda—that is, an agenda of issues that emerge from existing policy or programs and crowd out new problems.

To summarize:

1. The model party responsibility election is a relatively infrequent occurrence.
2. It is questionable whether those that come closest to meeting the criteria are, in fact, suited to the full policy implications of the model.
3. The policy production of party responsibility administrations has been significant, tending to dominate the subsequent agenda.

Alternative Thinking about Presidents, Congresses, and Agendas

The period from 1968 to 1988 should encourage us to think differently about presidents, Congresses, and agendas. The six presidential elections during that period produced one Democratic and five Republican victories. Three of the Republican wins were by Electoral College landslides, another was a sizable win (Bush's forty-state win in 1988). Not once did the Republicans begin a term with their party in a majority in both houses of Congress—a rare occurrence in the past. In the 1968–90 period, there have been eighteen years of split-party control between the White House and the House of Representatives (82 percent of the time) and twelve years of split control between the White House and the Senate (55 percent of the time).

The one Democratic win, in 1976, brought an outsider, Jimmy Carter, to the White House. He was joined by substantial Democratic majorities in both houses of Congress. But he won by the barest of margins, trailing all but one successful Democratic senator in his state and twenty-two successful House Democrats in their districts. There was no reason to believe that Carter was responsible for electing a Democratic Congress, nor did he welcome the credit for such an accomplishment given his anti-Washington campaign theme and his trusteeship style of governing.

These facts encourage consideration of a mixed representation or diffused responsibility perspective by which separated institutions compete for power, seeking to take credit and avoid blame. Elsewhere I speak of the "separated presidency"—a development in which the voters have detached the presidency from the rest of the political system.[7] Recent presidential elections display a combination of stalwart Republican voter support for their candidate, significant Democratic voter defection to and sizable independent voter support for the Republican candidate. Meanwhile, Democrats do well in Congress and in state and local elections. These developments encourage analysis of how it is that separated presidents seek to govern. Sounding the party responsibility theme that such an arrangement is bad for American democracy loses its utility when repeated over two decades. There must be some point in time when a perversion deserves relabeling as a commonality—possibly an event becomes a candidate for this conversion when it happens two-thirds of the time.

For present purposes, I recommend suspending expectations drawn from one-party control at both ends of the avenue. Concentrate instead on what one might expect politically and in policy terms from split-party control. This recommendation does not ask that the reader abandon preferences. It only encourages acceptance of contemporary developments and proposes evaluating political circumstances from the perspective of the separated president in a mixed representative system.

The most common form of mixed representation occurs when a president of one party faces a Congress in which the other party has majorities (typically a Republican president and Democratic Congress). In several instances the president received an overwhelming or substantial endorsement (as in 1956, 1972, 1984, and 1988), but his party in Congress failed to match his triumph. Policywise, the result is seemingly incongruous, in contrast to that of the "good" elections mentioned earlier.

Other elections, too, are difficult to interpret. Those won narrowly by a president whose party has congressional majorities are examples. Narrow Democratic White House wins in 1948, 1960, and 1976 displayed policy incongruities. Congressional Democrats had huge gains in 1948, recapturing control of both houses, while Harry S. Truman won narrowly and surprisingly. Democrats had a net loss of seats in the House and Senate when John F. Kennedy barely won in 1960. And congressional Democrats had almost no changes, but retained substantial majorities, in 1976 when Jimmy Carter won narrowly.

The point is that most post–World War II elections have sent mixed political, policy, and representational signals. Diffusion of responsibility is the result, and that outcome does not easily accommodate the concept of a mandate. Scholars such as Robert A. Dahl[8] and Raymond Wolfinger[9] raise serious questions about the plausibility of the mandate under any circumstances. It surely lacks bearing in the divided-government scenario. There may be congruent circumstantial evidence for a mandate, as in 1980. But normally the analyst is better prepared to describe outcomes by relying more on what is common than on what is exceptional.

I am aware that lack of a mandate by the criteria cited here need not paralyze a president. Perhaps, as George C. Edwards observes, a president may create "the perception of an electoral mandate, an impression that the voters want to see the winner's program implemented."[10] Or as a former aide to President Kennedy noted: "He [Kennedy] moved forward on the theory that he had a mandate whether he had a mandate or not.... If you have a program ... then you move forward to do it" (personal interview). A former Carter aide agreed, explaining that

> what is said and done in the campaign becomes part and parcel of the mandate.... Candidates do take their promises seriously; the groups to whom they are made take them seriously.... Having the ability to claim a mandate is crucial to governing. Without it, it is very difficult to convince other institutions ... that your program has public support and should be passed.... There are, however, conflicting mandates. Part of the ability of being president is to control the perception in your direction of what you want your election to be interpreted for. (personal interview)

This statement reveals the strategic use of mandates in building support for presidential programs, whether or not the empirical evidence meets the demanding tests of the party responsibility model. Unquestionably one may expect various strategies to be employed in acting on public problems absent from the stringent conditions of the classic mandate. How else are we to explain the passage of a federal highway act, tax reform, civil rights acts, trade and welfare reform, under conditions of split-party control?

Another feature of the diffusion of responsibility result is that of a continuing agenda—one so substantial that it is difficult for new issues to gain status. Further, the agenda is full of macro issues that do not lend themselves easily to ideological or partisan divisions. How the agenda and divided government interact causally, I am not prepared to say. I simply observe that many of the issues (e.g., trade, the deficit, environmental degradation, energy supply, role of defense in peacetime) cross partisan and ideological lines. And cross-party macro issues encourage a diffusion of responsibility (see below).

Given his role as chief executive—sitting atop one of the larger hierarchies in the world—the president may be expected to perform a certifying function for the agenda. Though it is unlikely that he can in fact prevent major issues from coming to the fore, much of the system depends on this certification function to trigger the development of proposals. If he fails to act or delays action, others in Washington and outside will act on compelling issues. And the policy proposals from any source will take their place in a continuous process of exploration and testing as the government seeks its role in social, economic, and political problem solving. But to have the president on board greatly facilitates the process.

One may even question how rational it is for any one person, institution, or party to seek or accept responsibility for the government's policy performance on mega issues. A self-generating agenda, split-party control, diffused responsibility, continuity of issues between administrations—these characteristics are not conducive to one party coming forward to make an accounting. Therefore look for what Kent Weaver refers to as "blame avoidance,"[11] as well as for a rush to symbolic issues (the flag, ethics in government, crime) for credit taking.

Diffusion of Responsibility and the Reagan-Bush Era

The Reagan-Bush era is a prime example of the application of party responsibility expectations to the reality of diffused responsibility. Begin with the 1980 election. It was widely interpreted as conveying a strong mandate to the new Reagan administration. The election results appeared to suit the conditions required for declaring a mandate. There was even talk of realignment—a requirement if party responsibility is to follow an electoral mandate for the minority party.

The actual evidence from the 1980 election, whether aggregate or survey data, was not encouraging for either declaring a mandate or projecting realignment. Ronald Reagan won by a huge Electoral

College margin—third highest in the century to that date (exceeded only by Nixon in 1972 and Roosevelt in 1936). But his percentage of the popular vote was the lowest of any of the major landslide elections in the century (including 1920, 1932, 1936, 1940, 1944, 1952, 1956, 1964 and 1972). Granted there was a third-party candidate in the 1980 election: John Anderson. The point is that Anderson voters were not voting for Reagan.

Then there is the issue of why those who voted for Reagan in 1980 did so. Were they endorsing Reagan's program? Were they particularly pleased with Ronald Reagan as a candidate? Were they rejecting Jimmy Carter? According to Martin Wattenberg, the negativism exceeded positivism among voters. In fact, many voters did not like Reagan but they were adamantly opposed to returning Jimmy Carter to the White House.

> Prior to the Reagan elections, the average voter expressed an average of 0.77 more reasons for voting for the winning candidate than reasons for voting against him. Yet for Reagan in 1980, the sample actually had more to say about why they would not vote for him than for why they would! Of all the candidates prior to 1980, only Barry Goldwater in 1964 and George McGovern in 1972—each the victim of a landslide against them—received lower ratings than Reagan. The difference of course is that Reagan's 1980 opponent, Jimmy Carter, was seen even less favorably by a substantial margin.[12]

These results illustrate the hazards of declaring policy mandates from Electoral College landslides, whether or not they exceed expectations. Yet spurious conclusions are difficult to quash in the rush to analysis following an election, particularly if election results appear to support preconceived judgments about what is best for making the political system work. As one prominent journalist put it: "Elections should be a mandate for something. If elections aren't a mandate for something, then what do they [elections] mean?" (personal interview). Mandates are just plain handy for explaining what has happened in an election and for testing a campaign during an election.

Congressional results in 1980 were dramatic, especially those in the Senate. Yet, as it turned out, there was reason to be as cautious as normal in interpreting the returns as reflecting presidential coattails. Declaring mandates solely on the basis of congressional returns is even more problematic than doing so on the basis of presidential returns. And yet connections between the two (presidential and congressional returns) were made by postelection analysts in 1980. Were they justified in doing so?

For the House, the results showed a substantial increase for the Republicans, the greatest in a presidential election since 1920. But their numbers going into the 1980 election were low. House Republicans had still not fully recovered from the devastating losses in the Watergate election of 1974. Therefore even with a thirty-three-seat net increase, the House Republicans only matched their numbers from the 91st and 93d Congresses. Richard Nixon, with a razor-thin margin in 1968, was able to work with exactly the same number of House Republicans as Ronald Reagan with his landslide of 1980. Mandate was not a word used to describe the 1968 election. The percentage of the popular vote received by House Republican candidates in 1980 was impressive—48 percent. It was, in fact, 0.2 percent less than that received by Republican candidates in 1968. Reagan ran behind most Republican candidates in their districts, not an unusual result these days, but he ran ahead of Ford in most districts. The latter is some evidence for his impact, perhaps, more for the members themselves in judging whether and when to follow the president's lead on policy than as an actual indication of policy signals from the voters.[13]

Of course, for purposes of immediate postelection analysis, the House results complemented those for the Senate. The net increase for Republicans was impressive—a gain of twelve seats. It was an extraordinary result—stunning to both parties. Unquestionably the Senate results contributed as much as Reagan's victory to the interpretation of a mandate. It added the special surprise that encouraged the media to identify a policy message in the election returns.

Closer examination of the returns, however, would have muted that message considerably. Thus, for example, the victory margins for the new Republican senators were extremely narrow: eight won with 51 percent or less. In fact, the Democratic candidates for the Senate received a larger proportion of the vote in 1980 than did the Republican candidates for the Senate. An even more curious result, but one that emphasizes the competitiveness of Senate races these days, is that the total vote for Senate Republican candidates in 1986 exceeded that of 1980. Yet in 1986 the Republicans had a net loss of eight seats. For present purposes, the point is that a gain of twelve Senate seats is circumstantial evidence of a policy mandate and that is sufficient in the postelection analyses for declaring it to exist. It provides a convincing justification for an administration to move ahead boldly as though the electorate had, in fact, endorsed the specific policy proposals of the campaign.

None of this is to suggest that a president with a declared or circumstantial mandate will somehow lounge about, awaiting the analysis of the survey data from the Center for Political Studies at the University of Michigan. He may be expected to move quickly to take advantage of the declaration. *A president is never so in control of the agenda than when observers detect congruity between the messages of presidential and congressional returns.* He is advised to "hit the ground running" under these conditions.

What then? Well, of course, the midterm election occurs and presumably has policy implications for the party responsibility advocates. Yet nasty, complicating things happen in these elections. By the model, the elections are tests of how well the administration is doing in fulfilling the mandate. But there are the problems of low turnout, no national-level candidate, the happenstance of whatever third of the Senate happens to be up for reelection, the high return of House incumbents, and the matter of which party is more "exposed," as one group of scholars puts it.[14]

It is a risky enterprise to read the raw results for their policy meanings, though many try to do so. Consider the following: Comparatively speaking, the Democrats did well in 1978—a net loss of just fifteen House and three Senate seats. Did that mean the public approved of Carter's presidency? Carter himself did not draw that conclusion. In fact, he detached himself from the 1978 returns. The Democrats did even better in 1962, a net loss of just four House seats and a gain of three Senate seats. Was that a referendum on the Kennedy presidency? If so, it did not seem to contribute substantially to the president's bargaining advantages. The Republicans had a net loss of twenty-six House seats in 1982 and a net gain of one Senate seat. What did it mean in policy agenda terms? Based on economic indicators alone, the predicted Republican House losses were for forty seats or more. And what about 1986? The Senate Republicans suffered significant losses, but the House Republicans had the smallest net loss during a Republican administration in this century (save for 1906 when Republicans had a net gain but the Democrats had a much larger gain among the new representatives added in that year). Reading midterm election results for the policy messages they contain requires more care than is normally exercised.

What about the reelection? Is it reasonable to expect an administration to seek a new mandate? Or is it a question of seeking confirmation of the original mandate? How may we expect the president to run his campaign? And how do we then interpret the results? It seems that recent reelections—Eisenhower in 1956, Nixon in 1972, and Reagan in 1984—have certain characteristics in common. The incumbents run on their records, they return to face very much the same Democratic Congresses. Based on post–World War II experience, it seems that voters convey approval to the whole government. They reelect the president by landslide proportions and they return congressional incumbents at a high rate (almost 95 percent in the House). The message, if not the mandate, for each party seems to be: "Carry on."

What of the incumbent who loses a reelection bid? I discussed the matter of campaign themes and second-term plans with a former member of Carter's White House staff.

> One of the things we struggled with with the '80 campaign was: could we run, in a sense, as a challenger. That is to say, promise a whole new agenda of items to break away from what had gone on. We basically felt that that was impossible to do. You do want to give a sense of where you will go in a second term but inevitably a reelection is a referendum on the success of the president.
>
> Even with successful presidents, Reagan being an example in '84, there was no real content to the '84 campaign. He didn't seek the kind of mandate for change that he ran on in 1980. He inevitably ran on his record.
>
> In our situation we were better off since people were not satisfied with what we were doing in saying "here are ways in which we are going to change." That never came to fruition in part because of the preoccupation of the president and all of us with just the daily governing crises that we had. It was very difficult to step back and say: "Look here are the things we did wrong and we are going to break from the past." And, indeed, if you do that, it's almost an indictment of what you have been doing. (personal interview)

Among other points made by this person is that of the continuity of an agenda and how that agenda comes to influence political and electoral decision making. Presidents, whether mandated or not, do play an important certifying role in the agenda. That point is unarguable. But issues carry through both elections and presidential administrations, thus confounding the policy demands of a party responsibility model. However much we may wish for policy clarity and responsibility, they are not natural products of a diffuse and separated political system or an electoral system that runs on the clock (or calendar) rather than on the agenda (or policy crises).

One extraordinary feature of the Reagan-Bush administration is that it continued beyond the two-term limit. It was as though Reagan had run for a third term. In fact, he campaigned actively, much more so than did Eisenhower in 1960. From the Republican perspective, the 1988 campaign had features of a reelection and therefore the campaign advisers treated it as such in developing their strategy: defend the record, offer few new initiatives, rely heavily on symbolic issues. Since economic indicators were strong and international tension reduced, there was no need to run defensively as a "challenger" (the option considered by Carter's aides in 1980). The post-Reagan, deficit-driven agenda carried through. It would be hard to claim that President Bush was defining the agenda as he entered office; in fact, many critics claimed just the opposite.

And what if Michael Dukakis had won? He too would have had to cope with the legacy of the Reagan years. There would have been differences to be sure. But it would not have been any easier to identify a mandate for Dukakis. His winning margin would have been small had he won and his campaign lacked a unifying theme (characteristics not unlike those of the Carter win in 1976).

To summarize: The Reagan-Bush period is a classic case of the diffused responsibility perspective. If we allow ourselves to do so, we can understand how it comes about. Separation of power and politics (mostly of the presidency from the rest of the political system) has been endorsed again and again. Should we expect clear accountability under these conditions? Woodrow Wilson argued in *Congressional Government* that "somebody must be trusted, in order that when things go wrong it may be quite plain who should be punished." He recommended that power be distributed so that "abundant honor" would be bestowed for the just use of power and "full retribution" for every abuse.[15] But the American voters are not willing to entrust a president to that extent or provide the clarity in accountability that Wilson sought. What are we to do? We can't fire them—they are doing the hiring. Some analysts are led to constitutional and other types of tinkering, typically to make the separated system work differently, not better.

Diffused Responsibility and the Issues

Many of the domestic issues in a deficit-driven agenda involve reform. This is a natural outcome from the increased attention to program evaluation and congressional oversight that tends to accompany an era of policy consolidation or contraction. Among the larger of these issues are reforms in taxing, welfare, social security, health care, trade, and budgeting. It is unlikely that such reforms can be enacted if one side has to bear the full responsibility for the changes. Certainly many reform proposals prepared by Democratic presidents for Democratic Congresses have failed in the past. Diffusion of responsibility may be essential at certain points in a policy's history if large-scale change is to occur.

One may even raise a question of how fair it is to hold one party accountable for a program that has grown incrementally through decades of single-party and split-party control of the White House and Congress. Yet displays of reform proposals are bound to be occasions for holding one or the other of the branches accountable for the wrongs being righted by the proposals. If, however, politics allows crossing over a partisan threshold to place both parties on the same side, then agreements can be reached that will permit blame avoidance, credit taking, and significant policy change. This threshold has obviously varied among policy issues. But it is apparent that it has been crossed several times in *producing legislation that one simply could not predict from any version of the party responsibility model with which I am familiar.*

Attention to recent administrations and the issues with which they have had to deal also encourages analysis of political party adaptation to their institutional locus. The congressional Democrats have gotten used to being the opposition party to the White House Republicans. They have provided themselves with the resources needed to play that role aggressively. It is not at all certain that they would now work well with a Democratic president (as they did not with Carter and may well not have with Dukakis). One can make a persuasive case that the present Democratic leaders in Congress like their jobs as spokesmen for a legislative party whose cooperation is needed by a Republican president.

Likewise, an experienced group of White House Republicans have accommodated themselves to executive life. Despairing of ever controlling the whole Congress, they work to sustain their strong foothold on the presidency. It is equally uncertain that they work well with Republican majorities in the House and Senate. At the least, they would have to learn how that is to be done—at every stage of the policy process. For the fact is that White House Republicans have become quite accomplished at managing Democratic Congresses. They have no such experience with a Republican Congress.

Unquestionably the most frustrated in this maturing system of separated politics and diffused responsibility are the House Republicans. In fact, some, like the Conservative Opportunity Society, have turned to classic party responsibility arguments in proposing change. They argue for ideology, for clearly stated policy positions, for damning the Democrats, and against bipartisan coalition building. Interestingly enough, however, their devotion to partisanship led to the resignation of the highly partisan House leaders (Jim Wright and Tony Coelho), who were then replaced by more moderate leaders suited to a diffusion of responsibility that may keep the House Republicans in the minority.

It should be noted that the interpretation here is uncommon. Many observers despair of the conditions fostering divided government. With Sundquist, they predict stalemate and are anxious to make changes that will unify our government. Benjamin Ginsberg and Martin Shefter, in *Politics by Other Means,* conclude that electoral competition has been replaced by "institutional combat," a pattern that "undermines the governing capacities of the nation's institutions, diminishing the ability of America's government to manage domestic and foreign affairs, and contributing to the erosion of the nation's international political and economic standing."[16]

Ginsberg and Shefter identify several cases of institutional combat: the deficit, aid to the *contras* (and the Iran-*contra* scandal), certain court appointments, and other political and policy conflicts. Unquestionably their cases do illustrate the difficulties of a divided government in which each institution seeks to protect its advantages, sometimes at a high cost. But there are other stories they do not tell—stories of agreements reached between the contending institutions, even after the Democrats recaptured the Senate in 1986. The policy product of the 100th Congress cannot be explained by their highly pessimistic scenario, nor do they attempt an explanation. The policy bargaining on many issues between the Bush White House and Democratic leaders in Congress also confounds expectations derived from the Ginsberg-Shefter analysis (see chapter 10).

Sustaining the Power of Office

In recent times the American voters have frequently separated the presidency from the rest of the political system. Many do not like that outcome, but it is a fact of contemporary political life. Presidents have had to construct and reconstruct their presidencies to suit changing political conditions and sustain the advantages of office. Meanwhile, the agenda is essentially self-generating, full of continuing issues associated with the commitments inherent in defense and entitlements. Choices are often structured in the context of ongoing commitments. The president plays an important certifying role in regard to the agenda—a role that can assist the Congress in setting priorities. Deficit politics spawns reform proposals, which typically require bipartisan, interinstitutional cooperation.

The party responsibility model is of little or no explanatory or predictive value in contemporary politics, for all the reasons Sundquist identifies. A mixed representative or diffusion of responsibility perspective is proposed here as suited to present circumstances. In this view, we are led to expect a separated presidency, an expansive Congress, and competition between the branches. Policy success, by standard measures, will be characterized by diffused responsibility, for it is neither rational nor fair to assign credit or blame to one party. Each political party will tend to harden its hold on its institution (the White House for the Republicans, Congress for the Democrats), unwilling to take risks to make inroads at the other end of Pennsylvania Avenue. Thus, far from making the political corrections necessary to meet the demands of the party responsibility advocates, the political parties are likely to protect current strengths. In so doing, they contribute to the diffusion that then tends to perpetuate the mixed representation of divided government.

At the least, these conclusions are instructive for those who propose reforms. If nothing else, they will understand why their changes are resisted. At the more hopeful most, this perspective will provide a more constructive evaluation of current agenda politics as it is played out between Republicans and Democrats in the White House and on Capitol Hill.

NOTES

1. James L. Sundquist, "The New Era of Coalition Government in the United States," *Political Science Quarterly* 103 (1988–89): 629.
2. Ibid.
3. Ibid., 629–30.
4. *Wall Street Journal,* 9 November 1988, A39.
5. Raymond E. Wolfinger, "Dealignment, Realignment, and Mandates in the 1984 Election," in *The American Elections of 1984,* ed. Austin Ranney (Washington, D.C.: American Enterprise Institute, 1985), 293.
6. Robert S. Erikson and Gerald C. Wright, "Voters, Candidates, and Issues in Congressional Elections," in *Congress Reconsidered,* 4th ed., ed. Lawrence C. Dodd and Bruce I. Oppenheimer (Washington, D.C.: CQ Press, 1989), 97.

7. Anthony King, ed., *The New American Political System*. Revised Edition (Washington, D.C.: American Enterprise Institute, 1990), chap. 1.
8. Robert A. Dahl, *A Preface to Democratic Theory* (Chicago: University of Chicago Press, 1956), 127.
9. Wolfinger, "Dealignment, Realignment, and Mandates," 293.
10. George C. Edwards III, *At the Margins: Presidential Leadership of Congress* (New Haven: Yale University Press, 1989), 147.
11. Kent Weaver, *Automatic Government: The Politics of Indexation* (Washington, D.C.: Brookings Institution, 1988).
12. Martin Wattenberg, "The Reagan Polarization Phenomenon and the Continuing Downward Slide in Presidential Candidate Popularity," *American Politics Quarterly* 14 (1986): 223.
13. Lester Salamon and Michael Lund, eds., *The Reagan Presidency and the Governing of America* (Washington, D.C.: Urban Institute, 1985), 261–87.
14. Bruce I. Oppenheimer, James Stimson, and Richard Waterman, "Interpreting U.S. Congressional Elections: The Exposure Thesis," *Legislative Studies Quarterly* 11 (1986): 227–48.
15. Woodrow Wilson, *Congressional Government* (Boston: Houghton Mifflin, 1885), 283–84.
16. Benjamin Ginsberg and Martin Shefter, *Politics by Other Means: The Declining Importance of Elections in America* (New York: Basic Books, 1990), 161.

5

Presidents and Agendas

It is not surprising that analyses of national policymaking stress the role of the president. The media focus attention on the White House as the center of decision making. Presidents represent the nation in international negotiations. And much of the national policy process is designed to flow to and through the White House. But it stands to reason that presidential participation in national policymaking and implementation will vary with changing political, policy, and personal conditions. Therefore it is not sufficient simply to declare that the president is important. That we know. Instead, we need to understand the varying conditions under which the president participates in the policy process.

In this chapter I concentrate on agenda setting, a crucial activity in which presidents presumably are heavily engaged. One major purpose of the analysis is to place the president in a broader policy context. An associated purpose is to explore agenda setting and related concepts.

Here is the problem. Conventional wisdom on the role of the president in agenda setting does not always accommodate common knowledge about the workings of our government. The standard view stresses presidential preeminence in determining the policy agenda. Richard Neustadt states that "congressmen need an agenda from outside, something with high status to respond to or react against. What provides it better than the program of the president?"[1] John W. Kingdon concludes that "there is plenty of confirmation in [my] interviews that the president can singlehandedly set the agendas, not only of people in the executive branch, but also of people in Congress and outside of government."[2] And Paul C. Light, in the most comprehensive analysis of presidential agendas, finds that the president's agenda "determines the distribution of political benefits; it is a signal to the Congress and the public of national needs; it carries the president's vision of the past and the future."[3] One might also observe that the Constitution calls on the president "from time to time" to "give to the Congress information of the State of the Union"—a natural occasion for agenda setting.

Yet, as with the presidential role in the policy process, it is apparent that the president's agenda-setting function varies considerably over time and across issues. Presidents surely lead governments, but governments carry on with business even when presidents are crippled by scandal, disability, or loss of power. Many policy activities, expectations, and forces have a momentum of their own. In fact, presidents enter a government already at work. Our task as political scientists is to determine the variable role they play within ongoing governing and policy processes.

The literature on agenda setting (as distinct from that on the presidency) also encourages one to place the president into the broader context of an ongoing process. Various studies emphasize that agenda setting at any level is a complex process involving events, organization, pressure, expertise, choices, and bargaining.[4] The role of presidents in this process can not be understood merely by studying what they do but by clarifying what else is going on that may have an impact on agenda formation. The trick then is to fit presidents into this complex set of activities, not to paste them in at the top of the organizational chart and conclude by that exercise that they are in charge.

A Conceptualization

I propose three concepts to encourage anchoring the president in the flow of political and policy events: *agenda orientation, agenda alternatives,* and *agenda congruity.* Following a discussion of each, I offer a scheme to display their applicability for analyzing presidential-congressional relationships. Then I discuss five recent presidential successions (from Kennedy through four other presidents to Reagan) as an exploratory test of the model.

AGENDA ORIENTATION

This concept refers to the broader issue developments, interpretation, and rhetoric within which specific problems are identified and defined. It draws attention to broad trends in the role of government, either across policy issues, as with the budget-cutting, contractive phase of current policymaking or within specific policy areas, as with developments, say, in agriculture, health, or defense (essentially tracking policy orientations over time). My illustrations and analysis are restricted to domestic policy (and drawn more from social welfare than social-control issues), though I assume such a concept is relevant as well to foreign policy. Typically the orientation is associated with the effects of previous government action. For example, in figure 5.1 I propose a sequence of orientations from expansive to consolidative to contractive to fiscal. In the past we have witnessed cycles of expansiveness followed by consolidation (the Wilson administration followed by the more consolidative Harding, Coolidge, and Hoover administrations; the Roosevelt and Truman administrations followed by the Eisenhower administration). The period since the 1960s is particularly interesting because contraction followed the cycle of expansion and consolidation. Then, having discovered the limits of contraction, a fiscal agenda orientation was introduced. Each of these orientations is discussed in more detail when I discuss presidential administrations.

One may legitimately inquire whether "conservative" and "liberal" suffice as labels for agenda orientation. I do not find them to do so. I detect developments that are less ideological and partisan in the period examined (1961–89). Thus in each phase one finds bipartisan support for programmatic expansion, consolidation, even contraction. I expect a similar development in the emerging fiscal orientation. Ideological labels may find use within each phase, but they are insufficient to denote agenda or issue differences between the phases.

AGENDA ALTERNATIVES

This concept refers to specific policy proposals designed to treat problems on the agenda. Kingdon distinguishes between agenda and alternatives, finding the distinction to be "quite useful analytically."[5] I agree. He also concludes that "presidents can dominate the congressional agenda ... but they have much less control over the alternatives members of Congress consider."[6] Yet, as we see, presidents differ on the degree of control over alternatives. Thus, with this concept we can identify significant differences among presidents, differences associated with variations in agenda congruity.

AGENDA CONGRUITY

This concept refers to the extent of agreement among major policymakers in regard to agenda orientation and agenda alternatives. Principal interest here is in the president and members of Congress. Congruity is influenced by election results or significant events (e.g., the Kennedy assassination). Where congruity is high, one may expect

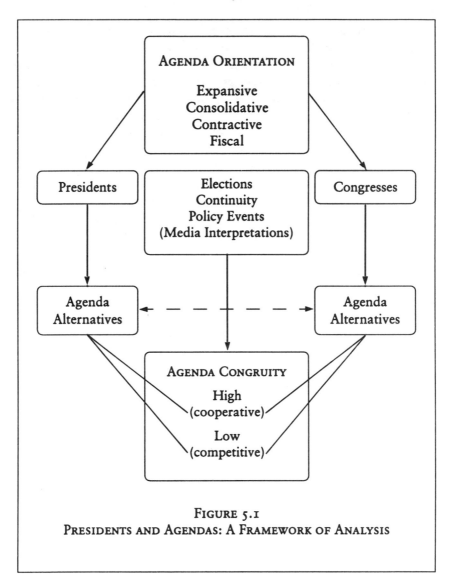

FIGURE 5.1
PRESIDENTS AND AGENDAS: A FRAMEWORK OF ANALYSIS

substantial presidential influence in proposing policy alternatives; where congruity is low, the president is forced to compete with many other sources of policy alternatives. We never expect congruity between the White House and Congress to be 1.0. But we do expect it to vary between and within presidential administrations, as is illustrated in the following pages.

Figure 5.1 (page 80) displays these concepts in schematic form. The agenda orientation within which issues are shaped forms the core. Agenda alternatives are offered by the president and members of Congress under varying conditions of agenda congruity. Congruity is assumed to be influenced by elections, leadership and membership continuity, and events—often with the media as issue or agenda carriers and interpreters. I turn next to consider the five successions from Kennedy to Reagan, concentrating on the transition and first year of each administration, presumably the time of greatest impact on the agenda for a president.

Six Administrations, Five Successions — Kennedy to Reagan

The years from 1961 to 1989 are particularly interesting for this inquiry because of the frequent changes in administration, as well as the astonishing variation in political conditions represented by the various changes. Table 5.1 (page 82) shows presidential succession and party changes in this century, then identifies the number of presidential and party changes in twenty-six-year segments. The two most recent periods register the highest number of presidential and party changes. These latter two periods also show an unprecedented sequence of landslide and marginal election victories starting in 1956 (landslides in 1956, 1964, 1972, 1980; narrow margins in 1960, 1968, 1976). As is discussed in the following pages, the landslide has special implications for presidential control of the agenda.

I turn then to consider each presidential transition, beginning with Kennedy to Johnson in 1963. In each case I review the carryover agenda as suggested by items considered but not resolved in Congress at the time of the succession; the continuity, or lack thereof, of membership and leadership; and the extent to which the carryover agenda is likely to be reinforced by events (including the election).

KENNEDY TO JOHNSON

In his careful analysis in *Politics and Policy* (1968) during the 1953 to 1966 period, James L. Sundquist recounts the emergence of a Democratic Party program to cope with domestic policy problems. He shows how it was that activist Democrats in Congress identified these problems and introduced remedial legislation. Lyndon B. Johnson, then Senate majority leader, is described as the classic "middleman" leader—a facilitator of coalition building once policy direction was clear.

TABLE 5.1
PRESIDENTIAL SUCCESSION IN THE TWENTIETH CENTURY

Presidents	Year of change	Party change
McKinley to Roosevelt	1901	R → R
Roosevelt to Taft	1909	R → R
Taft to Wilson	1913	R → D*
Wilson to Harding	1921	D → R*
Harding to Coolidge	1923	R → R
Coolidge to Hoover	1929	R → R
Hoover to Roosevelt	1933	R → D*
Roosevelt to Truman	1945	D → D
Truman to Eisenhower	1953	D → R*
Eisenhower to Kennedy	1961	R → D*
Kennedy to Johnson	1963	D → D
Johnson to Nixon	1969	D → R*
Nixon to Ford	1974	R → R
Ford to Carter	1977	R → D*
Carter to Reagan	1981	D → R*
Reagan to Bush	1989	R → R

Changes in twenty-six-year periods

	Presidential changes	Party changes
1901–27	5	2
1909–35	6	3
1913–39	5	3
1921–47	5	2
1923–49	4	1
1929–55	4	2
1933–59	3	2
1945–71	5	3
1953–79	6	4
1961–87	6	4
1963–89	6	3

* Indicates change in party control.

The senator who held the title of Democratic leader was in many respects a follower. Others made the program and initially mobilized the support; the leader joined the movement only after it was well underway. But this may be in the nature of legislative leadership in the party that does not hold the White House. Power comes only from those who are led; the party leader must stand somewhere near the middle of the party spectrum in his legislative body if he is both to gain and hold power and to use that power effectively.[7]

Sundquist then outlines the development of New Deal–like proposals thwarted by a Republican president during the 1950s that came to be the basis of the Democratic Party platform in 1960. The 1960 election results were rather ambiguous, however. Sundquist believes that the election "was a clear endorsement of an approach to domestic problems, of a governing temper—and tempo," but he also noted that

> the voters' mandate to the Democratic Party in 1960 was not one that could be promptly and smoothly executed. The election had been one of the closest in American history. What Kennedy had gained on the domestic issues he had all but lost on the other factors that influenced the voting—on his Catholicism surely, and probably on issues of foreign policy as well. In the House of Representatives the Democratic Party actually had won twenty-one fewer seats than it had carried two years earlier.[8]

> [The] election did not resolve the partisan conflict between the executive and legislative branches that had wracked the Eisenhower administration in its last two years.... The voters were hardly more decisive in 1962 than they had been two years earlier.[9]

A review of the congressional agenda at the time of President Kennedy's assassination confirms Sundquist's analysis. Much of the Democratic Party's program remained bottled up in Congress. The end-of-session review by the *Congressional Quarterly* identified these items as pending: a tax cut, civil rights, medical care for the aged, general school aid, domestic peace corps, an interest-equalization tax, area-redevelopment increase, mass transit aid, youth employment, civil defense shelters, a wilderness system, minimum wage increase, a land-conservation fund. All but one of these issues was acted on during the next two years. Two major events carried the agenda forward: the assassination and the landslide election of Lyndon B. Johnson in 1964 (together with the overwhelming Democratic majorities in the House and Senate).

A review of congressional election results and leadership continuity during the critical first two years of the Johnson administration (1964–65) shows unusual reinforcement for the president in getting action on the agenda. Table 5.2 shows the percentage of House and Senate incumbents who sought reelection for each party and the percentage of those who won. The figures demonstrate the remarkable return rates for Democrats–a high percentage seeking and gaining reelection. Meanwhile, of course, Republican incumbents were devastated by voters–only 71 percent were returned in the House, 63 percent in the Senate.

TABLE 5.2
INCUMBENT RETURN, 1964

	House		*Senate*	
	Democrats	*Republicans*	*Democrats*	*Republicans*
Percent seeking reelection	89	95	96	89
Percent reelected	98	71	92	63
Percent returning	87	67	88	56

Leadership continuity in both party and committee positions was very high during 1964–65. House and Senate party leaders remained the same during the period with the exception of the substitution of Russell Long (D-La.) as whip when Hubert H. Humphrey (D-Minn.) was chosen by Johnson to be his running mate in 1964. The changes in important committee chairmanships were either neutral in their effect or supportive of the president. Senator Harry Flood Byrd (D-Va.) retired and Russell Long took over as chairman of the Committee on Finance. In the House, Clarence Cannon (D-Mo.) died in 1964 and was succeeded as chairman of the Committee on Appropriations by Johnson's fellow Texan, George Mahon, and Carl Vinson (D-Ga.) retired and was succeeded by Mendel Rivers (D-S.C.).

The conclusion is this: The bulk of the evidence points to the fact that an agenda was already in place in 1964 when Lyndon Johnson gave it a name. Johnson helped facilitate the development of the agenda during the 1950s as Senate majority leader but was by no means its creator. The assassination of Kennedy, the landslide election of 1964, and the continuity of congressional leadership contributed to a high degree of agenda continuity and thus support for programmatic alternatives offered by the Kennedy-Johnson administrations. In fact, it is likely that these events encouraged greater acquiescence to these alternatives than could have been expected had Kennedy completed his term. I have more to say about this matter of a "program beyond mandate" when I discuss the Reagan administration. Suffice it for now to point out that President Johnson knew precisely how to take advantage of the coincidence of favorable conditions for getting Congress to act.

JOHNSON TO NIXON

Not surprisingly, the record-setting legislative actions of the Johnson administration left little on the agenda for a subsequent administration. Even had Hubert Humphrey, the quintessential Democratic liberal, won the 1968 election, he would have found it difficult to repeat Johnson's performance. Quite simply the agenda orientation shifted in the direction of consolidative and regulatory matters. The *Congressional Quarterly* review of Congress in 1968 observed that

> Congress was in a conservative mood in 1968, preoccupied chiefly with inflation and crime and disorders in the street and on the campus. It was divided on how to respond to rioting and the multiple problems of the cities which riots had highlighted—unemployment, poor education and inadequate housing—and the underlying racial issues.[10]

Many of those issues left unresolved by Congress in 1968 carried over to the new year, but virtually none of them was acted on in 1969 either. Paul Light shows that only 12 percent of President Nixon's requests, which were few, were made during the first three months in 1969. Light explains that

> Nixon's postelection planning was somewhat haphazard. Though he appointed a number of postelection task forces, he was not particularly interested in the findings. Nixon preferred to concentrate his energies on foreign policy. The problem was partly the complexity of the domestic issues ... and partly the absence of an interested hand in the Oval Office....

Nixon's first hundred days may also have reflected a deliberate decision to slow down the domestic process. That is the opinion of several former aides.[11]

The Nixon administration has been referred to as an "administrative presidency,"[12] in part because of the president's suspicion that civil servants were unlikely to be loyal to him. One might have expected an emphasis on administration and consolidation following the extraordinary policy achievements of the Johnson administration, even had a president been elected who was less seemingly paranoid. In fact, Erwin C. Hargrove and Michael Nelson classify Nixon as a "president of consolidation" and argue that such a style was suited to the agenda of the time.

> Presidents of consolidation seldom are elected on the basis of positive policy proposals. They can, however, play a constructive role in rationalizing and legitimizing the programs of achievement presidents. Nixon and a number of his appointees brought a managerial style to government. They did not formally reject the purpose of the Great Society—an ambivalent public could not be said to be any more squarely against these programs than for them, and program beneficiaries and administrators had come to constitute a powerful lobby in Congress on their behalf. But the Nixon administration did search for ways to change the way programs worked.[13]

If it is correct that the consolidative agenda dominated congressional action even before the election of Richard Nixon, then the data in table 5.3 are particularly relevant for carrying that agenda forward into the new year. On the House side, a very high proportion of incumbents sought reelection (94 percent for each party), and the percentage of incumbents winning reelection was the highest in

TABLE 5.3
INCUMBENT RETURN, 1968

	House		Senate	
	Democrats	Republicans	Democrats	Republicans
Percent seeking reelection	94	94	87	73
Percent reelected	96	98	65	100
Percent returning	90	93	57	73

the post–World War II period. Only 13 incumbents of the 409 running were defeated (4 of these lost in primaries). A record-setting 91 percent of the total House returned in 1969. The situation was a bit different in the Senate, where the Republicans had a net gain of six seats. The effect was to draw Senate Republicans somewhat closer to the Democrats after the devastating results in 1964.

Leadership continuity in the House was also extraordinarily high between the 90th and 91st Congresses. There were no changes in party leadership (Gerald Ford of Michigan had taken over from Charles Halleck of Indiana as minority floor leader in 1965). Committee leadership changes were limited to one minor chairmanship and two minor ranking minority positions. On the Senate side, there were changes in both party and committee leadership. Edward Kennedy (Massachusetts) defeated Russell Long (Louisiana) for Democratic Party whip. Hugh Scott (Pennsylvania) succeeded Thomas Kuchel (California) as Republican whip, then succeeded Everett Dirksen (Illinois) as minority leader when Dirksen died on 7 September 1969. Robert Griffin (Michigan) was the new Republican Party whip. Scott was not a particularly happy choice for Nixon. John Ehrlichman may well have spoken for Nixon when he said about Scott:

> He could explain at length the reasons he could not get his colleagues in the Senate to support the president's legislation. I saw more of this hack than I wanted to.[14]

Ehrlichman was more generous in his assessment of Ford, whom he described as working hard "to win the loyalty of his Congressional troops."[15]

Surely conditions associated with the transition from Johnson to Nixon supported a less active president. One would expect a pause in the expansive agenda setting of the late Eisenhower and early Kennedy years. Thus, Nixon as president is fitted into a policy context well suited to his predisposition. This is not to say that any president would be as basically suspicious, even antithetical, to the rest of government as Nixon showed himself to be. Instead, it is to emphasize the nature of the domestic agenda constraints operating at the time and to observe that they suited the incumbent.

Nixon to Ford

In truly classic understatement, Gerald R. Ford points out in his autobiography that he "took office with a set of unique disadvantages."

Most vice presidents who become president have buried their predecessors and then gone on to reassure the people by wrapping
themselves in the mantle of the men they followed. ("Let us continue," LBJ said after Kennedy's death.) At the time of *his* departure, *Nixon had no mantle left.* Then, too, I had been a congressman for a long time. The White House press corps doesn't take
members of Congress very seriously. To many of those reporters,
my vice presidency had seemed disorganized, so they harbored a
natural skepticism about my talents and skills. Finally, I had no
mandate from the people, and the Congress understood that.[16]

Surely President Ford is correct in the weaknesses he identifies. His
subsequent list of advantages was very brief, primarily emphasizing
his penchant for openness in governing.

Hargrove and Nelson identify Ford's administration as "a presidency of status."[17] For present purposes, it is unquestionably true
that President Ford was in no position to propose a new agenda. He
was very weak by all of the standard Neustadtian measures of presidential power. His one principal source of power was that derived
from comparing his political ethics with those of Nixon, and this advantage was compromised when he pardoned Nixon. Meanwhile,
congressional Democrats had become considerably more assertive
during the Nixon years, even to the point of proposing large-scale
energy and economic programs.

A review of presidential-congressional interaction on domestic
issues in 1974 and 1975 shows an agenda driven primarily by energy
and economic events. A breakdown in presidential leadership because of Watergate and Nixon's resignation led to much greater congressional involvement in agenda setting and program formulation.
The *Congressional Quarterly* annual review concluded in 1974:

> With the Nixon Administration engrossed in Watergate and the
> Ford Administration beset by faltering leadership, Congress oper-
> ated with an unusually free hand in 1974. In many cases it oper-
> ated effectively....
>
> What Congress failed to do demonstrated some of the weak-
> nesses in congressional government.[18]

Congressional government could not produce large-scale, coor-
dinated energy, economic, and tax-reform packages. But it was not
for lack of trying. Congressional Democrats offered alternatives to
presidential initiatives in each of these areas. An effort was also

made by Democrats to enact a national health plan—the one large social welfare benefit remaining from the Great Society agenda. The limited control exercised by President Ford is illustrated by the fact that he was forced to rely heavily on the veto to thwart congressional initiatives not acceptable to him.

Table 5.4 displays the familiar evidence of the 1974 election. As in 1968, a high percentage of House Democrats sought reelection, and they had a 96 percent reelection rate. The proportion of Senate Democrats returning was smaller but quite high compared to 1968, 1976, and 1980. Thus, congressional Democrats were encouraged to continue their agenda-forcing actions. Meanwhile, many House Republicans decided not to seek reelection, and the election results suggest their decision was wise. The return rate of incumbents seeking reelection was higher than in 1964, but with the greater number of retirements in 1974 the overall House Republican incumbent return rate was the same. A relatively large number of Senate Republicans also retired; thus the overall Senate Republican incumbent return rate was just 57 percent.

TABLE 5.4
INCUMBENT RETURN, 1974

	House		*Senate*	
	Democrats	*Republicans*	*Democrats*	*Republicans*
Percent seeking reelection	93	87	85	71
Percent reelected	96	77	88	80
Percent returning	89	67	75	57

Party leadership continuity was high between 1974 and 1975. There were no changes in the Senate and two shifts in the House. Thomas ("Tip") O'Neill won the majority leadership post to fill the vacancy caused by the death of Hale Boggs, and John McFall (D-Calif.) was appointed to the Democratic whip position.

By contrast, the combination of Republican losses and Democratic Party reforms (primarily in the House) resulted in much higher than usual turnover in committee leadership. In the House, there were chairmanship changes in six major and three minor committees. In addition, a Budget Committee came into existence as a result of the Budget and Impoundment Control Act of 1974. In three instances, House Democrats even defied the seniority principle in selecting chairmen for important committees. Defeats and retirements on the Republican side resulted in an equal number of changes in ranking minority positions on committees—five for major committees, four for minor committees. There were also important changes on the Senate side, primarily the result of retirements (new Democratic chairmen for three important committees, new ranking Republicans for four important committees). A new Senate Budget Committee was also put in place.

In summary, conditions severely limited President Ford's agenda-setting capabilities as well as his control of alternatives. The combination of political and policy circumstances encouraged congressional Democrats to participate actively in the full range of policy functions. They were even moved to propose broad-scale consolidative and regulatory programs to cope with energy and economic issues. The president was frequently in a reactive position, relying on the veto and other defensive maneuvers to thwart Democratic initiatives.

FORD TO CARTER

Elsewhere I have identified the Carter administration as a "trusteeship presidency."[19] As a Democrat and the first elected president following Watergate, Jimmy Carter was bound to interpret his mandate as that of improving politics in Washington. It so happened that the mood of the times suited his own predispositions and personal experience. Thus he interpreted his victory as having entrusted him "to do the right thing" while in the White House. As regards agenda setting and program formulation, the trustee president is likely to exhibit considerable independence. After all, for such a president Congress is populated with delegate politicians primarily interested in reelection.

Regarding the agenda itself, the stalemate on many issues during the 94th Congress naturally produced a full policy slate for the 95th Congress. President Carter was criticized for overloading the congressional agenda in 1977. Yet it seems that there was a full agenda awaiting the new Congress *had there been no president elected at all in 1976!* Many energy and environmental issues required action—in some cases authorizations had expired for important programs. In addition, certain other major items were bound to carry over—a consumer protection agency, national health insurance, social security increases, criminal code revision, and food stamp revision. Further, legislation to stimulate a sluggish economy was guaranteed.

Thus the first point to make about President Carter and the agenda is that many issues were carried over from 1976 to 1977. Was the president able to manage the alternatives or to control policy development? Several points are relevant. First, it seemed clear that Carter understood the agenda shift that had taken place since the enactment of the Great Society programs. Even during the campaign he spoke frequently about the need for balancing the budget. In his acceptance speech at the Democratic National Convention, he struck a number of consolidative themes: "It is time for the people to run the government, and not the other way around." "As president, I want you to help me evolve an efficient, economical, purposeful and manageable government for our nation." "We Democrats believe that competition is better than regulation." Following his first State of the Union message, it was reported that "frequently ... applause was led by the Republicans in the House chamber, who obviously found much in the speech that could be applauded."[20] Thus it was unsurprising that many congressional Democrats countered with alternatives to proposals offered by the president.

Second, the president's own negative attitudes toward legislators did not invite either loyalty or acquiescence. And as a third, related point, Congress had just enacted more reform than in any time in its history. Congressional Democrats had grown used to opposing the president during the Nixon and Ford administrations. And they had expanded the policy-analysis capabilities of Congress by a quantum amount. Leading such a group would have been difficult for a skilled legislative politician like Lyndon Johnson; it was a supreme challenge for Jimmy Carter. But he was unlikely to want to meet the challenge anyway. As a trustee president, he wished to preserve distance between himself and congressional Democrats. It is not apparent that Jimmy Carter had substantial control of either the agenda or programmatic alternatives.

What of membership and leadership continuity between 1976 and 1977? As shown in table 5.5 (page 92), House incumbents in both parties were returned at a very high rate. Only sixteen incumbents were defeated in 1976, three in primaries, thirteen in the general election. On the other hand, a record number (to that date) of incumbents decided not to seek reelection. Thus the overall return rate was not as high as 1968. Remarkably, a very high percentage of the 1974 Watergate Democrats were returned—seventy-six of the seventy-eight who sought reelection won.

The situation in the Senate was very different. The 1976 election was the first of three that ousted a high percentage of incumbents.

TABLE 5.5
INCUMBENT RETURN, 1976

	House		Senate	
	Democrats	Republicans	Democrats	Republicans
Percent seeking reelection	87	90	82	64
Percent reelected	96	95	72	43
Percent returning	84	85	59	27

The number of retirements was higher than usual, and many incumbents were defeated. The overall return rate (counting both retirements and defeats) for the Democrats was 59 percent, for Republicans it was 27 percent (just three of eleven senators returned).

Leadership change in 1977 was extraordinary. Speaker Carl Albert (D-Okla.), Senator Majority Leader Mike Mansfield (D-Mont.), and Senate Minority Leader Hugh Scott (R-Pa.) all stepped down. Thus, three of the four leadership teams in Congress were changed. Neither of the changes on the Democratic side were likely to improve Carter's chances of developing an easy working partnership with Congress. The new speaker, Thomas P. O'Neill of Massachusetts, was an old-line partisan urban Democrat from the Kennedy wing of the party. The new Senate majority leader, Robert F. Byrd of West Virginia, was a strong institutionalist, very likely to resent Carter's attitude and approach toward Congress.

The changes in committee leadership were minimal. Only two House committee chairmen stepped down and only one Senate committee changed its chairman; however, the Senate did make other important changes in its committees. The Stevenson Committee reforms were put into effect in 1977. Several minor committees were abolished, and other committees experienced jurisdictional shifts. None of these changes could be said to have had a major affect on agenda setting. They were designed primarily to streamline procedures and to reduce the number of committee assignments for senators.

The Carter administration is one of the most interesting for any study of presidents and agendas. It demonstrates the continuity of the consolidative agenda orientation. We can never know, of course, what might have happened with another president. And it is conceded that various personal and political circumstances led Carter to a style that was unattractive to congressional Democrats. Still there appeared to be considerable continuity of consolidative issues between the Nixon-Ford and Carter administrations—surely enough to question the extent to which President Carter set the agenda. Further, like Ford, Carter was unable fully to manage the alternatives. Agenda congruity was low even with a Democratic president and Congress. Whatever was sent to the Hill by the Carter White House often had to compete with proposals prepared by others.

CARTER TO REAGAN

To this point I have examined the last year of the previous administration as partial evidence for the carryover of issues. In 1980 there was no question that the state of the economy and budget growth were major domestic issues. Leadership was also an important topic in the 1980 presidential campaign, but leadership is not an agenda item—it is the means by which the agenda is specified and acted on. In his end-of-session review, Irwin B. Arieff of the *Congressional Quarterly* concluded that

> the 96th Congress spent the first half of 1980 confronting economic issues and the second half of the year avoiding them.
> It was not a fruitful combination.
> Congress found little it could do to combat the nation's fiscal woes....
> A recession combined with spiraling inflation soon dashed the Democrats' balanced-budget hopes. But these new economic woes also did nothing to encourage the Democrats to resume pushing for some of their favorite programs. In addition, because of escalating campaign pressures, Democratic leaders delayed until after the election consideration of the budget and a number of other key bills.[21]

What Arieff's review suggests is that an agenda of economic and budgetary issues was already in place for the new president. That really is the point of this reading. An agenda was set—the question then was the extent to which the president acknowledged this agenda and was successful in managing the alternatives. Elsewhere I have argued that electoral and policy conditions "locked Congress into the consolidative agenda ... new social programs were no longer entertained or even proposed."[22] Congressional Democrats did not expect to have their way with Reagan. Thus, ironically, there was not the same disappointment that had characterized their relations with Carter. Indeed, it seemed apparent that many congressional Democrats were more content with presidential-congressional relations in 1981 in spite of the fact that Reagan was the most conservative president elected since the 1920s.

Further, not since the 1964 elections had political conditions so favored the attentiveness to and enactment of a president's program. Just as Johnson was able to formulate the Kennedy program of expansive government into a legislative whole with the Great Society, so too was Reagan able to fashion the consolidative, even contractive, elements of the Nixon, Ford, and Carter efforts into a legislative package. And one might argue that in both cases, the election results were "overinterpreted," as Adam Clymer put it in reviewing the 1980 election.[23] But that is an important matter to be treated separately in the following pages.

Table 5.6 shows why it is that one might be led to overinterpret the results. Reagan's overwhelming victory over an incumbent Democratic president—the first for a Republican since Benjamin Harrison defeated Grover Cleveland in 1888—was complemented by stunning victories for Republicans in the Senate and the House. A high percentage of House Republican incumbents sought reelection, and 97 percent of those members were reelected (only five were defeated). The thirty-three-seat increase for House Republicans was the greatest in a presidential election since 1920. But it was in the Senate that the Republicans really made an impression on the national Democratic Party. Less than half of the incumbent Democrats were reelected, and the overall return rate (counting defeats and retirements) was just 38 percent. The gain of twelve Senate Republicans was the third greatest since the founding of the party.

TABLE 5.6
INCUMBENT RETURN, 1980

	House		Senate	
	Democrats	*Republicans*	*Democrats*	*Republicans*
Percent seeking reelection	91	92	92	70
Percent reelected	87	97	46	100
Percent returning	80	89	38	70

It was not surprising, then, that the media and the members themselves interpreted the results as possibly presaging a realignment. It is true, of course, that the dramatic nature of the results invited misinterpretations. More sober academic analysts pointed out that

Reagan's election represented a strong call for moderate change. Far from signaling a sharp departure in voter preferences, it built upon two key developments of the preceding decade: (1) electoral dealignment, the weakening of party loyalties, and the diminishment of public confidence in traditional partisan answers; and (2) growing public ambivalence on many major policy questions, especially on the role of government itself. While these developments did not augur a "new Republican majority," their extension and elaboration in the 1980 balloting further weakened the New Deal Democratic coalition and ended its status as a reliable national majority.[24]

It was even true that the Senate Democrats slightly outpolled the Senate Republicans in 1980—many Republicans won by very narrow margins (sixteen by 55 percent or less, eleven by 52 percent or less).

As it happens, scholarly analysis, however sound, is typically received too late and with too little volume to have a major impact on the immediate interpretations by journalists and politicians. The prevailing view was that Ronald Reagan had scored a dramatic triumph and that his proposals for solving the major economic and budget problems should therefore be enacted into law. Even House Speaker O'Neill conceded in regard to the proposed tax cut: "We will ultimately send a bill to the president that he will be satisfied with."[25] The first session of the 97th Congress confirmed the consolidative-contractive agenda and included decisions that would lock it firmly into place for the remainder of the Reagan administration.

The many changes in party and committee leadership in the House and Senate tended to reinforce President Reagan's control of policy alternatives for economic and budget issues. In the House a somewhat more aggressive Republican floor leader, Robert Michel of Illinois, replaced the retiring John Rhodes of Arizona. Two very effective members took over as party whips for their respective parties—Thomas Foley of Washington for the Democrats, Trent Lott of Mississippi for the Republicans. There were no changes in Senate party leadership, but the two teams changed sides and that was of major importance for enacting the Reagan program. For the first time since 1953 and only the second time since 1933, a Republican president could rely on a majority party in the Senate for forming legislative strategies. And he was likely to find favor among those in this majority since he ran ahead of thirty of the thirty-four Republican Senate candidates in 1980 (counting the two-party vote only).[26]

On the House side, a combination of retirements and defeats resulted in an unusually high turnover of committee chairmanships. Five major committees changed hands: Agriculture; Banking, Finance, and Urban Affairs; Budget; Energy and Commerce; and Ways and Means. Seven other committees also got new chairmen in 1981—an overall turnover rate of 55 percent. There were, as well, a number of changes among ranking minority members—turnover on seven committees in all.

Of course, the more important changes occurred in the Senate, again resulting from the Republicans winning a majority. Republicans would chair all standing committees and subcommittees and the long-suffering minority staff would now serve in the majority. There were eight shifts in Republican committee leadership positions because of retirements. Of these, only that of Mark Hatfield of Oregon taking over for Milton Young of North Dakota on the Appropriations Committee was likely to cause problems for Reagan.

As in 1964, the 1980 election results confirmed an existing agenda orientation—the 1964 election encouraged expansion of government; the 1980 election favored further consolidation and even contraction. In each case, the magnitude of the president's victory was enhanced by strong showings of the president's party in Congress, leading to high agenda congruity. As a result, Reagan, like Johnson, was in an excellent position to control alternatives and thus manage program formulation and legitimation. It is equally true, however, that neither Johnson nor Reagan was able to sustain this control throughout his presidency.

The President's Role in Agenda Setting

Several observations can be made as a result of this brief review of recent presidential administrations.

1. Both logic and the facts seem to support the view that new presidents must cope with an existing agenda. Their role as agenda setters should be evaluated within the context of a rather impressive list of items carried over from the previous administration. Further, this agenda can be identified with a particular orientation that reflects the issues of the time.

2. Presidents vary considerably in the extent to which they are able or permitted to manage the policy process when they first take office—a difference in agenda congruity as identified here. Some are perceived as deserving to be in charge; others

are constrained by the initiative, even pretentiousness, of members of Congress.

3. Those presidents with high agenda congruity will experience extraordinary legislative success. Further, under these circumstances one may expect a reorientation of the agenda.

Each of these observations merits more detailed discussion.

The Continuing Agenda

The simple exercise of examining what remained on the congressional agenda prior to an incoming presidential administration establishes the nature of the agenda orientation within which presidents offer their programs and indicates the range of policy alternatives being considered at the time. It leads one to question the extent to which presidents are agenda setters. Further, it encourages analysis of the policy process as continuous, not segmented by presidential administrations.

Actually, much of what I have suggested is unsurprising if one stands back to consider the broader political and policy environment within which presidents do their jobs. If representative government is working at all well, then presidents and Congresses are likely to be attending to many of those issues that are on the so-called systemic agenda.[27] We can hardly expect to see the policy slate wiped clean at the end of each presidential administration. Further, presidential campaigns and elections tend to focus on current issues, which in turn are associated with the agenda orientation as defined earlier. Incoming presidents, then, are products of those debates and normally feel instructed by election results.

Another way to state the obvious is this: it truly would be surprising for a president to enter office and try to establish an agenda orientation out of sync with that of recent policymaking and the just-concluded campaign and election. Thus, at the least our judgment that the president controls the agenda must be modified to account for the constraint of existing issues.

Variation among Presidents

Saying that the president is constrained by what has gone on before is not to suggest that all presidents are alike in their agenda-setting roles. It is, I trust, evident from the review of six administrations that political and policy conditions vary considerably from one administration to the next. Two differences are particularly striking (and relevant for present purposes):

1. Administrations differ in the extent to which the agenda orientation is confirmed and supported by events. The election, of course, is the most visible such event. Of the set included here, the 1964 and 1980 elections provided strong endorsements for the agenda orientation; the 1968, 1974, and 1976 elections provided weak or mixed endorsements. Where the message is strong, one may expect a high degree of agenda congruity. Other events at the point of presidential succession may also have an impact on the agenda. The assassination of Kennedy enhanced the expansive agenda for Johnson; Watergate and the eventual resignation of Nixon had an adverse impact on Ford's management of the consolidative, post–Great Society agenda.

2. As a part of the preceding effects, presidents also vary in the extent to which they can control policy alternatives. Presidents are in an excellent position to dominate program formulation when the election or other events can be interpreted as supporting their views. That is not to say others in Congress and elsewhere are excluded from developing counter proposals. Instead, it is to stress that the president's alternatives will form the central core of the debate. Presidents elected by landslides will be perceived as being in charge, as deserving a chance to do it their way. Other presidents, of course, have no such advantage. Their proposals are competitive with those from other sources.

The five succeeding presidents in the set of six administrations can therefore be classified into two groups. Johnson and Reagan were favored by strong endorsements of the agenda orientation, dominant control of the policy alternatives, and a high degree of agenda congruity. Nixon, Ford, and Carter were much less favored. Each had to compete with alternative interpretations of the agenda orientation. Even when there was apparent agreement on a consolidative agenda, the president's policy alternatives were met with counterproposals because of the low degree of agenda congruity. Members of Congress may have agreed that it was time to make government work better, not more, and yet disagreed with the president's proposals for reaching that goal.

It should be noted in passing that presidents in each of the two groups differ in various ways that are relevant to this discussion. Thus, for example, Johnson and Reagan differ in the extent to which viable policy alternatives were available when they took office. Johnson was in a position to enact much of the Kennedy program. Reagan, on the other hand, had to supply new proposals. He was unlikely to turn to those proposals Carter had devised (though some proposals were carried forward from the Nixon and Ford administrations). Then, too, the limited agenda congruity and competing policy alternatives during the Nixon and Ford administrations can be explained in partisan terms—Democratic majorities in Congress facing Republican presidents. For Carter, however, the conflict was somewhat more complicated. Large Democratic majorities were returned to Congress but Carter himself won narrowly. Further, the president's incompatibility with Congress seemingly suited his political beliefs and style.

Also, presidents cannot expect to dominate agenda alternatives through their entire administrations. What Kingdon reports as a typical limitation for a president eventually restricts the presidents of achievement—the president "is unable to dominate [the key word] the alternatives that are seriously considered and is unable to determine the final outcome."[28] Paul Light also prepares us to accept the fact that even presidents who get their way early in an administration must face stiff competition later on.[29] This point is confirmed by Jon R. Bond and Richard Fleisher in their measures of actual and predicted presidential success. They base their analysis on measures of potential advantages that a president has in working with Congress—the partisan balance, level of public approval of the president, and time in office. Bond and Fleisher have identified measures associated with agenda congruity. In the case of Johnson they find that he did better than expected in the first year only. For present purposes we may interpret these findings as supporting the amplification of the policy message from the two elections.[30]

PRESIDENTS AND HIGH AGENDA CONGRUITY

The Johnson and Reagan presidencies deserve special attention given their importance to agenda setting. First note that congruity in presidential and congressional election results tends to amplify the policy message of the campaign. Those interpreting the results—other elected policymakers and the media—tend to overstate the mandate. A landslide may well represent voters' preferences as to who should run the government, but often, it seems, landslides do not reflect deeply felt support for specific policy alternatives.

In both 1964 and 1980, the president and his party in Congress did remarkably well. Subsequent analysis cast doubt on the extent to which voters were sending policy messages, yet the mood at the time was in favor of granting each president the right to enact his pro-gram. Contrast these outcomes with the victory for Nixon in 1972. Though he won overwhelmingly, congressional Republicans made only modest gains. The election was widely interpreted as a personal triumph of an incumbent president over a weak challenger from a di-vided party. Though the president himself interpreted the result as conveying a mandate (as well as vindication), the pundits in the me-dia and elsewhere did not.

Second, the 1964 and 1980 elections appear to satisfy many of the conditions associated with *ambitious decision making,* leading to *speculative augmentation.* In elaborating on Lindblom's four quad-rants of decision making, I identified the following: integrative deci-sion making (large change, high estimate of capacities), administra-tive or technical decision making (small change, high estimate of capacities), incremental decision making (small change, low estimate of capacities), and ambitious decision making (large change, low esti-mate of capacities).[31] Many of the achievements of the Johnson and Reagan administrations during the first few months fit into this fourth quadrant. Grand intentions were facilitated by an opportunity to act, even while acknowledging that the consequences of these ac-tions were not known and that policy analytical capacities remained weak. Thus the analytical method associated with this quadrant is that of "speculative augmentation," as contrasted to the "disjoint incrementalism" of the third quadrant.

Third, the policy breakthroughs resulting from speculative aug-mentation will have an impact on the subsequent agenda orientation. A sizable semi-coordinated program is put into place—one with sig-nificant effects on the agenda. Future presidents will have to respond to the new context—to the Great Society of Lyndon Johnson, to the Great Deficit of Ronald Reagan. In these two cases, we observe an agenda shift from expansiveness to consolidation, then from consoli-dation to contraction. Thus, for Nixon, Ford, and Carter (or other presidents who might have served during this period), further gov-ernment expansion in social welfare was unlikely; the challenge was to make government work more effectively.

For President Bush, the challenge was *fiscal* in nature (i.e., to provide more resources). The efforts to shrink government had been only marginally successful despite the stimulus to act created by enormous deficits. Therefore, one was justified in concluding that the Reagan era had revealed the political limits for reducing government. Not all remaining programs were essential or efficiently managed, but the president and Congress working together and in competition could not make further substantial cuts that would be politically acceptable. Having thus identified irreducible government programs or functions, we might then expect a fiscal agenda orientation so as to pay the bills. In this connection, it is particularly interesting that a tax-reform package was enacted in 1986. It may be viewed as facilitating the fiscal agenda, since it is easier to reform a reform than to make significant changes in an existing tax code.

Conclusions

I offer the following recapitulation of the principal points emphasized in this chapter:

1. Greater precision is needed in the study of presidents and agendas. The concepts of agenda orientation, alternatives, and congruity are seen as contributing to that end.
2. The president's role in agenda setting is influenced by the agenda orientation of the time and further shaped by the electoral or other events associated with succession.
3. Presidents differ in the extent to which they are able to control policy alternatives.
4. Landslide elections with seemingly congruent presidential and congressional outcomes tend to be interpreted as carrying strong policy messages, thus enhancing presidential control of policy alternatives.
5. Control of policy alternatives and agenda congruity can contribute to ambitious decision making through speculative augmentation, which can in turn alter the agenda orientation for future presidents.
6. A progression of agenda orientations is observed for the period studied—from expansive to consolidative to contractive, possibly to fiscal.

NOTES

1. Richard E. Neustadt, *Presidential Power: The Politics of Leadership* (New York: Wiley, 1960), 6–7.
2. John W. Kingdon, *Agendas, Alternatives, and Public Policies* (Boston: Little, Brown, 1984), 25.
3. Paul C. Light, *The President's Agenda: Domestic Policy Choice from Kennedy to Carter* (Baltimore: Johns Hopkins University Press, 1982), 233.

4. See Roger Cobb and Charles Elder, *Participation in American Politics: The Dynamics of Agenda-Building* (Boston: Allyn and Bacon, 1972).

5. Kingdon, *Agendas, Alternatives,* 4.

6. Ibid.

7. James Sundquist, *Politics and Policy: The Eisenhower, Kennedy, and Johnson Years* (Washington, D.C.: Brookings Institution, 1968), 402.

8. Ibid., 471.

9. Ibid., 480.

10. "Congress 1968—The Year in Review," *Congressional Quarterly Weekly Review,* 18 October 1968, 2813.

11. Light, *The President's Agenda,* 47.

12. Richard P. Nathan, *The Plot That Failed: Nixon and the Administrative Presidency* (New York: Wiley, 1975).

13. Erwin C. Hargrove and Michael Nelson, *Presidents, Politics, and Policy* (New York: Knopf, 1984), 74.

14. John Ehrlichman, *Witness to Power: The Nixon Years* (New York: Simon and Schuster, 1982), 198.

15. Ibid.

16. Gerald R. Ford, *A Time to Heal* (New York: Harper & Row, 1979), 125–26. Second emphasis mine.

17. Hargrove and Nelson, *Presidents, Politics,* 75.

18. "Congress Strives to Fill Leadership Vacuum," *Congressional Quarterly Weekly Report,* 28 December 1974, 3415–16.

19. Charles O. Jones, *The Trusteeship Presidency: Jimmy Carter and the U.S. Congress* (Baton Rouge: Louisiana State University Press, 1988).

20. Barry M. Hager, "Carter's State of the Union," *Congressional Quarterly Weekly Report,* 21 January 1978, 100.

21. Irwin B. Arieff, "Congress in 1980: Big Turnover, Little Action," *Congressional Quarterly Weekly Report,* 6 December 1980, 3491.

22. Lester Salamon and Michael Lund, eds., *The Reagan Presidency and the Governing of America* (Washington, D.C.: Urban Institute, 1985), 285.

23. Ibid., 222.

24. Ibid.

25. Gail Gregg, "Reagan Proposes Dramatic Reduction in Federal Role," *Congressional Quarterly Weekly Report,* 14 March 1981, 445.

26. Salamon and Lund, *The Reagan Presidency,* 267.

27. Term used by Cobb and Elder, *Participation in American Politics.*

28. Kingdon, *Agendas, Alternatives,* 26.

29. Light, *The President's Agenda,* chap. 1.

30. Jon R. Bond and Richard Fleisher, *The President and the Legislative Arena* (Chicago: University of Chicago Press, 1990), chap. 9.

31. Charles O. Jones, *An Introduction to the Study of Public Policy,* 3d ed. (Pacific Grove, Calif.: Brooks/Cole, 1984), chap. 10.

Part II

Presidents Working with Congresses

6

The Pendulum of Power

In his classic work comparing forms of government, Woodrow Wilson stressed the absence of organic connections between the legislature and the executive in the United States. "In all other modern governments," he wrote,

> the heads of the administrative departments are given the right to sit in the legislative body and to take part in its proceedings. The legislature and executive are thus associated in such a way that the ministers of state can lead the houses without dictating to them, and the ministers themselves be controlled without being misunderstood—in such a way that the two parts of the government which should be most closely coordinated, the part, namely, by which the laws are made and the part by which the laws are executed, may be kept in close harmony and intimate cooperation, with the result of giving coherence to the action of the one and energy to the action of the other.[1]

The large majority of governments continue to foster executive-legislative relations by the constitutional connections referred to by Wilson. Not so the United States, which severed the executive from the legislature in its Constitution.

The principal purpose of this chapter is to explore recent developments in congressional-presidential relations. William J. Keefe concludes that "presidential-congressional relations . . . are often unpredictable, sometimes unfathomable, and always complex."[2] "It all depends" appears to be the principal generalization one is led to by an attempt at fathoming these institutional associations. But on what does it all depend? It is argued here that relations between Congress and the presidency depend substantially on how each judges the legitimacy and competency of the other.

This chapter is organized to treat the following questions: What appear to be the principal determinants of relations between the two branches? What difference does it make when each challenges the legitimacy or competency of the other? What happens when a Richard M. Nixon becomes president? What happens when a Jimmy Carter becomes president? Can we expect conditions to change? But before we examine these questions, it is useful to set the stage with a brief discussion of constitutional structures and contemporary events.

One President and Two Legislative Bodies in an Age of Disrespect

One cannot begin an analysis of the connections between Congress and presidents without acknowledging their context. First, the constitutional setting. The investment of executive power in a single, independently elected individual tends to focus public and media attention on that person as representing all government. There he is—a Franklin D. Roosevelt or Dwight D. Eisenhower or Lyndon B. Johnson or James Earl Carter. We study his intentions and goals, watch for his reactions to events, discuss his appointments, critically analyze his statements and initiatives. Students of the American system argue that our balance of powers among the three branches surely demands more balanced reporting than a Washington press corps preoccupied with the White House seems ready to provide. But let's face it, Congresses are known by the presidents they keep, not the leaders they select, the constituents they serve, or the reforms they enact.[3] Madison interpreted Article II as restraining the executive "within a narrower compass." In an active government, however, the presidency "being more simple in its nature"[4] was bound to receive a degree of public attention that, itself, guaranteed active participation by the president in decision making. As Keefe observes: "The president's advantages begin with the expectations that others have about his leadership role in the nation's political life."[5] At no time is this more obvious than when a crisis develops, as with the taking of hostages in Iran and the invasion of Afghanistan by the Soviet Union.

The two legislative bodies called Congress, separated from each other and from the executive, also must be comprehended as constitutional structures in this exercise. At the most basic level, Article I reminds us that presidential-congressional relations are not relations between one person (and his appointed aides) and one body of persons organized hierarchically. Instead, the president, acting through aides, must negotiate with a variable set of congressional actors through time, through legislative stages, across issues, and for two legislative bodies. To be sure, patterns emerge that provide continuity and stability to the connections. But the complexity of the relationship has often been dealt with by oversimplification.

Another basic contextual matter is that of the disruptive issues of the recent past. These issues have been described and analyzed in many works and do not require special review here. Our interest is in their effects on the political context of presidential-congressional contact. Among these effects are the following:

- ☐ A decline in trust and respect for governmental institutions and political leaders
- ☐ A demand for reform of governmental structures and political (including policy) processes
- ☐ A melding of what were formerly distinctive issue types—foreign and domestic; national, state, and local; the three "E's," energy, environment, economy; and so on
- ☐ A shift from the more expansive to the more consolidative programs—from new thrusts to more effective means to achieve existing goals

This brief review reminds us of the importance and difficulty of understanding Congress and the presidency. It also urges us to form a simple model that will aid in understanding.

What Determines Congressional-Presidential Relations?

Legitimacy and *competency* are two of the most important standards by which actors in each branch judge each other. Legitimacy refers to whether persons have the right to be involved in decision making. Judgments about this right may be based on such factors as an interpretation of proper constitutional authority, the means by which a person assumes an office, and personal conduct in the office. Competency refers to whether persons have the capabilities required to be effective in decision making. Judgments about competency may rely on such factors as experience, training, expertise, commitments, and availability of staff.

Judgments are made about whole institutions or about parts thereof. For example, the president and his aides may question the legitimacy of the House Committee on Rules without doubting the right of the House itself to act (as seemed to be the case during the Kennedy administration when the coalition of southern Democrats and Republicans on the Rules Committee threatened to kill important domestic legislation). Similarly, questions of legitimacy or competency may be raised about a particular action (such as the impoundment of funds in the Nixon administration) or about action within a particular issue area (such as a highly technical or sensitive foreign policy issue being dealt with by Congress)—without implying doubt about the legitimacy or competency of the presidency or Congress.

Many of the traditional determinants of congressional-presidential relations—constitutional prerogatives, political party, personality, electoral margins, media expectations—influence how congressional and presidential actors view one another. Accordingly, changes in these actors may alter interbranch evaluations. But the argument here simply is that the assessments themselves provide a useful entry point for explaining, perhaps even predicting, how the two branches get along.

If they react positively toward the other branch, members of Congress or the president and his aides will also have opinions about the policy activities proper for that branch. For example, assuming that a congressional committee chairman pictures the president and his aides as legitimately and competently involved in an issue area, he or she may have in mind specific activities that they can perform properly. Should the president engage in activities other than those deemed proper, the committee chairman may reevaluate the president's legitimacy or competency in dealing with the issue at hand. Members of one branch may be expected to have opinions about the legitimacy and competency of the other branch to perform each of the following policy activities:

- Agenda setting (including problem identification and definition)
- Program development (including planning, choice among alternatives, building support, funding)
- Program implementation (including interpretation and application)
- Program evaluation (including specification of goals, measurement, and recommendation for change)
- Program coordination (including comparative analysis)

To summarize, I have argued that it is useful for understanding relationships between the branches to explore how actors in Congress and the presidency view one another's legitimacy and competency to cope generally and to cope with specific issues. These estimates of institutional and individual capabilities are influenced by political and personal factors and, when positive, lead to judgments about the specific policy role to be played by each branch.

WHAT ABOUT NEGATIVE EVALUATIONS?

When a presidential-congressional partnership is successful, presidential and congressional actors respect one another's position, talent, and specialized capacities. Their partnership is defined and circumscribed by estimates of what each does well. This situation by no means eliminates conflict, but disagreements tend to focus on substance rather than process, structure, or constitutional position.

What happens when those in one branch challenge the legitimacy and competency of those in the other? Negative evaluations set the stage for the encroachments that so concerned Madison. *The really significant effect of one institution's disparaging view of the other is its effect on the behavior of the viewer.* If one branch sees the other as neither trustworthy nor dependable, it will see itself as called on to assume full responsibility. Ernest Barker worried that such encroachments sprang from the very nature of institutions:

> Every human institution tends naturally to institutionalism. It exaggerates itself. Not content with discharging its specific function, it readily seeks to encroach. . . Instead of seeing itself as a part, which must play its function as such, and claim no more than that, each institution is prone to see itself as a whole, *to regard itself as a rounded O,* and to claim a total sovereignty. That is an aberration.[6]

What I suggest is that proneness to "rounded O's" is directly related to negative interbranch evaluations. Rounding the "O" is more than a pleasant little redundancy. It means creating a total policy process within one branch of government.

A basic challenge to the integrity of either branch naturally elicits a response. With the partnership dissolved, one may expect the challenged branch to react like the challenger—by expanding its activities. The encroachments of the challenging branch will be the basis for expansion by the challenged branch. Ironically, the same rationale will be used—loss of legitimacy and competency by the other branch.

Negative evaluations of legitimacy and competency can have important consequences in the national policy process. Stalemate is one of the more immediate effects (as in the last two years of the Bush administration). But other, potentially more serious, results may occur. Public apathy, even alienation, may follow stalemate, with low turnout in elections casting doubt on the legitimacy of those elected. Under these circumstances negative interbranch evaluations result in a self-fulfilling illegitimacy. Meanwhile, where complex social, economic, and defense-related programs are already in place, the bureaucracy may be expected to assume the tasks of governing—essentially through rational increments to existing policy. This outcome is not a result of some devious bureaucratic design. Instead, it stems from the decline of trust between separated partners.

The Nixon Presidency

Presidents, Congresses, and their various components can be rated by applying the tests of legitimacy and competency—both as an impressionistic exercise and as a much more particular scientific endeavor. Accomplishing the latter requires elaborate explication of criteria, specification of sources, collection of data for several administrations, and careful analysis of findings and is, therefore, beyond the scope of this chapter. At the level of educated impressions, however, one can do quite well with this scheme in explaining the relations with Congress of Presidents Franklin Roosevelt, Harry Truman, Dwight Eisenhower, John Kennedy, and Lyndon Johnson, both in general and on various issues. Each of these administrations was characterized by both branches' doubts about each other's legitimacy and competency to deal with particular issues. One only need mention Roosevelt's Court-packing plan, the Taft-Hartley Act of the 80th Congress, the many budgetary and domestic policy conflicts during the Eisenhower administrations, the Bay of Pigs disaster of the Kennedy administration, and, of course, Vietnam. Further, it has been characteristic of all administrations that relations deteriorate over time. President Roosevelt's relations with Congress were going from bad to worse before World War II. Truman's conflicts with Congress were legendary throughout his presidency and became extremely trying toward the end of his elected term. Eisenhower had to deal with a Democratic Congress for six of his eight years in office, and his successes on Capitol Hill showed a steady decline. Neither Kennedy nor Johnson served a second term, and the former was in office less than three years. In Johnson's case, an initial period of harmony between the branches on domestic issues was followed by intense conflict over the proper course of action in Vietnam.

It is not surprising to find conflict and competition between the two major policymaking branches of the national government. In general, however, these challenges have tended to be program directed; that is, those in one branch have doubted the legitimacy or competency of those in the other branch to cope with an issue. Occasionally challenges were made to the whole institution—the legitimacy of third and fourth terms for Roosevelt was questioned, as was the competency of the "do-nothing" 80th Congress. But in most cases judgments have been policy specific and, as composite evaluations, more positive than negative.

The case of the Nixon administrations, particularly the second administration, appears to be quite different. Here is an instance of interbranch evaluations that were more negative than positive and applied to a whole institution, not just parts thereof. With all that has been written on the Nixon administration, one finds relatively little systematic analysis of congressional relations—particularly those of the president's staff.[7] But what analysis there is confirms the negative valence of congressional-presidential evaluations. I have selected two particularly cogent accounts to illustrate this tendency. The first, by Nelson W. Polsby, describes the conditions leading to the executive's negative evaluations of Congress. The second, by Ralph K. Huitt, goes more directly to Nixon's dealings with Congress. Here is how Polsby describes the Nixon terms:

> It was a strong presidency, strong in the sense of setting and achieving goals. Yet it achieved its ends principally through the device of attacking, crippling, neutralizing, and diminishing the powers of other legitimate power centers in the political system. Underpinning this approach to presidential government were two articles of belief, frequently stated by Mr. Nixon or one or another of his spokesmen. The first held that the accountability of the president ran solely to his electoral majority. Politics for Mr. Nixon was electoral politics, campaign politics. Election conferred a mandate, an entitlement for him to act in office as his predecessors had acted—in small ways as well as large ways.[8]

The second article of belief, according to Polsby, followed logically from the first and directly supports the argument here. As a Republican with a Democratic Congress and a New Deal bureaucracy, Nixon was, in his view, mandated to fight the good fight, against overwhelming odds. He believed that

> the elite political stratum in this country ... was out of step with the dominant mood of conservatism in the country at large. Thus,

in his view, his election conferred not only an extraordinary measure of legitimacy upon him, but also a kind of illegitimacy upon
many of the very people with whom a president ordinarily does
business—the bureaucrats, interest-group leaders, and journalists,
congressmen and party leaders of official Washington. These after
all, had for the most part been elected neither in the close election
of 1968 nor in his landslide of 1972 [or, if they had, they came
from constituencies made safe from the ebb and flow of American
politics].[9]

In a most interesting practical review of "White House Channels to
the Hill," Huitt uses a marriage analogy to analyze successful presidential-congressional relations. He identifies two elements as indispensable to the partnership between the president and Congress:
"that both parties want it to succeed and ... that workable arrangements be established which make the crucial day-to-day lives flow
together easily without letting every chore or responsibility become a
possible confrontation."[10] Workable arrangements are the natural
means of accommodation once goodwill and good intentions exist.
"But what if a president does not want a marriage with Congress?"
With this question, Huitt turns to the extraordinary Nixon years.

> The Constitution does not say that he must [marry Congress].
> Nixon did not seem titillated by the prospect. In fact, he seemed to
> balk Congress by turning the relationship upside down. Histori-
> cally, the principal checks Congress has had on the president came
> from maintaining control of the negatives—that is, the president
> asks for what he wants, and congressional power comes from the
> liberty to decide how much of it to let him have or what to give
> him in its place. But Nixon did not seem to want anything from
> Congress. To be sure, he initiated domestic programs and pro-
> claimed priorities, but he seemed to lose interest in them
> quickly....
>
> Trying to oppose Nixon on domestic programs was, as some
> congressmen put it, like "pushing on a string." There was no resist-
> ance. Instead, *Nixon tried to run things without Congress.*
> Impounding funds, deferring the spending of them, shifting money
> from one purpose to another—these gave him control of what re-
> ally mattered, the allocation of government resources. He had ef-
> fectively got control of the negatives, a role reversal that seemed for
> a time to bemuse Congress.[11]

We see in these statements precisely the developments described earlier as associated with negative evaluations. If a competing institution—Congress in this case—is of dubious legitimacy, then the country must be run without it. This conclusion of Nixon's was facilitated by his priorities—foreign policy and the reduction of domestic programs. Had Nixon wished to enact an elaborate domestic program, he would have been less free to exclude Congress.

So far the discussion of the Nixon presidency has proceeded without mention of Watergate. Negative evaluations of Congress by the president and his aides preceded Watergate and surely would have been present had Watergate not occurred. Counterevaluations of President Nixon by members of Congress would have challenged his legitimacy anyway—on the basis of Nixon's excesses.[12] Watergate simply speeded up the process, as the president's unlawful acts provided the ultimate evidence for illegitimacy, the symbolic "smoking gun."

THE CONGRESS REACTS

I have argued that an institution that has been challenged on so basic a matter as its legitimacy to make decisions will respond with a challenge of its own. The challenge to Congress came from Nixon, and the "new Congress" we hear about might well be labeled the "Nixon Congress." Certainly Nixon's actions and attitudes stimulated many of the changes that have taken place on Capitol Hill.

Elsewhere I have identified three roles for Congress in the policy process as an *initiator* of comprehensive policies, as a *reserved partner* to the executive, and as a *facilitator* of interests.[13] That Congress should assume any of these roles may be the view of the whole membership, of the members of each house, or of the leadership. The most pretentious role is that of initiator because it is based on the belief that the House, the Senate, or both working together, can define problems, set priorities, identify options, and analyze effects. In other words, Congress can govern.

> Presumably this need for independent analysis results from executive incapacity to analyze the problem and develop proposals and/or the production of "wrong results" by the executive.... Thus, the Congress-as-initiator model may be said to assume an organizational contretemps between the two branches, resulting from substantive or partisan considerations or both.[14]

Stimulated in large measure by Nixon's negative evaluations, many important members of Congress assumed the pretentious role of initiators of comprehensive policies. Yet substantial reform was needed in order for Congress to acquire the full capacity for comprehensive policy initiation. And so we witnessed a period of unprecedented reform on Capitol Hill during the 1970s. Three definite phases of the reform decade can be identified:

> *Phase 1: before the Nixon challenge.* The principal reform in this phase was the Legislative Reorganization Act of 1970. This act had its roots in the work of the Joint Committee on the Organization of Congress created in 1965. Most of the changes were minor organizational and administrative ones. Though enacted in the first Nixon administration, this act presumably would have been passed even if Hubert Humphrey had been elected president in 1968.
>
> *Phase 2: response to the Nixon challenge.* This group of reforms is by far the most extensive and is associated with Nixon's stated and implied challenges to the legitimacy and competency of Congress. These reforms followed the bolstering of Nixon's self-image as a result of the 1972 election. Among the most important were the War Powers Act of 1973, the Budget and Impoundment Control Act of 1974, the several changes in the party and committee systems (particularly in the House), and the expansion of congressional staff.
>
> *Phase 3: after Watergate.* This last set of reforms grew out of the excesses of the Committee to Re-elect the President in handling campaign funds and, of course, the focus on ethics in government following the Watergate revelations and the president's resignation. The Federal Election Campaign Act of 1974, ethics codes, more streamlining of the committee systems, and the demands for sunset legislation and greater use of the congressional veto are all included.

I have used the word "pretentious" to characterize the initiator role because I believe it is inordinately ambitious for Congress to prepare itself to initiate comprehensive policy programs. Having undertaken such a complex assignment, a legislature may not know where to stop imitating the executive. Thus, one may expect to witness an escalation of congressional involvement in more policy activities for more issues which in turn demands more staff, greater organizational articulation, and an expansion in the number of congressional participants for any one issue. Given the fragmented and representative nature of Congress, a generous degree of pretension is required to pursue the initiator role.

These are interesting developments, but ambition is not sufficient to ensure effective and efficient policy dominance by Congress. Increased policy involvement by an expanding legislative population by no means implies integrated lawmaking. In fact, without leadership, quite the reverse result may occur. In short, reactive efforts by a challenged institution to expand its functions—to "round its O"—may produce a highly diversified, even chaotic policy system.

One other piece of business must be attended to before we turn from the Nixon Congress to the Carter presidency. Gerald R. Ford became president after Nixon's resignation. But Ford was a product of Congress, having served in the House for twenty-five years. More important, his legitimacy as president was traceable to his selection by a vote in Congress, not by a vote among the people. As Ford himself observed at his swearing-in:

> I am acutely aware that you, the voters, have not elected me as your president by your ballots ... I have not sought this enormous responsibility, but I will not shirk it. Those who nominated and confirmed me as vice-president were my friends and are my friends. They were of both parties, elected by all the people, and acting under the Constitution in their name. It is only fitting, then, that I should pledge to them and to you that I will be president of all the people.[15]

What an extraordinary turnabout! The new president drew his approval from the very institution whose legitimacy had been challenged by his predecessor. Moreover, the Republican Ford was dependent on a Democratic Congress.

The Carter Presidency

What was required in 1977 for amicable and effective presidential-congressional relations? In the abstract, it seems that the following conditions would improve the chances for reestablishing reliable connections between the separated partners:

Conditions in the Executive Branch

1. A president from the party that holds a majority in Congress

2. A president familiar with and attuned to the changes in national politics and policies of the last decade
3. A president appreciative of the inner workings of Congress—the important differences between the chambers, for example, or the operations of committees and subcommittees and their connections with the political party structure
4. A White House staff equally sensitive to and appreciative of Congress and how it has changed
5. Coherent presidential programs developed in cooperation or communication with appropriate congressional leaders

Conditions in Congress

1. Party leadership familiar with and attuned to changes in national politics and policies of the last decade
2. Party leadership willing to cooperate or communicate with the president and his staff in the development and promotion of programs
3. Consolidation of the many reforms of the past decade so as to achieve the traditional functions of representation and lawmaking
4. Growth of electoral connections between the president and his party's members in Congress (such as perception by the members that the president's electoral success and theirs bear some relationship to each other)

On the presidential side it is apparent that the election of Jimmy Carter satisfied the first condition—he was a Democrat. Also he was aware of the shifts in public mood in the years prior to his election. His capabilities as a campaigner were considerable, as demonstrated in his winning the nomination and election. He had less luck in building grassroots support for his programs, but in general it can be said that Carter's election satisfied the second presidential condition too, a president who understood national change.

But President Carter came to Washington with a limited knowledge of the inner workings of Congress, "never having lived or served in the federal government in Washington." Moreover, the politics of accommodation and compromise so characteristic of the operations on the Hill somehow were unsatisfying to this engineer. What was second nature to Lyndon B. Johnson seemed neither natural nor right to Jimmy Carter.

Substantial failure to meet the third condition need not be fatal to effective congressional-presidential relations. In fact, one might expect a president who admits his own unfamiliarity with Congress to surround himself with experts in legislative liaison. Not wishing to succumb to the Washington establishment, however, Carter chose instead to rely on those who had worked with him in the campaign and earlier when he had served as governor of Georgia. As a consequence, congressional liaison from the White House was viewed by many on Capitol Hill with skepticism and even ridicule.

Meeting the fifth condition is highly unlikely if neither the third nor the fourth condition is satisfied. After a difficult beginning, however, Carter and his aides acknowledged the necessity of congressional contact in program development. Individuals with Hill savvy, such as William H. Cable, were added to the staff. But the communication and clearance with Congress so characteristic of other Democratic administrations emerged slowly in the Carter administration.

On the congressional side, the change of party leaders in 1977 provided an unusual opportunity for the president. The new Speaker, Thomas P. ("Tip") O'Neill (D-Mass.), and the new majority leader in the Senate, Robert C. Byrd (D-W.Va.), announced their willingness to cooperate with the new president. Both had served in congressional party positions previously—O'Neill as whip and majority leader, Byrd as caucus secretary and whip. Both had been involved in the turbulent issues and politics of the 1960s and 1970s. Thus the first two congressional conditions for effective congressional-presidential relations, cooperative and aware party leaders, were satisfied as fully as at any time in recent history.

President Carter had it within his power to make the two leaders look good in Congress by consulting them, providing them with favors and support in their dealings with the membership, and relying on them as principal sources of information about the mood and interests of the membership. As new leaders themselves, they were naturally anxious to look good before their own party colleagues. And, of course, their effectiveness with the House and Senate Democrats was important to the success of the president's program. Unquestionably, a new partnership could have been forged in the 95th Congress between the president and the party leaders in Congress.

Far from making them look good, President Carter and his staff seemed intent at first on making congressional leaders look bad. The president pressed for decisions such as the reduction of water projects that were bound to cause problems for Democratic leaders. He sometimes ignored the courtesy of informing members about appointments within their states or districts. He formulated a major energy program with little or no consultation with the party and committee leaders who would have to manage it through Congress—and then announced it to the people first, the Congress second. He altered proposals or dropped them altogether (the fifty-dollar rebate, for example)—sometimes after leaders had already committed themselves and their resources to enactment. Byrd and O'Neill consolidated their leadership positions during the first year of the Carter administration. But essentially they did it on their own, often in spite of the problems created for them by the president. Thus they owed no particular allegiance to the president. It was, in fact, quite remarkable that they remained as outwardly loyal to the president as they did during this first troubled year.[16]

The third and fourth congressional conditions, consolidation of reforms and growth of electoral connections, were not met to any substantial degree. Congress continued the process of consolidating the reforms of the 1970s. It is still not altogether clear what the full range of their effects will be. Subcommittees have more staff and have increased their functions in the policy process. Members too have more staff, and many have expanded their legislative activities. In some cases, committee chairmen play a different role than before, perhaps a more managerial or brokerage role. The reforms seem to have embroiled members in comprehensive budget games. And party leaders have increased responsibilities, particularly in the House. The reforms appear to have expanded, but not shaped, congressional participation in the policy process.

The fourth condition assumes that a vital link is necessary between the processes by which the president and Congress come to be in Washington. This connection has never been strong. The framers of the Constitution did not intend it to be—indeed they rejected the direct link of having the president selected by Congress. But there have been times in the recent past when members of Congress had reason to believe that their electoral fate was positively connected to that of the president. The Johnson landslide of 1964 is the principal case in point.

In the 1976 election, Jimmy Carter won the presidency by a very narrow margin (50.1 percent of the total vote). Meanwhile, Democratic candidates for the House polled 56.2 percent of the total vote. They led the president in every region—by 5.3 percentage points in the East, 8.3 points in the South, 4 points in the Midwest, and 9 points in the West. Senate Democratic candidates also outpolled the president (54.4 percent to 50.1 percent). In two cases Carter ran behind Senate Democratic incumbents who were defeated, and he lost all five of the states in which Senate Democratic incumbents were defeated.[17] Small wonder that, in the words of a Washington journalist, "the members think that what happens to the president doesn't happen to them as members of Congress."[18] A member of Congress put it this way: "The relationship between the president and Congress is partly a result of how well the president is doing politically. Congress is better behaved when he does well.... Right now, it's almost as if Congress is not paying attention to him."[19]

One does not get a very encouraging picture of the prospects for productive congressional-presidential relationships from this brief review. It should be noted, however, that the conditions I have described are demanding. They reflect the changes in both institutions—a more dependent presidency and a more independent Congress—and taken together they allow perhaps less room for miscalculation than there was in the past. As Eric L. Davis rightly observes: "If Carter and his associates were to attempt to replicate their predecessors' approaches to legislative relations, they would be using an entirely inappropriate set of strategies and tactics."[20] So the challenge to any new president in 1977 was considerable; for Jimmy Carter it was monumental.

In summary, in 1977 the occupant of the White House was an intelligent and socially aware Democrat without either Washington experience or any apparent interest in acquiring it. At the other end of Pennsylvania Avenue was a Congress with able but uncertain leadership seeking to consolidate a plethora of democratizing internal reforms. More bluntly, a dependent president, demonstrating artless policy behavior, faced an independent Congress, anxious to assume a pretentious policymaking role.

How does each evaluate the other? Neither set of actors—presidential or congressional—seriously questioned the institutional legitimacy of the other set. To be sure, there were individual cases where both were charged with having exceeded their authority, but no more perhaps than in other administrations before Nixon. For the most part, the evaluations were positive on the legitimacy test.

The same cannot be said for the competency test. The president seemed to have had to learn about the capabilities of individual members, the committees and subcommittees, and the institution as a whole. By his own admission, he "got a growing understanding of Congress." Carter appeared to rely on his experience in Georgia in evaluating congressional competence, and generalizing from this experience did not help him establish workable relationships with Congress.

Meanwhile, many members of Congress believed that the reforms of the past decade increased their competence—not only to perform the traditional functions of representing constituents and participating actively in lawmaking, but to expand their involvement to program development and evaluation, foreign and domestic. Thus it was particularly unfortunate that this renewed Congress faced a president less able than most to appreciate the increased self-confidence on Capitol Hill. No doubt we all have experienced similar deflations—failing to have an accomplishment applauded, understood, appreciated, or even acknowledged by a person who counts. It should not be difficult for one who has had such an experience to understand how disappointed some members of Congress were with the new president.

Negative evaluations of competency, like negative assessments of legitimacy, prompt the challenged institution to return the insult. Further, each appraisal has its most important effect on those who do the evaluating. Carter's hesitancy about the capabilities of Congress led him to formulate programs within his own family of advisers and then to assume they would be enacted because they were intelligently or logically drafted (assigning to Congress the reserved partner role). This very approach confirmed for many members of Congress that Carter himself lacked the capacity to lead. The president's failure to acknowledge the growth of Congress's ambitions and capabilities in the area of policy formation showed a lack of political judgment on his part, according to some. Lack of political judgment is as serious an indictment as can be made of a politician's competence. How should one expect members of Congress to react under these circumstances? It was predictable that many would seek to outdo the president. This solution is not a very firm foundation for amicable presidential-congressional relations. Thus, one found commentators making assessments like these:

> In the battery of attacks President Carter has received recently from Congress, one conclusion stands out: There is a massive gap in communication and coordination between the White House and Congress and nothing short of a Carter reelection is likely to heal the breach.[21]

> With the 96th Congress scheduled to convene January 15, President Carter may find it easier to normalize relations with 900 million Chinese than to establish harmonious operations on Capitol Hill.[22]

Perhaps a Carter was inevitable after the events of the mid-1970s. It does seem apparent that a weakened presidency was desired by many.

Carter was attractive to those desiring a weak presidency in large part because of his unfamiliarity with the Washington scene. But Carter's narrow victory at the polls in 1976 was by no means inevitable. What if Gerald Ford had won? He, too, would have been constrained in his exercise of the office. But the checks would have been more political, less personal. Ford would have had to cope with large Democratic majorities in both houses of Congress, and a quite different congressional-presidential relationship could have been expected.

What about the Future?

In his eloquent essay on the parliamentary system of government, Ernest Barker specified the conditions he regarded as essential to effective government in a free society. He said:

> How do men act—or rather, how do they plan and determine their action ...? The answer is that they "get together." They pool their minds: each puts forward his point of view, and all discuss and compare their different points of view. That ... is what happens everywhere, in any living, reasoning, free society. It happened in tribal gatherings and folkmoots, thousands of years ago; and it happens still today. That is parliament, or "parley": that is the use of "the Word," which, as the Evangelist tells us, "was in the beginning," and which ... will be with us to all eternity. But no parley or use of the Word, stops short at mere parley or words.... We seek by all our talk, and by all our comparison of points of view, to discover a common point of view which will satisfy us all, and on which we can all agree to act.... Our search is a search for the common—for a *modus convivendi*—for what the politicians call a "compromise."... It is not an easy thing do.... Any society, to be worthy of the name, must consist of *partners,* who enjoy a say in the affairs of the society. When a society ceases to be that, it ceases to be a society! It becomes a mere heap of the leader and his followers—followers strung together, like so many dead birds on a string, by the compulsion of leadership.[23]

This statement serves the dual purposes of reminding us of what must be preserved and warning us of the consequences of failing to preserve it. The Nixon Watergate interlude did not exactly produce "a mere heap of the leader and his followers," but it is fair to say that it contributed to conditions that directed us away from, not toward, partnership in governing.

"Congress is supposed to represent the voters, and if our assembly does not work with the chief executive, the battle for democracy is lost before a shot is fired."[24] The constitutional structure creates special demands on the American partnership. Any union or "search for the common" will be influenced by structure. In Britain, the process is facilitated by the party system, particularly when one party can command a majority in the House of Commons. In the United States, separate elections create special requirements if a partnership between executive and legislature is to develop and be maintained. The most severe test comes when the voters select a president, like Nixon, of one party to serve with a Congress in which the other party has a majority; at the opposite extreme, conditions are most propitious for partnership when a majority-party leader in Congress—a Lyndon Johnson—is elected president. Party has the potential to facilitate the partnership between the branches in the United States. Its decline, therefore, takes on special significance for the topic under discussion.

So a first order of business is for the leadership on both sides to recognize the attitudinal and structural effects of these turbulent times and reevaluate the strengths and weaknesses of their present circumstances. What do we want a president to do? What do we want a Congress to be? Until these questions are treated in a serious and comprehensive manner, the kind of active, vibrant, and productive partnership Barker describes will be far off.

The debate on these questions cannot proceed as though the 1964–80 period had never happened. During that period changes occurred that must influence the analysis and expectations of each branch. For example, the expansion of congressional and presidential staffs, much of it designed to counter the perceived inadequacies of other institutions, is now an integral part of each institution. The faces will change but the positions will not disappear. The question is not, Will these staffs continue to be there? They most assuredly will. It is rather, What will they be doing? Even more important is the question, How will the president and members of Congress use or relate to these new bureaucracies? Each branch must decide what it can do well, so that this vast new technical staff apparatus can be shaped accordingly. Each branch's attempts to do everything probably hasten the day when elected officials will be no more than honorary resident managers of an ever expanding group of technicians.

James S. Young believes that "to recapture that tenuous harmony between constitutionalism and presidentialism" the president must assume a special, very public, leadership role.

> It means getting the presidency substantially out of the business of managing the executive branch: ceding large parts of that domain to Congress, courts, and Cabinet, but not ceding the president's power to preempt or intervene when reasons of state require. It means putting distance between the presidency and the permanent government in Washington—distance enough to enable a president to watch the Government as the outsider he really is, to know when it is getting the country into serious trouble and when it isn't, to know when to step in and when to stay out.
>
> It also means regaining the ability, within the presidency at least, to distinguish between true and pseudo crises, real alarms and false ones, threats to the Republic and mere problems for the Administration.[25]

According to Young, this "statecraft" requires "reconstituting the institutionalized presidency" to curb its tendency to expand the scope of the president's activities. Young does not submit to the temptation of recommending a reduction in the institutional paraphernalia of the presidency. Instead, he is interested in more clearly specifying the president's responsibilities—as he puts it, "retrenching presidential power in order to preserve it." In this spirit, Young proposes that the president make the rest of the government—Congress and the bureaucracy—"come up with solutions to pressing public problems."

Of course, this reversal of aggrandizement, or encroachment, is easier prescribed than realized. It obviously depends to a considerable extent on how the incumbent views the job. What is called for is a president who respects the legitimacy and competency of the national government in Washington. This simple requirement must be met, it would seem, before the president can expect to make the system work for him and the nation.

I have started with the president because he remains so vital for directing and influencing the work of Congress and the bureaucracy. Just as both resonated to the vibrations of disdain and distrust in the Nixon and Carter administrations, so we may expect them to react positively to an administration supportive of their capabilities. The president can stimulate, if not totally manage, the rest of the policy system.

But just as the government is "too big, too complex, and too pervasive in its influence" for the president "to direct the details of its important and critical programming,"[26] it is also too big for the members of Congress to command fully. It seems clear, to paraphrase Greenstein, that today's Congress is an institution in search of new role definitions. Much of Young's analysis of the president applies as well to members of Congress. They may have to retrench in order to preserve, to wind down (or at least redefine) in order to save themselves for what they can do well.

The traditional functions of Congress in the policy process have been representing interests, serving constituents, and finding bases for compromise, albeit with notable differences in style and organization between the House and Senate. Staff increases have made Congress better able to accomplish the first two functions, not the third. But the really important development is that the reforms of the 1970s, including staff increases, have encouraged the members of Congress to expand their functions to those less suited to legislative organization, such as program development, coordination, and evaluation, all of which are associated with the initiator role. However justifiable the changes were as a counterforce to Nixon's presidential performance, their consequence is an overextended Congress.

A change of presidents can accomplish the kind of transformation Young speaks of. It is not so simple for Congress to reorient itself. Bicameralism, limited leadership, complex committee organization, and a high return of incumbents constrain its capacity to adjust quickly. It seems apparent, however, that members must reevaluate what it is they want Congress to do. I argue that party and committee leaders in each house must develop means for taking charge of their own organization and processes. It is particularly important that leaders direct the work of the committee and research support staffs (such as the Congressional Budget Office, the Office of Technology Assessment, and the Congressional Research Service).

I am not proposing the reduction or elimination of staff. Instead, I am stressing the need for congressional leaders to emulate Young's revitalized president by reducing the policy functions of the staff so that Congress can recapture its proper political role. How can that happen in our Congress? It probably will not happen unless the presidency changes along the lines suggested by Young. Congress probably will try to broaden its policymaking role as long as the president fails to command the presidency.

"Any society, to be worthy of the name, must consist of *partners.*" The framers of our Constitution created a structure that tests our capacity to form a partnership between the legislature and the executive. In the Nixon period each branch sought to go it alone. So extensive were the consequences that a return to former times is not realistic. Nixon did give us a new kind of government in Washington! But partnership still is possible—if it is adapted to the important structural changes of the recent past. The way to start may well be to reestablish trust and respect between the president and Congress. A change in attitudes, not further organizational reform, is what is now required.

NOTES

1. Woodrow Wilson, *The State,* rev. ed. (Boston: Heath, 1904), 546.
2. William J. Keefe, *Congress and the American People* (Englewood Cliffs, N.J.: Prentice Hall, 1980), 120.
3. This attention to the president has advantages and disadvantages. As Bert A. Rockman observed in comments on this chapter, presidents pay a particularly high price for the decline in institutional respect. "Presidents are seen as the institution, i.e., the presidency is far less disengaged from the president than Congress is from its members."
4. Both quotations from *The Federalist* (New York: Modern Library, 1937), 323.
5. Keefe, *Congress,* 108.
6. Ernest Barker, *Essays on Government,* 2d ed. (Oxford: Clarendon Press, 1951), 70, 71; emphasis added.
7. See John H. Kessel, *The Domestic Presidency: Decision Making in the White House* (North Scituate, Mass.: Duxbury Press, 1975), where he analyzes the internal workings of the Domestic Council, including some material on how the staff members viewed Congress. "[The members] were seen as advocates for constituency interests, and while they were respected in that capacity, this very advocacy limited their ability to determine overall priorities" (p. 69). There are many journalistic accounts of Nixon's White House staff.
8. Nelson W. Polsby, *Congress and the Presidency,* 3d ed. (Englewood Cliffs, N.J.: Prentice Hall, 1976), 51. I must acknowledge a larger debt to Professor Polsby. We often discussed the Nixon presidency during the period 1971–74. I learned a great deal from him and have no doubt that some of the ideas expressed here are traceable to that education.
9. Ibid.
10. Ralph K. Huitt, "White House Channels to the Hill," in *Congress Against the President,* ed. Harvey C. Mansfield, Sr. (New York: Praeger, 1975), 71.
11. Ibid., 76; emphasis added.
12. It is relevant in this connection that a conference on "The Constitu-

tional Crisis: Congress vs. the Executive" was held on Capitol Hill, 7–8 March 1973, after the Watergate event but before the Watergate revelations. Many members of Congress were in attendance. The discussion topics included impoundment, war powers, executive agreements and treaties, executive privilege, and impeachment. See *New Priorities* 2, no. 1 (Fall 1973). The whole issue is devoted to a summary of the conference.

13. Charles O. Jones, "Congress and the Making of Energy Policy," in *New Dimensions to Energy Policy,* ed. Robert Lawrence (Lexington, Mass.: Lexington Books, 1979), 162–65.

14. Ibid., 163–64.

15. *Congressional Quarterly Weekly Report,* 17 August 1975, 2211.

16. For a review of this first year see *Congressional Quarterly Weekly Report,* 24 December 1977, 2637–42. President Carter's presidential support scores in Congress for the first three years of his administration were closer to those of Nixon than to those of either Kennedy or Johnson. The average presidential support scores for the first three years after election were Eisenhower, 82 percent; Kennedy, 84.5 percent; Johnson, 84 percent; Nixon, 78 percent; and Carter, 77 percent. *Congressional Quarterly Weekly Report,* 12 January 1980, 91. See the analysis by George C. Edwards III on what presidential support scores reveal and hide: Edwards, *Presidential Influence in Congress* (San Francisco: Freeman, 1980), chap. 7.

17. Data taken from *Congressional Quarterly Weekly Report,* 10 March 1977, 488–89.

18. Taken from an interview for the author's paper entitled, "Can Our Parties Survive Our Politics?" prepared for a conference on "The Role of the Legislature in Western Democracies," Selsdon Park, England, 20–22 April 1979.

19. Statement by Representative Richard B. Cheney (R-Wyo.), a former White House staff aide, in Richard E. Cohen, "The President's Problems," in *The Carter Presidency under Pressure,* ed. Thomas E. Cronin (Washington, D.C.: National Journal Reprint Series, 1979), 35.

20. Quoted in Dom Bonafede, "The Tough Job of Normalizing Relations with Capitol Hill," in Cronin, *Carter Presidency,* 37. Amitai Etzioni agrees with this point, noting that "all the talk about a return to a LBJ-mastery of Congress disregards both the unconstitutional nature of a domination by the executive, and that forces in Congress, more than in the White House, make such a return quite impossible." Etzioni, "The Lack of Leadership: We Found It in Us," *National Journal* 12 (23 February 1980): 335.

21. Cohen, "The President's Problems," 35.

22. Bonafede, "The Tough Job of Normalizing Relations with Capitol

Hill," 36. For a more sympathetic evaluation of the Carter administration from one who worked in it, see Etzioni, "Lack of Leadership," 334–37.

23. Barker, *Essays on Government,* 67–68.
24. E. Pendleton Herring, *Presidential Leadership* (New York: Rinehart, 1940), 45.
25. James S. Young, "The Troubled Presidency: II," *New York Times,* 7 December 1978, 23.
26. Statement by Dwight D. Eisenhower, quoted in Fred I. Greenstein, "Change and Continuity in the Modern Presidency," in *The New American Political System,* ed. Anthony King (Washington, D.C.: American Enterprise Institute, 1978), 84.

7

Presidential Negotiating Styles with Congress

In his book *The Vantage Point,* Lyndon Johnson relates an important lesson taught to him by a Texas state senator, Alvin Wirtz. Senator Wirtz had arranged a meeting of private utility company owners, trying to persuade them to make electric power available to small farmers. Johnson got upset with one of the company presidents, "and in the course of our discussion I told the man that he could 'go to hell.'" Later Senator Wirtz called Johnson aside and said: "Listen, Lyndon, I've been around this business for a long time.... If I have learned anything at all in these years, it is this: You can tell a man to go to hell, but you can't make him go." That bit of advice was offered to Johnson in 1937. He never forgot it.

> I thought of that story many times during my presidency. It seemed particularly apt when I found myself in a struggle with the House or the Senate. I would start to speak out, then I would think of Senator Wirtz and remember that no matter how many times I told the Congress to do something, I could never force it to act.[1]

The Founding Fathers were determined that the president should not command Congress. Even the master congressional tactician, Lyndon Johnson, knew that success depended on his understanding the limits on the presidency. The two institutions have been described as being like "two gears, each whirling at its own rate of speed. It is not surprising that, on coming together, they often clash."[2]

This chapter describes and analyzes this coming together of the president with Congress. Normally the relationship tends to be activated by the president because he wants something. He is forced to acknowledge, however, that members of Congress also have needs. The trick is to make his wants mesh with their needs. Since theirs is a dependent relationship, the president and Congress negotiate. What is the nature of these negotiations? How do negotiating conditions vary from one administration to the next? What are the different styles and techniques of negotiation associated with recent presidents? Which are most successful, and why? These are the questions to be treated here.

The Nature and Conditions of Negotiation

Negotiation is a process by which contending parties seek agreement on an issue of importance to each. It is characterized by various means of persuasion; those used typically depend on the resources available, including the estimates each side makes of the strength and capabilities of the other. Many social scientists use the word "bargaining" as synonymous with "negotiation." Strictly speaking, however, a bargain involves a transaction or trade: something for you in exchange for your giving something to me. It is good to remember, therefore, that presidents engage in a wide range of negotiating strategies in addition to the classic bargain—for example, those designed to convince the members of Congress that cooperation is in their own best interest or those based on an interpretation of what is good for the nation at a particular time.[3] Note that bargaining is typically a form of negotiation that brings the president in close contact with the members of Congress; other forms allow greater distance between the two. As we later see, presidents differ in their choice of and preferences for various negotiating strategies, as well as in their resources (including personal capabilities) for implementing preferred strategies.

Robert A. Dahl and Charles E. Lindblom are among those who define bargaining as more or less synonymous with negotiation. Nevertheless, their excellent analysis suits present purposes by stressing the importance of the classic bargain in American politics. For them, bargaining is "a form of reciprocal control among leaders."[4] It is characteristic of a society that wants to get something done but has distributed the power to do that something among a variety of groups in and out of government. Dahl and Lindblom argue: "Leaders bargain because they disagree and expect that further agreement is possible and will be profitable.... Hence bargaining takes place because it is necessary, possible, and thought to be profitable."[5]

The "human embodiment of a bargaining society" is the politician, "whose career depends upon successful negotiation of bargains."[6] The skill involved in successfully negotiating bargains tends to be more procedural than substantive. The politician may have substantive commitments, but these commitments are often compromised in the pursuit of a majority.

> Because he is a bargainer, a negotiator, the politician does not often give orders. He can rarely employ unilateral controls. Even as a chief executive or a cabinet official he soon discovers that his control depends on his skill in bargaining.... The role calls for actions such as compromise, renunciation, face-saving of oneself, which are morally ambiguous or even downright immoral to people with morally rigorous standards.[7]

Presidents uncomfortable with bargaining in its classic form are, according to this analysis, in a somewhat odd position.

Dahl and Lindblom observe that the U.S. Constitution established multiple conditions for bargaining. Vertical and horizontal controls and checks operate to prevent the realization of a national majority even if it exists. The result is often three- or four-dimensional bargaining within and between branches in program development, and bargaining may even carry over into program implementation. Congress and the president are at the center of this complex set of policy relationships. And as Nelson W. Polsby points out: "If the Constitution can be said to grant legitimacy to anything, surely it legitimizes conflict between Congress and the president."[8]

Saying that negotiation is ubiquitous in American politics is not to say that it always looks the same or is well managed. Three principal factors appear to condition presidential-congressional negotiations:

- □ *The issues:* Who wants what? How do decision makers in each branch define social, economic, and political needs? Who controls the agenda?
- □ *The president:* What does he want? What are his resources? How does he view the presidency? the Congress?
- □ *Congress:* Which party is in the majority? What is the dominant congressional view of the presidency? of the role of Congress?

This list is brief, but one should not be misled into believing that the task of classification is thereby made simple. Even cursory reflection on the conditions reveals the challenge faced by scholars in seeking to generalize about presidents and Congresses. Perhaps we can do no more than characterize the relationships of each administration. Surely we are unlikely to do more unless we specify significant conditions and identify applications.

Presidential-Congressional Conversation

Before making applications to four recent administrations, I need to say something general about what Anthony King refers to as "presidential-congressional conversation." By this he means both the talk itself and the bargaining counters or "chips" that presidents rely on.

The talk itself appears to differ in amount, volume, and intensity, but not in type. That is, some presidents hardly make a move without congressional involvement; others find it almost unnatural to include members of Congress in their ordinary decisional discourse. Yet all presidents engage in formal and informal talk, which may be directly or indirectly targeted at Capitol Hill. Formal talk includes the State of the Union and other messages, press conferences, radio and television addresses, and so on. Words on these occasions may be aimed directly at the members or filtered through others —the press, interest groups, or constituents. Informal talk includes the less public discourse of the president and his aides—the daily contact between the White House and members or between the White House and those who may be expected to influence the members.

Formal and informal words on a topic do not always bear the same messages. The more public exhortations are typically expected to satisfy the expectations of diverse groups and thus must be prepared with great care and attention. Often members of Congress understand and are tolerant of the demands being met in formal talk, even when they are themselves the objects of criticism or ridicule. Their tolerance may be nurtured by simultaneous or subsequent informal conversation of a reassuring nature.

What is behind the talk? What do presidents have to offer? And how do the offerings change? Conditions vary and what is, or is deemed to be, appropriate in one administration is judged inappropriate in another. Still, one can prepare a catalogue of appeals and rewards, as George C. Edwards III has done in *Presidential Influence in Congress*.[9] The more positive inducements on the standard list for the president include knowledge of Capitol Hill, respect for the legislative process, persistence, public standing, interpretations of the national interest, projects and services, personal amenities, and political and campaign support. Negative appeals include threats, penalties, withholding political or campaign support, and excluding members from benefits enjoyed by others.

Beyond saying that the standard list is differentially applied across issues and through time, one can also observe that certain of these appeals are more associated with formal talk (e.g., interpretations of the national interest, veto threats), others with informal talk (e.g., projects, amenities, campaign support). Further, it appears that changes have occurred in what constitutes an acceptable trade between the president and Congress. As unfolds in the cases presented below, bargaining (in the narrow sense of trading) appears to have come into disrepute in recent years, either because the president wants less from Congress, as with Nixon, or because he personally eschews that form of negotiation, as with Carter. The Reagan administration is the subject of final comment. Suffice it to say at this point that he evidenced a style not unlike a president he professed to admire—Franklin D. Roosevelt.

Four Administrations

It is instructive to examine different presidencies to illustrate the variation in negotiating conditions. My plan is to analyze the administrations of four presidents—Lyndon Johnson, Richard Nixon, Gerald Ford, and Jimmy Carter. They represent a remarkably diverse sample of conditions, styles, and techniques. In the course of preparing this chapter, I became convinced that political and personal *conditions* help to explain presidential *styles* of relating to Congress, and these styles in turn contribute to determining which *techniques* are used to get the legislative program enacted.

Table 7.1 presents basic election information about the four presidents. Clearly Lyndon Johnson assumed office with great advantages—an impressive nationally based victory and a better than two-thirds Democratic majority in each house of Congress. Nixon had an equally impressive victory in 1972 but lacked the congressional advantage. His 1968 victory was much less impressive. Carter had a very narrow victory, but his party won sizable majorities in both houses of Congress. And Gerald Ford had to govern without electoral support and was faced with large Democratic majorities in Congress. The contrast between Johnson and Ford is particularly dramatic. As an official of the Office of Management and Budget (OMB) observed:

TABLE 7.1
ELECTION RESULTS AS POLITICAL CHARACTERISTICS OF FOUR ADMINISTRATIONS

Adminis-tration	Year	President			House		Senate	
		Popular vote %	Electoral vote %	Electoral base	Margin %	Change[a] %	Margin %	Change[a] %
Johnson	1964	61.1	90.3	National (outside Deep South)	67.8 D	+8.5	68 D	+1
	1966				56.8 D	−11.0	64 D	−4
Nixon	1968	43.4	55.9	Regional (West, Midwest, Border South)	55.9 D	+0.9	57 D	+7
	1970				58.4 D	−2.5	54 D	+1 [b]
	1972	60.7 c	96.6 c	National c	54.9 D	+3.5	56 D	−2
Ford	1974				66.9 D	−12.0	60 D	−4
Carter	1976	50.1	55.2	Regional (South, East)	67.1 D	+0.2	61 D	+1
	1978				63.4 D	−3.7	58 D	−3

SOURCE: Compiled by the author from data in U.S. Bureau of the Census, *Statistical Abstract of the United States* (Washington, D.C, 1979), 497–507.

a. Refers to percentage change for president's party from previous Congress; D indicates the Democratic Party.
b. Two senators were not in either of the major parties.
c. Nominated by Nixon in 1973 to be vice-president; approved by the Senate 92-3, and by the House 387-5.

TABLE 7.2
ISSUES EMPHASIZED IN PRESIDENTIAL STATE OF THE UNION
MESSAGES FOR SELECTED YEARS, 1965–80

Administration	Major issues	Other important issues
Johnson		
1965	Great Society programs	Foreign, defense policy
1966	Vietnam, foreign, defense policy	Poverty, taxes, crime, urban development, clean rivers, civil rights
1968	Vietnam, foreign, defense policy	Employment, cities, housing, health, consumer protection, crime
Nixon		
1970	Vietnam, foreign, defense policy	Environment, government reform, welfare reform, inflation, crime, cities/rural areas
1972	Foreign, defense policy	Economy (employment, inflation); (Congress urged to enact earlier requests)
1974	Energy	Health, revenue sharing, transportation, education, privacy, welfare reform, trade, veterans' benefits
Ford		
1976	Economy (employment, inflation), energy	Health, social security, welfare reform, crime, national security
Carter		
1978	Energy, economy (employment, inflation)	Government reform, foreign and defense policy, Panama Canal
1980	Foreign, defense policy	Energy, economy (employment, inflation)

SOURCE: Compiled by author from State of the Union messages and from reports on them in the *Congressional Quarterly Weekly Reports.*

> You ought to think of the presidency as an engine. Each president enters office facing the same model—the horsepower is generally stable and the gears are all there. What differs is the *fuel*. Different presidents enter with different fuel. Lyndon Johnson entered office with a full tank, while Ford entered on empty.[10]

Political and personal advantages or limitations stem from more than election returns, however. Also involved are the factors mentioned earlier—the issues as well as presidential and congressional images of how the system ought to work. One of the more reliable inventories of issue priorities is the presidential State of the Union message. Table 7.2 (page 134) displays the range of issues identified as important by the presidents in the years selected. Most obvious is the shift from foreign to domestic priorities (and back again in 1980). Less obvious, perhaps, is the fact that many of the domestic requests by Nixon, Ford, and Carter were reform measures seeking to reshape the structure and substance of programs enacted during the 1960s, a shift from issues requiring expansion of government to those demanding consolidation or even contraction of government.

The broad developments on issues are summarized in the second column of table 7.3 (page 136). Columns 3 and 4 provide general responses to the questions of how the president and Congress viewed their own responsibilities and those of the other branch. Thus, for example, compare the characteristics of the first Johnson administration with those of the Carter years. With Johnson, a full agenda of expansive domestic issues was aggressively presented by a president with impressive resources. Johnson had a "mixed government" view of national policymaking. For him, both the president and Congress had legitimate authority to be involved. He got support from a Democratic majority, most of whom appeared to believe that the president should rule.

With Carter, in contrast, a less comprehensive agenda contained many consolidative and even contractive proposals. Demands were being heard to coordinate existing government programs or eliminate them altogether. Carter himself had fewer resources and appeared to believe in an executive-centered government (a president working with an efficient bureaucracy). The Democrats were in the majority in Congress but were highly critical of the president and demanded at least equal involvement in the full range of activities associated with the policy process.

These impressive variations in the work to be done, the political resources available to do the work, and the impressions in each

TABLE 7.3
CHARACTERISTICS OF FOUR ADMINISTRATIONS,
1964–80

Adminis- tration	Issues	Presidential characteristics	Congressional characteristics
Johnson			
1964–66	Domestic, expansive	Full agenda, assert- ive, impressive re- sources, mixed government	Democratic majority, supportive, presi- dential government
1967–68	Foreign, expansive	Reduced agenda, as- sertive, limited re- sources, presiden- tial government	Democratic majority, critical, mixed gov- ernment
Nixon			
1969–72	Foreign, consoli- dative	Moderate agenda, moderately assert- ive, mixed re- sources, presiden- tial government	Democratic majority, critical, mixed gov- ernment
1973–74	Domestic, consoli- dative	Moderate agenda, assertive, mixed to limited resources, presidential gov- ernment	Democratic majority, aggressively critical, congressional gov- ernment
Ford			
1974–76	Domestic, consoli- dative	Moderate agenda, moderately assert- ive, limited re- sources, mixed government	Democratic majority, critical, congres- sional government
Carter			
1977–80	Domestic, consolida- tive to contrac- tive	Moderate agenda, less assertive, mixed resources, executive gov- ernment	Democratic majority, critical, mixed gov- ernment

SOURCE: Compiled by author.

branch as to who should do what work, lead us to expect different behavior in presidential-congressional relations. But there is more. The personal backgrounds and qualities of the individual presidents may also be expected to have an effect. Politically Lyndon Johnson was born and raised in the U.S. Congress. He began his political career working on the staff of a member of the House in 1931 and was himself later elected to the House and then the Senate. He served as Senate Democratic whip and floor leader during the 1950s. Johnson's strength and resourcefulness in Congress and in the South led to his being selected as Kennedy's running mate in 1960. Not surprisingly, Johnson's style of dealing with Congress was that of the *majority leader as president*.

Richard Nixon also served in Congress, but only briefly. He was elected twice to the House of Representatives and once to the Senate. He resigned his Senate seat after two years in office when he was elected vice-president. His total congressional service was just six years. Nixon's eight years as vice-president and his experience in running for president in 1960 contributed to an interest in foreign policy. Henry Kissinger reports that he was struck by Nixon's "perceptiveness and knowledge" of foreign policy when he first met him. At that meeting Nixon indicated that "he was determined to run foreign policy from the White House."[11] Nixon's interest in international affairs, and possibly the reasons the subject fascinated him, influenced his relations with Congress. Perhaps it is not overstating the case to suggest that his style was that of the *foreign minister as president*.

Gerald Ford's career parallels that of Lyndon Johnson, but on the other side of the tracks. Ford was first elected to the House of Representatives in 1948 and became leader of the House Republicans in 1965. As Kennedy had selected Johnson, Nixon chose Ford to serve with him as vice-president in part because of Ford's knowledge of Capitol Hill and the respect he commanded there. We are safe, then, in identifying Ford's style of congressional relations as that of the *minority leader as president*.

Jimmy Carter had virtually no national political experience prior to his election as president. He served two terms in the Georgia State Senate (1963–67), ran for and lost the governorship in 1966, ran again in 1970 and won. Interestingly, Carter was forty-six years old before he won major elective office, whereas Johnson was twenty-nine, Nixon was thirty-three, and Ford was thirty-five. Carter's 1976 nomination and election are explained in large part by his lack of Washington-based experience. Indeed, he campaigned on this theme, seeking to capitalize on the post-Watergate public mood of distrust of politics. Once in office, therefore, Carter's methods of dealing with Congress were those of the *political layman as president*.

Lyndon Johnson — Majority Leader as President

If I were to name the one factor above all others that helped me in dealing with the Congress, I would say it was the genuine friendship and rapport I had with most Congressmen and Senators. I understood and respected men who dedicated their lives to elective office. Most politicians are men of principle dedicated to the national interest. I believed that I, as president, had the responsibility to appeal to that dedication, to outline what I considered the national interest required, to lay out the alternatives, and to hope that a reasonable man would understand and accept his duty.[12]

Winston Churchill once observed that he was a "child of the House of Commons." In like manner, Lyndon Johnson was a child of Congress. In several recent works on presidential-congressional relations, Johnson has received considerably more attention than any of the other presidents, often twice as much as the rest combined. One also finds in reading presidential memoirs that Johnson himself liked talking about how he dealt with Congress; other presidents in the modern era (including Ford) have little to say on the subject. Much of our current lore about presidential legislative style therefore comes from the Johnson administration, particularly from the first three years (1964–66). It should be noted that Johnson's behavior also influenced expectations on Capitol Hill, setting the standard by which other presidents would be measured, regardless of changes in political conditions.

What was this "majority leader style"? And what techniques were employed? Understanding the style, as exercised by Lyndon Johnson, begins with acknowledging a consummate interest in and knowledge of Congress. To like anything is to enjoy seeing it work. And Johnson liked to make Congress work. While serving as Democratic floor leader in the Senate, "he wanted the bills to become laws."[13] His move to the White House did not change this goal. Nothing about Congress seemed to bore Johnson. By all accounts, as president he wanted a daily accounting of Capitol Hill activities, particularly before the Vietnam war came to dominate and frustrate his political life.

Complementing this presidential desire for legislative production were the several favorable political conditions cited in table 7.1. Even before his landslide victory in 1964, Johnson was in a position to capitalize on the progressive mood of Congress following the tragedy of John F. Kennedy's assassination. Further, much preliminary work on developing social programs had been completed by the Democrats in the Eisenhower and Kennedy years. James L. Sundquist described the situation as follows:

> During the early years of the period [1953–56] ... the problems were being identified and the initial forms of remedial action were being devised. In the middle years [1957–61] ... political support was being mobilized and the measures themselves were being refined in public debate....
>
> The late years of the period [1962–65] were a time of rounding out the program with additional proposals, of solidifying popular support, and of maneuvering the program through the policy-making institutions of government.[14]

Favorable political conditions, a full agenda, and a strongly motivated and interested president combined to produce "the Congress of fulfillment ... of accomplished hopes ... of realized dreams."[15] It is important to be reminded of this happy coincidence of factors when deciding whether to measure other presidents by the Johnson standard.

The various legislative strategies and techniques relied on by the Johnson administration during these early years follow from, in the sense of being logically derivative of, the developments above. And they tended to be positive in nature—after all, the president was trying to enact an extensive legislative program. "Many carrots and a few sticks, these were the tools of O'Brien's men" (Lawrence O'Brien headed Johnson's liaison office).[16] Based on several accounts of Johnson's relations with Congress, I have compiled the following list of techniques or strategies.

Know what is going on. Johnson wanted to know everything that affected or might potentially affect his legislative program. Not only was the knowledge itself important to him in judging what to do, how, and when, but he had a reputation to uphold. "The foundation of Johnson's involvement was intimate knowledge of Congress, knowledge that came from beyond even his own vast experience."[17] He wanted the members to think that he knew even more than he actually knew. The illusion of knowledge can be created by organization and activity. Anyone observing the amount of legislative-directed activity in the Johnson White House would draw the conclusion that the legislative liaison team (which included the president) must surely know everything about everyone. And that is exactly the impression Johnson wanted to create.

Know thyself. It is a commonplace that the national legislative process extends beyond the halls of Congress. Much of what happens in the executive branch affects legislation and legislators, either by design or by circumstance. Departments and agencies want existing programs authorized and funded. Many of these programs involve contracts, construction, projects of various kinds, services, and so on, that will benefit the constituents of representatives and senators. And new programs proposed by the president or the departments and agencies require legislative approval. It was Johnson's style to adopt a congressional perspective in the preparation of programs for approval and in the administration of programs in the states and districts. He accomplished these goals by ensuring that "the liaison staff had a substantial involvement in the formulation of policy."[18] The staff used the Bureau of the Budget (now the Office of Management and Budget) to track legislation. And according to Stephen J. Wayne, "the agenda of every cabinet meeting included an item on legislative activities."[19] The president was also anxious to know about all appointments, contracts, and projects so that he and the appropriate members of Congress could take credit. Knowing thyself, then, is simply being aware of what is going on within the administration that is pertinent (1) to what you send to Capitol Hill for approval and (2) to what you do by way of administering programs that affect the members in their states and districts.

Act fast. Lyndon Johnson was extraordinarily anxious about moving quickly early in his term. He believed that a president's impact is very short-lived. Here is how he put it in his memoirs:

> The president and the Congress run on separate clocks. The occupant of the White House has a strict tenancy. . . .
> A president must always reckon that this mandate will proved short-lived. . . . For me, as for most active presidents, popularity proved elusive.[20]

Be persistent. Doris Kearns quotes Johnson as saying:

There is but one way for a president to deal with the Congress, and that is continuously, incessantly, and without interruption. If it's really going to work, the relationship between the president and the Congress has got to be almost incestuous. He's got to know them even better than they know themselves. And then, on the basis of this knowledge, he's got to build a system that stretches from the cradle to the grave, from the moment a bill is introduced to the moment it is officially enrolled as the law of the land.[21]

At least two forms of persistence are suggested in this quotation. First is that associated with a particular bill—making contact with members over time, not being discouraged by setbacks, maintaining continuous pursuit. Second is the more general persistence characterized by habitual communication and contact on Capitol Hill. Though this second brand of persistence is less focused, it supplies the foundation for more specific requests.

Set priorities. In his description of presidential lobbying by Kennedy and Johnson, John F. Manley speaks of "superintending the legislative process."[22] Surely a part of "superintending" is to be sensitive to the pace and workload of Congress. Johnson had an enormous legislative program, but he was aware that he should not overload the system.

He sent bills one by one rather than in a clump.... Also, he sent them when the agendas of the receiving committees were clear so that they could be considered right away, without time for opposition to develop and when the members most intensely concerned about the bills would be most likely to support them.[23]

One begins to understand the importance of Johnson's intimate knowledge of the workings of the Hill. A president must either know about committee and subcommittee schedules or establish a mechanism for finding out. Johnson had both advantages—a sort of failsafe system. As noted later, Carter had neither.

Be accessible. Accessibility of the president to members of Congress must start with the president's inviting contact between himself and his own liaison people. He cannot possibly maintain close communication with all 535 members, but it is important that the members know that they can get to the president if they need to. Johnson's passionate interest in the legislative process once again led him

quite naturally to establish means for two-way congressional contact. The liaison officers could make commitments for the president.
"Johnson had even issued a standing order with the switchboard that
any time O'Brien called, he was to be put through regardless of the
hour. The calls went in both directions."[24]

Implicate the members. In describing Johnson's philosophy and
approach to Senate floor leadership, Ralph K. Huitt observed:

> Johnson was a legislative pragmatist. He believed it possible to do
> anything that was worth the effort and the price, and *so considered
> every problem from the standpoint of what was necessary to
> achieve the desired objective, and whether the objective was worth
> the cost.* He learned early and never forgot the basic skill of the
> politician: the ability to divide any number by two and add one.[25]

Johnson carried this approach to the White House. He wanted the
Congress to work on his bills, but he understood the importance of
finding a basis for compromise. He employed the time-honored
method of implicating the members through consultations, appointments to "secret task forces," and advance notice.[26] Such methods
helped him build support but also informed him about the limits of
his support.

Make party leaders look good. Polsby reminds us that there are
forces encouraging cooperation between the president and Congress
and "high on any list ... would be the effects of party membership."[27] Not unexpectedly, it was Johnson's style to work with party
leaders—almost to incorporate them into his daily operations. Manley points out that the House and Senate Democratic Party leaders
"worked so closely with the White House during the 1960s that the
system more resembled the parliamentary form of executive-legislative relations than the presidential."[28] The executive branch lobbyists
conducted their own legislative head counts. These polls were combined with those of the party leadership to produce reliable information on probable outcomes. All this activity was good business for
the president, but it also made party leaders look good.

Go to the public last. "I sometimes felt that Congress was like a
sensitive animal—if pushed gently it would go my way, but if pushed
too hard it would balk." Lyndon Johnson "preferred to work from
within, knowing that good legislation is the product not of public

rhetoric but of private negotiations and compromise." But his objections to the public opinion route to Congress involved more than the immediate effect on a piece of legislation. He believed that taking an issue to the people typically involved picking "a fight with the Congress." It was not enough to state one's position on the issue. That would not get press or public attention. The president also had "to say mean words and show [his] temper."[29] Thus, there are possible long-run effects of going to the people—in essence going over the heads of the members of Congress, who, after all, also believe they represent the people. These views of Johnson illustrate the problems in managing continuity between formal and informal talk. Perhaps it goes without saying that Johnson also considered arm twisting a last resort.

Summary. These several guidelines to White House lobbying on Capitol Hill are all consistent with the majority leader style of building coalitions. They worked extraordinarily well for enacting Johnson's domestic program, 1964–66. Such complete management of congressional relations, however, demands a great deal of the president's time. It so happens that President Johnson wanted to use his time in this way. By 1966 the Vietnam war required his full attention, and from that point on the president had to concentrate on foreign and defense issues that were less familiar and more frustrating to him. His congressional relations deteriorated rapidly, since he seemed to be incapable of applying to foreign issues the guidelines that worked so effectively for him on domestic programs. The 1968 presidential election brought to the White House a person with impressive interest and expertise in foreign and defense policy, and variable interest in domestic issues.

Richard Nixon—Foreign Minister as President

Nixon had no more stomach for face-to-face confrontations with members of Congress than for those with anyone else. When he did invite a member into the Oval Office to ask his help, the personal Nixon pressure was mild indeed—the antithesis of the insistent Johnson treatment. "I know you have your problems with this," the president would say, "and I will completely understand if you can't come with me, but if you can I'd appreciate it." ... Although no contest with Congress engaged Nixon so viscerally as his humiliating failure in the spring of 1970 to win Senate confirmation of

Judge G. Harrold Carswell to the Supreme Court, he never personally demanded or pleaded for any senator's vote.[30]

It would be difficult to imagine a more striking contrast in congressional styles than that between Lyndon Johnson and Richard Nixon. As noted earlier, the explanation lies in large part with personal and political factors. These were two very different men belonging to different political parties and facing different sets of issues. A review of the data on Nixon in tables 7.1 to 7.3 illustrates some of the more important changes. Certainly most notable among these was the fact that Nixon faced a Democratic Congress. But this condition by no means explains the problems that developed. Both Eisenhower and Ford also faced Democratic Congresses and yet avoided the animosities that developed in the Nixon administration. For reasons too complicated to explore here, Nixon came to question the legitimacy and competency of Congress, particularly after his landslide victory in 1972. Therefore, whereas Johnson's interest in and knowledge of Congress were the most important determinants of his relations with that institution, Nixon's interest in nonlegislative issues and his basic distrust of Congress were important in explaining his approach to the institution.

This lack of motivation and involvement was reflected in the organization of Nixon's legislative liaison arrangements. Most significantly, the legislative liaison staff "appeared to become distanced from the president."[31] Bryce Harlow first headed the office. He had served in a similar post under Eisenhower and was very close to Nixon. After Harlow changed jobs in early 1970, none of the operational persons in the office had intimate, daily contact with the president.

Nixon himself "seemed to lose interest in programs quickly and was frequently upbraided in Congress for not trying to get his programs passed."[32] He was also not above publicly upbraiding Congress, something that Johnson avoided if at all possible. Before delivering his State of the Union message in 1971, for example, Nixon issued a statement criticizing the record of the previous Congress. Here is some of what he had to say:

> In the final month and weeks of 1970, especially in the Senate of the United States, the nation was presented with the spectacle of a legislative body that had seemingly lost the capacity to decide and the will to act. When the path was finally cleared, vital days had been lost, and major failures insured.

In probably no month in recent memory did the reputation of the whole Congress suffer more in the eyes of the American people, than in the month of December, 1970. In these times when the need to build confidence in government is so transparent, that was good neither for the Congress nor the country. Let us hope that it never takes place again.[33]

That the president may have been right about his observations was even more reason not to make them public. It was unusual to have the president humiliate Congress just weeks before presenting his legislative program.

We begin our review of strategies or guidelines by noting that the Nixon agenda in the early years differed markedly from that of Johnson in his early years. First, of course, was the dominance of foreign and defense matters—a condition that suited Nixon and that could be used with good effect in dealing with Congress (that is, Vietnam created the priorities). Second, many of the most important domestic requests were designed to reform and reorganize the Great Society programs—a goal not likely to be warmly accepted by the members who had enacted these programs a few years earlier. We should not therefore be particularly surprised to find that many of the guidelines for congressional contact produced conflict rather than harmony.

Why, then, have we labeled his style as that of the foreign minister as president? Simply because a president faced with international crises is generally acknowledged to be performing a virtuous role. And in Nixon's case it gave him a legitimate excuse for rising above the fray, coping with problems more important than those associated with getting a legislative program through Congress. It also provided a basis for Nixon to criticize Congress. Surely legislators could be expected to cooperate at the domestic level if the president is ending wars and establishing communication (as with China) to prevent future wars. Now one can see how President Nixon believed himself justified in chastising the naughty 91st Congress and admonishing them, like a scolding father: "Let us hope that it never takes place again."

The guidelines, too, become comprehensible even though they are antithetical to those espoused by President Johnson. For the fact is that they suited Nixon's evaluation of his political situation and the role he chose to play as a response. Here are some of them:

Don't involve the president in lobbying. As indicated in the opening quotation, Nixon simply would not display his commitments in face-to-face encounters with members. He did not like the contact, and he would seldom ask, plead, or cajole in order to get a vote. This work was to be done by others. At the same time, Nixon made judgments about those who supported and opposed him, and he would reward his friends and seek reprisals against his opponents.

Reduce accessibility. If the president did not want to bargain personally with the members, he likewise did not want them to come to him. Stephen J. Wayne quotes a House Republican as saying that "I pretty well concluded that there was almost no way to contact him except if you had a personal relationship."[34] This distance between the president and the members was lengthened as a result of the reduced role of the liaison people in White House decision making. Though Harlow had the ear of the president, his successor, William Timmons, did not, and neither was as close to Nixon as O'Brien was to Johnson.

Work with your friends. Although the Democrats were in the majority throughout Nixon's five and one-half years in office, there was surprisingly little reaching out to Democrats by the president. His personal contacts with members were with those he knew. His meetings with congressional leaders were not particularly productive. Naturally this separation and distance made the job of the liaison people especially difficult.

Steer the proper course. In his memoirs, Nixon states:

> I was determined to be an activist president in domestic affairs. I had a definite agenda in mind, and I was prepared to knock heads together in order to get things done.... But it didn't take long to discover that enthusiasm and determination could not overcome the reality that I was still the first president in 120 years to begin his term with both houses of Congress controlled by the opposition party.[35]

Perhaps because of Democratic control of Congress, more likely because of his own demeanor, Nixon was never prepared "to knock heads together." It was more convenient for him personally to rely on the force of the idea and a steadiness in purpose. This is not to say that the White House staff did not engage in arm twisting—only that it was not the style of Nixon himself. He believed that "if a president is sufficiently forceful, sufficiently sound in his policies and sure of his purpose, and able to take his argument persuasively, to the people, Congress will go along a good deal of the time."[36]

Summary. In a manner of speaking, Nixon's style did not facilitate legislative lobbying at all. Instead, it contributed a rationale for the distance he wanted between himself and Congress. And, of course, much of what he personally wanted the government to do could be accomplished with limited legislative involvement (at least as contrasted to Johnson). Interestingly enough, Nixon's separation from Congress and his own legislative liaison personnel apparently reduced the effect of Watergate on the president's legislative program. "Despite the awesome political and personal consequences of the congressional investigation and legal controversies, Timmons [successor to Harlow as head of legislative liaison] believed the effect of Watergate on pending legislation was minimal."[37]

Gerald Ford — Minority Leader as President

I think the president has to accept the fact that he must spend more time personally with members of Congress, and he must work with the leaders of both parties to enhance their strength and influence. *Members of Congress are important.* The president cannot spend too much time with them.... I think a president has to give the leaders in the Congress and influential members of both parties an open door to come and take part in policy decisions. He doesn't have to guarantee that he will do what they say, but at least they have to have the feeling that their views are considered before the fact, and not after.[38]

Gerald R. Ford served in the House of Representatives for twenty-five years before being nominated by Nixon to serve as the first vice-president selected under the procedures of the Twenty-fifth Amendment. During his long congressional service, Ford was in the majority for just two years, 1953–54, when the Republicans held a narrow eight-seat majority in the House. Thus, for twenty-three of his twenty-five years in the House, Ford learned well the problems associated with minority status. As a member, chairman of the Republican conference (1963–65), a senior member of the Committee on Appropriations, and Republican floor leader (1965–73), Ford experienced the frustrations of trying to fashion majorities either in support of Republican initiatives or against Democratic programs. His rise to a leadership position largely resulted from his capacity to work well with others—to make accommodations without losing a sense of purpose. When Ford defeated Charles Halleck for the floor leadership in 1965, Halleck commented: "It's the only election I've ever lost and it was because I got myself involved in a beauty contest."[39] Robert L. Peabody suggests that much more than "age and physical appearance" were at stake, however: "the activists were able to convince a majority of their colleagues that Ford would project a more positive image to the nation and work toward more constructive alternative programs within the House of Representatives."[40]

As minority leader, Ford had to work with a Democratic administration for four years and Democratic Party leaders in Congress for over eight years. He also had to coexist for four years with his counterpart in the Senate, Everett McKinley Dirksen. Sometimes working with Dirksen was as difficult as working with the Democrats. For example, when Ford tried to criticize President Johnson's handling of the Vietnam war, Dirksen rebuked him: "You don't demean the chief magistrate of your country at a time when a war is on."[41] The point is that Ford developed a style for coping with those likely to upstage him, either because they had the votes or because they commanded the audience. When Nixon entered the White House, Ford was also put in the position of having to lead under severely limiting conditions. During the Johnson administration at least he was not responsible for enacting the president's program, though, as noted, he had to be careful in his criticisms, given Dirksen's close association with the president. With a Republican in the White House, however, the situation changed, and Ford was made responsible for enacting the president's program. In the 91st Congress, Republicans held 44 percent of the House seats; in the 92d Congress, they held 41 percent of the seats. And in doing his job Ford could not depend on consistent and attentive support from the president.

The techniques relied on by Ford were very much like those used by Johnson, but accommodated to a set of political circumstances that were severely limiting. After all, Ford was an unelected president.[42] He was nominated because of his congressional experience, and he was approved by bipartisan votes in the House and Senate. By experience, personality, and means of selection, then, one expected Ford to develop close working relationships with Congress. But his agenda of government programs was much more limited than that of Johnson. He therefore did not approach Congress with the same urgency. His requests tended to be more consolidative in nature—adjustments in existing programs, management of the economy and energy resources, executive reorganization.

As president, Ford relied on the legislative style he had learned so well in the House of Representatives. He was accessible, he worked closely with party leaders on Capitol Hill, he implicated members in his legislative program, he invited close contact with his legislative liaison people. Here is what Ford himself had to say about congressional relations:

> In dealing with the Congress, Nixon and some of his aides had tended to work with individual Senators and Representatives who they felt were loyal to him instead of working with the elected leadership. That strategy didn't help the legislation that Nixon was trying to push, and it infuriated Hugh Scott and John Rhodes [minority floor leaders in the Senate and House respectively] because it undercut their authority as party leaders. I assured both men that I considered them leaders in fact as well as in name, and I promised to pull no end runs. Indeed, from the moment I became president, I set aside several hours a week for any member of Congress who wanted to come and see me privately.[43]

This sensitivity to and interest in the members of Congress makes Ford sound like a relaxed Lyndon Johnson. Thus there is no point in providing a detailed description of the similar techniques he applied. Ford did successfully use one technique, however, that suited his political situation—a technique that Johnson had used only as a last resort.

Threaten a veto. The veto is definitely helpful to a minority president, particularly one with a limited program, who wants to resist expansion of government. After all, sustaining a veto only requires getting either 146 votes in the House or 34 votes in the Senate. Awareness of this advantage on Capitol Hill makes the threat of a veto a highly useful weapon for minority-party presidents. Nixon used the veto more than his Democratic predecessors but much less than Eisenhower. Ford, in contrast, relied heavily on the veto for getting what he wanted.

> In order to make the veto threat credible, the liaison staff had to be able to sustain presidential vetoes. This became the major strategic objective of the Ford liaison operation. The tactics used in this ef-

fort did not differ markedly from those employed in other legislative situations and by other administrations although the stakes from the president's point of view were higher.[44]

Summary. Ford's brief presidency was one of the most extraordinary in American history. Elected by Congress to the vice-presidency, Ford assumed office when the presidency itself had suffered incredible damage as a result of Watergate. His legislative experience in the minority served him well in restoring balance between the presidency and Congress. "Members of Congress are important." President Ford could say this convincingly, confident that the members themselves knew he meant it.

Jimmy Carter — Political Layman as President

I think I have found it is much easier for me in my own administration to evolve a very complex proposal for resolving a difficult issue than it is for Congress to pass legislation and to make that same decision.

The energy legislation is one example. I never dreamed ... when I proposed this matter to the Congress that a year later it still would not be resolved. I think I have got a growing understanding of the Congress, its limitations, and its capabilities and also its leadership, which was a new experience for me altogether, never having lived or served in the federal government in Washington.[45]

This statement by President Carter is remarkably candid and naive, but it is revealing of his approach to presidential-congressional relations. He seemed genuinely surprised and perplexed by the extent of congressional involvement in public policymaking. One wonders where he had been in the decade before his election, when Congress had thwarted presidential foreign policy, reshaped much of its own structure, and forced a president out of office. Where, indeed, was President Carter during these years? And how did this experience influence his behavior once in office?

In 1966 Carter ran for governor of Georgia and finished third in a crowded field. In 1970 he ran again—this time against former Governor Carl Sanders. He won the nomination in a bitter runoff primary.

Carter conducted what many observers said was reminiscent of the anti-desegregation campaign waged by former Gov. George C. Wallace ... of Alabama. But Carter's record before the primary indicated he was moderate and conciliatory toward racial matters.[46]

Former Governor Lester Maddox ran for lieutenant governor at the same time as Carter, though not necessarily with him. Carter and Maddox both won.

Carter's own view of his relationships with the Georgia legislature was that he "had to start from scratch." Few legislators had supported him in his campaign for governor, but, as he noted, "I had a heavy mandate from the Georgia people."[47] Unable to succeed himself as governor, Carter campaigned constantly for president in 1975 and 1976. Having sampled the anti-Washington mood of the nation during his travels in 1974, Carter settled on his campaign theme. In accepting the nomination, Carter emphasized his distance from the federal government: "I have never met a Democratic president, but I've always been a Democrat." He emphasized that his campaign had been a "humbling experience, reminding us that ultimate political influence rests not with the power brokers, but with the people." "It's time for the people to run the government" and, of course, he was the people's candidate.[48]

The legislative strategies and techniques relied on by the Carter White House are perplexing if one believes that the president ought to try to work with Congress as it is. They evidence considerably more coherence if one believes that national politics and policymaking should be changed. Carter was said to have a "'premeditated' purpose ... to wean the country away from" traditional leadership.

> Carter's purpose was "to try to get this country mature enough that people realize they're going to have to make decisions on their own and not listen to political leaders, because political leaders, under this Constitution, simply don't have the capacity to handle it all."[49]

The following techniques appear more rational if this view is correct.

Create a favorable climate. In his careful study of Carter's legislative liaison system, Eric L. Davis reports that the principal task of the White House team was to facilitate "the president's program, not so much by convincing members of Congress on the specific issues, but by creating a climate of favor conducive to the president and his ideas."[50] The president's senior assistant for public affairs, Anne Wexler, had the responsibility "to create an instant coalition for a specific presidential priority." She remarked in an interview: "Our job is to create lobbyists. We do that by educating people on the substance of the issues. We never ask a person to call a Congressman, but we will tell him when a vote is coming up or when a markup is due and give him a lot of information about it."[51] Unfortunately, effective coalition building among groups was not immediately translated into effective coalition building on Capitol Hill (though there were some notable successes in the last years of the Carter administration).[52]

Act fast; ask for a lot. Carter apparently believed with Johnson that a president needs to move quickly. He produced his complex energy proposal by April 1977. But he did not pace the proposals in sending them to the Hill and thus projected no sense of true priorities. Actually, with his penchant for hyperbole, everything was a priority. Either way, Congress was confused.

> The House Ways and Means Committee had, at the same time, the president's income tax, welfare, hospital cost control, and energy tax proposals. This legislative glut, it is said, has baffled Congress about his priorities and stretched his prestige too thin.[53]

Do not consult or notify in advance. Once in office, Carter tended to go it alone. For example, none of the congressional committee chairmen who would have to facilitate passage of the energy program was included in its development. Nor were members systematically informed of legislation, patronage appointments, or projects affecting their states and districts. Some of these initial problems were corrected, but terrible impressions were created.

Appeal on the merits. It seems apparent that Jimmy Carter believed the rhetoric of his campaign: "If I'm elected, it's going to be done, and you can depend on it." A man of impressive self-confidence, Carter wanted and expected Congress to adopt his programs because he had developed them. According to Thomas Cronin,

> Carter in office often acted as if he had some direct mandates to reshape domestic and foreign policy. Although not a populist by any stretch of the imagination, he tried nonetheless to be assertive, innovative, and purposeful.... He gave the impression that he was

the rational man and that Congress should deal with him and his programs completely on their merits.[54]

Pronounce first, compromise later. Consistent with the appeal to merits was a tendency by Carter to announce a program as meeting some great challenge, or declaring that a particular proposal was the centerpiece of a larger program, and then make major concessions—possibly even withdraw the proposal altogether. In part this behavior ignored Johnson's first principle: "Know what is going on." As Cronin points out, Carter failed to explore "the mine fields to see what traps and opposition he would encounter."[55]

> When he discovered that he did not have the necessary support, he would have to back down in public. . . . His compromises . . . came later in the game after damage had been done to his political reputation and his relationship with politically powerful others.[56]

Ignore traditional congressional politics. It is consistent with the political layman's role for Carter to have eschewed the amenities, announcements, favors, projects, and appointments associated with congressional politics. What president would have begun his term by cutting out water projects believed by members to be so vital to their districts (and their own future political careers)?

Summary. "It was as if he didn't like politics, and yearned to be above both politics and politicians."[57] This review of Carter's style and techniques suggests that his first instincts were to try to make Washington less political. Failing that, he was forced to engage in the very behavior that upset him. It is understandable that problems developed for him, both in pursuing his natural instincts and in trying to be somebody else.

Presidential Negotiation with Congress

I began this inquiry by emphasizing the role of negotiation and bargaining in a democratic society. Absolutely crucial transactions in national policymaking occur between the president and Congress. The precise nature of these transactions appears to depend heavily on the president. What this analysis of four presidents has shown, above all, is that a relationship dependent on the president is one subject to rather dramatic change (particularly in these times of high presidential turnover). Earlier I identified several forms of negotiation—from the classic bargain as an exchange, and characterized by close contact between the parties, to the more distant call for support associated with presidential interpretations of what is in the best interest of the members or the nation. Presidents Johnson and Ford understood and accepted classic bargaining (as defined by Dahl and Lindblom) but differed markedly in their political resources. Presidents Nixon and Carter were uncomfortable with the politics of exchange, depending instead on a form of persuasion that preserved distance between them and the members of Congress. Despite individual differences within this set of four presidents, at least we have spotted similarities among two pairs—Johnson and Ford accepting a partnership or inside model of congressional contact, Nixon and Carter preferring an independent or outside model.

Which model is the most successful? It is difficult to say because different measures of success may be employed for each. The partnership model is like a marriage. As Ralph K. Huitt describes it: "two elements seem to be indispensable: that both parties want it to succeed and (what is not so obvious) that workable arrangements be established which make the crucial day-to-day lives flow together easily without letting every chore or responsibility become a possible confrontation."[58] These elements are not unlike those identified by Dahl and Lindblom as crucial for bargaining. They occur because people "disagree and expect that further agreement is possible and will be profitable."[59]

"But," as Huitt notes, "what if a president does not want a marriage with Congress?"[60] What if the president seriously doubts that "further agreement is possible and will be profitable"? Or what if the president disagrees with Congress but expects that further agreement will be possible only on his terms or only if the members improve their politics? Clearly those accepting this more independent mode of behavior will rely on methods different from those above.

Now at least we are in a position to specify measures of success for each model. For the partnership model, one naturally looks for successful bargains. Were the bills passed? Did the president get what he wanted? Was the partnership personally profitable—was the president reelected? Taking into account the vast difference in political resources available to Johnson and Ford, it is fair to say that both were reasonably successful in making the partnership work, measured by the legislation produced. Johnson's production in the early years was phenomenal; Ford's consistently exceeded expectations. Johnson, however, got distracted by the intractable set of problems associated with Vietnam and did not even seek reelection. And Ford was narrowly defeated for reelection, though it may fairly be said that there was victory in defeat given his minority-party status.

For the independent model, the test would seem to be whether the president is able to produce on his own. Was he successful in doing those things to which he gave high priority? Before the Watergate debacle, Nixon scored quite well on this measure. He wanted relatively little from Congress. Above all, he wanted to be free to participate imaginatively in international affairs. He was also devising means for acting without Congress on many domestic matters. What we will never know for certain is how Congress would have reacted to his behavior had it not been for Watergate. There was evidence that they were determined to reduce his independence and that he might, therefore, have been much more constrained in his final three years even without the scandal that forced him out of office.

Carter did want something from Congress, and he was notably unsuccessful in employing the independent model for getting it. Carter was never free to produce on his own, and he was an unwilling and clumsy bargainer. Nixon's independent style was congruent with his goals and, up to a point, with the authority of the office (particularly in regard to foreign policy). Carter's independent style was incongruent with his goals and with presidential authority. Was their independence personally profitable? Nixon was reelected by a landslide, but was the first president in history forced to resign. Carter was defeated, also in a landslide.

The significant social, economic, and political changes in recent decades have resulted in highly unstable executive-legislative relations, which in turn have contributed to, if not caused, inconstancy in the national policy process. It is no doubt unfair to argue that this outcome is all the president's doing. Congress, too, has changed dramatically in recent years, sometimes in response to shifting presidential styles. My concluding point is not to judge who is to blame but to express concern about the effects of dramatically different presidential styles. I was able to pair off the four presidents—two each accepting the partnership and independent models. Still, there are significant differences in the conditions, styles, techniques, and effects within each pair. Interestingly some of these differences may be attributable to political party. Note that I have paired off a Democrat with a Republican in each case.

Though much remains to be said on this important topic, I have gone as far as I can comfortably go on the basis of available research. I cannot end, however, without commenting on relationships between President Ronald Reagan and Congress. There were signs even in the early months of his administration that he accepted the partnership model but was more prone than Johnson or Ford to rely on the full range of negotiating strategies—from classic bargaining to precise and resolute translations of the national interest.[61] Certainly Reagan's performance before Congress on 28 April 1981 in support of his economic program well illustrated the use of all available techniques.

It may be prosaic but appropriate to refer to Reagan's style simply as that of *actor as president*. Other labels to consider are communicator, personator, agent, or proxy. It happens that this style reflects a role-playing capacity consistent with the demands of representative democracy. Placing oneself in the position of another, communicating both the substance and style of the character, "enlisting the will and movements of others" (see below), predicting and translating audience reaction—these are commonplace responses in the theater, which serve the values of political representation. I am not making a judgment about whether Reagan was a good or bad actor as president (though the early reviews were favorable). I am simply observing that the style came naturally to him and was suited to some of the demands of the office.

Perhaps the president in this century whose style most closely resembled that of Reagan is Franklin D. Roosevelt. Again we have a pair drawn from the two parties and thus observe important differences in policy substance. But the emphasis on communication and role playing is surely there for both. In Roosevelt's case, the motivation for "acting by proxy" may have been his illness. Kenneth Burke persuasively makes this point:

> It is even conceivable that his illness contributed substantially as an important motive shaping the quality of his understanding, and thence the quality of his acts. For during the period of the attack and the slow recovery, he must have experienced most poignantly and forcibly a distinction between action and motion, since he could act only by proxy, through enlisting the will and movements of others. Thus, even down to the purely physiological level, he must have learned to make peace with a kind of dissociation between impulse and response rarely felt by men whose physical motions are in more spontaneous or naive relation to their thinking. Hence, it is conceivable that from this dissociation could arise a more patient attitude toward motives outside one's direct control than other men would naturally have. And from this could arise a sharpening of the administrative sense, which is decidedly that of

acting by proxy, and utilizing the differences among the agents through whom one acts.[62]

One is tempted to make something of the 1981 assassination attempt (or Reagan's age) at this point, but it is enough to take note of the similarity in styles of the two men and to speculate about the striking differences in motivation.

Finally, I am anxious to urge more research and analysis of presidential negotiation with Congress. Surely there are few better starting places for comprehending the political dynamics of recent decades. As Richard E. Neustadt concluded in 1960:

> The president's advantages are checked by the advantages of others. Continuing relationships will pull in both directions. These are relationships of mutual dependence. A president depends upon the men he would persuade; he has to reckon with his need or fear of them. They too will possess status, or authority, or both, else they would be of little use to him. Their vantage points confront his own; their power tempers his.[63]

Events of the past three decades have made this analysis even more appropriate today.

NOTES

1. Lyndon B. Johnson, *The Vantage Point* (New York: Holt, Rinehart and Winston, 1971), 461.
2. Nelson W. Polsby, *Congress and the Presidency* (Englewood Cliffs, N.J.: Prentice Hall, 1976), 198.
3. I am indebted to Anthony King for urging me to clarify the various forms of negotiation and bargaining.
4. Robert A. Dahl and Charles E. Lindblom, *Politics, Economics, and Welfare* (New York: Harper & Row, 1953), 324.
5. Ibid., 326.
6. Ibid., 333.
7. Ibid., 333–34.
8. Polsby, *Congress and the Presidency,* 191.
9. George C. Edwards III, *Presidential Influence in Congress* (San Francisco: Freeman, 1980), chaps. 5–7.
10. Quoted in Paul C. Light, "The President's Agenda: Notes on the

Timing of Domestic Choice," *Presidential Studies Quarterly* 11 (Winter 1981): 69.

11. Henry Kissinger, *White House Years* (Boston: Little, Brown, 1979), 11.

12. Johnson, *Vantage Point,* 459.

13. Ralph K. Huitt, "Democratic Party Leadership in the Senate," *American Political Science Review* 55 (June 1961): 337.

14. James L. Sundquist, *Politics and Policy: The Eisenhower, Kennedy, and Johnson Years* (Washington, D.C.: Brookings Institution, 1968), 506.

15. Statement by Speaker John W. McCormack, as quoted in Sundquist, *Politics and Policy,* 3.

16. Doris Kearns, *Lyndon Johnson and the American Dream* (New York: Harper & Row, 1976), 236.

17. Edwards, *Presidential Influence,* 117.

18. Stephen J. Wayne, *The Legislative Presidency* (New York: Harper & Row, 1978), 149.

19. Ibid., 150.

20. Johnson, *Vantage Point,* 441, 443. Johnson also said: "You've got just one year when they treat you right, and before they start worrying about themselves." Harry McPherson, *A Political Education* (Boston: Little, Brown, 1972), 268.

21. Kearns, *Johnson,* 236–37.

22. John F. Manley, "Presidential Power and White House Lobbying," *Political Science Quarterly* 93 (Summer 1978): 264.

23. Edwards, *Presidential Influence,* 119.

24. Wayne, *Legislative Presidency,* 148.

25. Huitt, "Democratic Leadership," 337; emphasis added.

26. Edwards, *Presidential Influence,* 119.

27. Polsby, *Congress and the Presidency,* 195.

28. Manley, "Presidential Power," 266.

29. All quotations from Johnson are taken from *Vantage Point,* 450–51.

30. Rowland Evans, Jr., and Robert D. Novak, *Nixon in the White House: The Frustration of Power* (New York: Random House, 1971), 107.

31. Wayne, *Legislative Presidency,* 156.

32. Edwards, *Presidential Influence,* 139.

33. Reprinted in Congressional Quarterly, Inc., *Nixon: The Third Year of His Presidency* (Washington, D.C., 1972), 5A.

34. Wayne, *Legislative Presidency,* 161.

35. Richard M. Nixon, *RN: The Memoirs of Richard Nixon* (New York: Warner Books, 1978), 1:512.

36. Richard M. Nixon, "Needed: Clarity of Purpose," *Time* 116 (10 November 1980), 32.

37. Wayne, *Legislative Presidency,* 163.

38. Gerald R. Ford, "Imperiled, Not Imperial," *Time* 116 (10 November 1980), 31; emphasis added.

39. Quoted in Robert L. Peabody, *Leadership in Congress* (Boston: Little, Brown, 1976), 137.

40. Ibid.

41. Quoted in Neil MacNeil, *Dirksen: Portrait of a Public Man* (New York: World, 1970), 291.

42. It is relevant that Ford was not Nixon's first choice. Ford reports that John Connally "had been Nixon's first choice." Rockefeller and Reagan were also considered but were rejected as possibly splitting the party. "That left me as the 'safest' choice." Gerald R. Ford, *A Time to Heal: The Autobiography of Gerald R. Ford* (New York: Harper & Row, 1979), 107.

43. Ibid., 140.

44. Wayne, *Legislative Presidency*, 159.

45. Congressional Quarterly, Inc., *President Carter—1978* (Washington, D.C., 1979), 92A.

46. "Election 1970: The South," *Congressional Quarterly Weekly Report*, 23 October 1970, 2592.

47. Donald Smith, "Carter Sees Ford as 'Not Leading Congress,'" *Congressional Quarterly Weekly Report*, 4 September 1976, 2382.

48. Acceptance speech reprinted in *Congressional Quarterly Weekly Report*, 17 July 1976, 1933–35.

49. Evan Dobelle, a Carter campaign aide, quoted in David S. Broder, *Changing of the Guard: Power and Leadership in America* (New York: Simon and Schuster, 1980), 128.

50. Eric L. Davis, "Legislative Liaison in the Carter Administration," *Political Science Quarterly* 94 (Summer 1979): 290.

51. Dom Bonafede, "To Anne Wexler, All the World Is a Potential Lobbyist," *National Journal*, 8 September 1979, 1476, 1478.

52. See Dom Bonafede, "The Tough Job of Normalizing Relations with Capitol Hill," *National Journal*, 13 January 1979, 54–57.

53. Edwards, *Presidential Influence*, 175.

54. Thomas E. Cronin, *The State of the Presidency*, 2d ed. (Boston: Little, Brown, 1980), 215.

55. Ibid., 174.

56. Statement by Betty Glad, quoted in ibid., 174.

57. Ibid., 216. Another useful review of Carter and Congress is that by Randall B. Ripley in *The Presidency: Studies in Policy Making*, ed. Steven A. Shull and Lance T. LeLoup (Brunswick, Ohio: Kings Court, 1979), 65–82.

58. Ralph K. Huitt, "White House Channels to the Hill," in *Congress against the President*, ed. Harvey C. Mansfield, Sr. (New York: Praeger, 1975), 71.

59. Dahl and Lindblom, *Politics,* 326.

60. Huitt, "White House Channels," 76.

61. For early reports and appraisals of Reagan's congressional liaison operations, led by Max L. Friedersdorf, see Judith Miller, "Reagan's Liaison Chief on Capitol Hill to Focus on Harmony as His Priority," *New York Times,* 6 January 1981, B8; and Helen Dewar and Lee Lescaze, "Reagan Hill Team Gets Rave Reviews," *Washington Post,* 17 March 1981, A5.

62. Kenneth Burke, *A Grammar of Motives* (Englewood Cliffs, N.J.: Prentice Hall, 1952), 391; emphasis added.

63. Richard E. Neustadt, *Presidential Power* (New York: Wiley, 1960), 35–36.

8

Carter and Congress

It seems a reasonable enough proposition that a president will organize his congressional relations to suit his political goals and his personal style. Available literature supports this expectation—at least before the administration of Jimmy Carter. But, of course, recent presidents have been wise in the ways of Washington as a consequence of lengthy experience in the nation's capital. In fact, most have served in Congress. Among post–World War II presidents before Carter, only Dwight Eisenhower lacked service on Capitol Hill (and Fred Greenstein now assures us that his political savvy was fine tuned).[1]

Having a president without Washington experience—or one intolerant of Washington ways of making policy—does not alter the basic proposition stated above. Instead, it encourages different expectations of how such a president will organize his congressional connections. Jimmy Carter was not reluctant to express his distaste for Washington politics during the 1976 campaign. He was expected, however, to ignore his anti-Washington campaign themes once in office. That he did not do so invited criticism of him for being inexperienced and naive. These judgments were based on tests drawn from a model of the president doing politics with Congress by time-honored methods, with the Johnson presidency often used as the basis for measurement. But, of course, Jimmy Carter was not Lyndon Johnson. And measuring his performance by the Johnson goals and style is not true to the opening proposition. In fact, it reshapes the proposition to read: a president who lacks Washington experience should organize his congressional relations in a manner that ignores (or changes) his policy goals and his personal style. The chapter is organized to treat the following topics:

1. The goals and style of the Carter administration
2. The organization of congressional relations as associated with Carter's goals and style
3. The test of achievement for his "outside-in" strategy

Goals and Style: From the Outside In

Analyzing Carter's approach to coping with Congress must begin with the president's ideas about politics.[2] There is abundant evidence that he eschewed his own profession. Beyond that, however, he appeared to espouse a not fully articulated separation between politics and governing. He worked with a concept of what was "right" for the American people—a concept that excluded both the fabled "special interests" and bargaining to accommodate those interests. One aide explained that Carter intended to be a different kind of president. For staff to argue the merits of a proposal on political grounds practically ensured its defeat in the Oval Office. For Carter, the options should be evaluated on substantive merit: what is best for the nation. Quite predictably, White House staff members with extensive Washington experience were frustrated by the president's methods. One aide offered this example:

> It was a matter of enormous frustration to some of us that the president didn't particularly like to hear ... that a decision was political. It was one of the first lessons that I learned in the White House. I can recall one of the first meetings I attended with the president when I went to the White House in the Cabinet Room with other members of the senior staff about a particular issue. The president went around the room asking each staff member what they thought he should do on this ... issue. When he got to me I started by saying, "Mr. President, I think that politically ..." I got about that far when he shut me up.... He put me down in front of the whole staff. So, I was very careful after that to make my arguments, but in a different way.... I could not believe that anybody who operated in an atmosphere where literally everything's political could take such a view.

Another aide with Washington experience explained the difficulty Carter encountered in seeking to avoid politics:

> I always had the sense of a man who was an engineer, who truly believed that if he knew enough about the details of a subject, he

could make a decision that was in the public interest rather than in the interest of particular groups. Therefore, you needed a lot of information; therefore, you needed substance; therefore, "don't bother me about the politics." But then suddenly, he would be forcibly jerked back from this position ... into a sort of purely political context in which a decision had to be made and I don't think that was ever resolved. I don't think it was ever integrated. I had the feeling of moving between the two [substance and politics] but never of pulling it together.

One aide who had served Carter throughout the campaign explained that the president's priorities changed after he entered the White House. This aide argued that Carter understood politics very well: "To say that he doesn't understand the political process is almost to ignore the phenomenally successful campaign out of which he rose from Georgian obscurity." But the reference in this statement is to electoral politics exclusively. The shift in priorities referred to by this aide can be translated as a change from campaign politics to presidential decision making. Apparently the president interpreted politics almost exclusively in electoral terms. Bargaining to build majorities for a legislative program was a type of politics that he "didn't want to hear" about, since he interpreted such behavior as campaign-related. But, of course, some presidents enjoy coalition building for its own sake, not just for how this or that coalition may contribute to reelection. The president's style was illustrated as follows:

[A congressional party leader] told me that Carter's knowledge was the most admirable thing about Carter, but was also obviously one of [his] weaknesses. He said that every time that he had ever been in the White House for a meeting with the president, the president was always well informed. The president was always on the high ground and was always talking or discussing the issue in terms of what was best for the country. But he said he never pulled me aside and said: "I've just got to have you as a Democrat on this vote." It was almost like the president was so preoccupied with the merits of the argument that he didn't approach these legislators with requests to congressmen in a personal or partisan sense.

Here, then, is a portrait of a president who sees himself as protecting the public interest against politics. Having won the office, his trust is then to prevent future electoral influence in policymaking. Is this a lonely quest? It seems so. Even trusted staff members must be corrected when they introduce political (i.e., future electoral) considerations. But beyond that, there is a whole institution at the other end of Pennsylvania Avenue that seemingly thrives on its identification with and representation of special interests. On this matter, President Carter can speak for himself. In evaluating his relations with Congress after he left the White House, he concluded: "My feelings toward Congress are mixed."

> On most issues, the lawmakers treated me well, sometimes under politically difficult circumstances. However, when the interests of powerful lobbyists were at stake, a majority of the members often yielded to a combination of political threats and the blandishments of heavy campaign contributions.
>
> Members of Congress, buffeted from all sides, are much more vulnerable to those groups than is the president. *One branch of government must stand fast on a particular issue to prevent the triumph of self-interest at the expense of the public.* Even when the system of checks and balances works, a price must sometimes be paid: beneficial legislation may be blocked by the threat of unacceptable amendments that cannot be stomached on both ends of Pennsylvania Avenue at the same time. When Congress and the president succumb to the same pressures and bad legislation is passed, the damage to our nation can be very serious.[3]

This is a highly pessimistic view of the capacity of the national policymaking system to reflect the public interest. And, indeed, President Carter was concerned about the strength of this system. "It is almost a miracle how well our nation survives and prospers."[4] In his speech to the nation on 15 July 1979, following the Camp David retreat, the president offered his gloomiest analysis. His comments on governmental capacities are particularly relevant. First the president observed that "Washington, D.C., has become an island." As a consequence, an unprecedented gap exists "between our citizens and our government."

> What you see too often in Washington and elsewhere around the country is a system of government that seems incapable of action.
>
> You see a Congress twisted and pulled in every direction by hundreds of well-financed and powerful special interests.
>
> You see every extreme position defended to the last vote, almost to the last breath by one unyielding group or another.

You often see a balanced and fair approach that demands sacrifice, a little sacrifice from everyone, abandoned like an orphan without support and without friends.[5]

This speech was very personal for the president. He was expressing his frustration in trying to make his approach work in Washington. The struggle for the nation was equally his struggle to implement a "balanced and fair approach" in the face of "well-financed and powerful special interests."

What I do promise you is that I will lead our fight and I will enforce fairness in our struggle and I will ensure honesty. And above all, I will act.

I will continue to travel this country, to hear the people of America. You can help me to develop a national agenda for the 1980s. I will listen and I will act. We will act together. These were promises I made three years ago and I intend to keep them.

The next sentence in this remarkable speech reads: "Little by little we can and we must rebuild *our* confidence" (emphasis added). Textually "our" refers to the nation. Yet it seems that a principal purpose of the speech was to rebuild *his* confidence—to reassert *his* mission and *his* determination to act after two difficult years in office. That is what makes this speech so useful for understanding Carter's political preferences.

An early section of the president's book *Keeping Faith* is entitled "An Outsider in Washington." A political outsider may be expected to conclude that the government is isolated from its people. That view was bolstered by Carter's own extraordinary triumph in winning the nomination and election, and it in turn influenced the president's analysis of his role and that of Congress.

Fortunately, we have available an interview with presidential candidate Carter concerning Congress.[6] Read at the time, the responses appeared to be rather standard, predictably stressing the conflict between President Ford and the Democratic Congress. Read now, they are revealing of the style identified above. Several topics were treated in the interview. Here is a sample:

1. *Proper roles for each institution.* Congress is inherently incapable of unified leadership. That leadership has got to come from the White House.... I believe ... that the Congress is looking for strong leadership in the White House to make

major comprehensive proposals on welfare reform, tax reform, health care, government organization, and so forth, and
then let the Congress in its legitimate constitutional authority
dispose of those proposals as it sees fit, working harmoni-
ously with the White House.

2. *Techniques of dealing with Congress.* One of the things that I
obviously learned while I was in the governor's office ... was
that the best way to avoid confrontations and showdown
votes and the necessity for major compromises is to work
with the members of the legislative branch in the initial stages
of the preparation of major proposals.... Also, to remind the
members ... that, to the extent that my election was successful, the American people join me in those commitments....
[Stresses the importance of open debate.] Now, if after all
those emphases are consummated and my voice to the American people is heard clearly, if we have a difference of opinion
in the Congress that I consider to be important, I would never
hesitate to go directly to the American people....

3. *Representation of constituents.* [Observes that he may go to
the Capitol "every now and then."] So I don't want to try to
dominate the Congress, or to have undue influence, but I
want them to know that we represent the same people.
There's no one in any congressional district in the nation that
won't be my constituent if I become president. And I want
that general sense of cooperation and mutual respect and mutual trust to pervade my whole attitude toward Congress
throughout the four years....the constituents of the congressman or congresswoman will also be my constituents. And I
want to do a good job for them.

4. *Personal contact.* I think just a few personal moves on my
part—treating Congress members as though they were presidents themselves, returning their telephone calls, letting my
staff members respect them thoroughly, dealing with the
problems that they present to me, making my own presence
felt in the Capitol building itself on occasion—would be con-
tributions that might alleviate the present disharmony and total separation of the White House on the one hand and the
Congress on the other.

While no doubt sincere and well intentioned, these views about
the two branches are not wholly consistent. For example, Congress
is incapable of unified leadership but members do not want "to go

back" to the "strong, dominant" (perhaps unified?) leadership of earlier eras. Members should participate in the initial stages of legislation but be reminded that the president has the backing of the American people. Throughout the interview, Carter stressed the importance of his role in representing the constituents of the members—a point he intended to make in dealing with Congress. Here was the true outsider's rationale and method for relating to Congress. The president must do what is right because of commitments made to the American people. Techniques for getting approval in Congress are primarily those designed to remind the members that the president represents their constituents. Bargaining and compromise are mentioned only as outcomes to be avoided. Essentially, harmony will result if Congress does what the president wants. An aide explained it this way:

> He believed 97 percent of the words that he uttered in those campaign speeches.... The man that believed those speeches believed ... that there's something kind of fundamentally corrupt about the governmental process in Washington.... *He was a common cause monarch.* He believed in procedural reform, he believed that we ought to be discussing the issues.

As with other administrations, analysis of congressional relations must begin with the president. Thus it is useful to review what President Carter relied on in setting his own personal agenda. He had a concept of presidential issues—issues that were his responsibility. He sought to master these matters, seeking to understand all the important details. He also made many campaign promises and judged that he had been elected to keep these promises. The combination of mastering the details and relying on the legitimacy of his election resulted in a confidence, perhaps even stubbornness, about what to do and how to do it. One of his close aides explained:

> A lot of folks ... used to ... say, "Look, he's not doing this right or not doing that right," and I'd say, "Look, there's no sense you being concerned about that. He's going to do it his way. That's the way he's going to do it."

Certain organizational and personal requirements are associated with the Carter approach. First, the president must have the time and the isolation to read. The White House is not a very good place for having either. Carter found the early morning hours and the weekends at Camp David useful for meeting this first requirement. Second, means must be found for maintaining contact with the people—Carter's constituents. An "outside in" president has to reassure others (and himself) of his legitimacy. The town meetings, the Patrick Caddell polls, and various White House communications operations (by the offices of Anne Wexler and Jody Powell) were important means to this end. Third, any political judgment that is to be offered must come from those close enough to be trusted implicitly. Even an antipolitical president understands the inevitability of political considerations. But he accepts advice only from those closest to him. Among those Carter relied on most were his wife, Rosalynn, and Hamilton Jordan. One aide went so far as to say: "I do not think he [Carter] ever made any basic decisions, [on issues] where he factored in the political." But his wife and Jordan were "very political."

> Now I think that when he listened to Rosalynn that he's no dummy by any means. He knows full well that Rosalynn has factored in the political aspects of it or Hamilton has factored in the political pluses and minuses. And frankly that's an awfully good position for somebody to be in. Because then he's true to his own being but he knows full well that [the political is] not being overlooked.[7]

This aide then allowed that he did not trust his own judgment on the "pluses and minuses" of certain issues. He therefore thought that having personal relationships with important congressional leaders (and even "obscure members") was very important. He doubted that the president "had any interest in that at all."

Organizing Outside

As pointed out earlier, doing "what's right not what's political" separates that which is normally joined in Washington: issues and politics, substance and process. It places emphasis on the issues—on developing and promoting the "right" solution. But what is "right"? The White House must be organized to answer that question; then a process must be created to build support for the decisions made. Almost by definition, that process excludes close contact with members of Congress, who are "political." Further, it is crucial that the Office of Congressional Liaison be integrated into this issue-based structure—a structure, one is reminded, directed toward doing what is "right," not what is "political."

What kind of organization is suited to the Carter style and priorities? Eric L. Davis points out that, lacking "cooperative lobbying relationships" with Congress, "the White House had to rely on its own resources to obtain legislative successes."[8] The approach to congressional relations was one of establishing confidence in and support for the right solutions to issues designated as high priority. What were the resources on which the White House might rely? They appear to have included the following:

1. President Carter himself as the chief interpreter of national needs and chief designator of priorities
2. A Domestic Affairs and Policy Staff as a source for the development of viable policy options
3. An Office of Management and Budget as a source for the relative cost of major programmatic initiatives, as well as for identifying the effects of choosing different options
4. A Public Liaison staff as a source for feedback on proposals and for building support among affected interest groups
5. A Congressional Liaison staff as a source of congressional reactions to presidential proposals and for creating a favorable climate on Capitol Hill
6. Departmental and agency congressional liaison staff as a source of lobbying on specific proposals

The order in which these sources are listed is important. What it suggests is a sequence of which is more important. One is reminded that we are speaking here of an *approach to Congress* and, for Carter, the approach begins with doing what is right. The congressional liaison operation, therefore, is to be evaluated in that context. One cannot limit analysis of Carter's relations with Congress to the activities of the liaison office since Carter himself did not view it in that way. *His integrative approach was from the outside in, not from the inside out.* And that emphasis relocated the congressional liaison operation when compared with that of other administrations, in particular that of the last Democratic administration (Lyndon B. Johnson's).

PROVIDING THE OPTIONS

The Domestic Affairs and Policy Staff (DPS), headed by Stuart E. Eizenstat, was charged with the responsibility of identifying major domestic policy issues and providing options to the president for dealing with them. The unit came to have a very important role in the Carter administration and was successful in avoiding the "incompetent" label pinned on so many other White House operations. Much of this success is attributed to the intelligence and staff skills of Eizenstat. As Dom Bonafede reported: "Throughout his White House tenure, Eizenstat has risen steadily in stature, and is recognized today within the departments and in Congress as a fair and able presidential emissary."[9]

DPS was strategically located to have impact. A president arrived in Washington with a large agenda derived from the campaign. Somehow these proposals had to be fitted into existing departmental and agency domestic planning agendas. What was going on elsewhere within the executive branch was of direct significance to what the president wanted to accomplish and therefore influenced his options. "We were the president's fingers out there in the government.... We operated on the narrow line between substance and tactics."

The work of the DPS was relevant to the president's relations with Congress in at least two important ways. In the early stages of decision making on domestic policy, the staff provided substantive support for presidential priorities, thus preparing him to deal with Congress on this or that issue. The staff also provided information on the status and conflicts of policy issues that were less important to the president but that might have an impact on his program or might be of significance to Congress.

In the later stages of decision making, this staff was often called on to work on Capitol Hill. Sometimes this activity was in the form of lobbying, though the DPS did not like to call it that. Often it was no more than a logical extension of earlier planning efforts. Major domestic proposals typically involved more than one department or agency. Interagency approval and support had to be orchestrated so as to produce a united front. Interagency lobbying of Congress followed. At this point the congressional liaison staff normally took over. But as with all high-level staff operations, the lines among functional units are not always crisply drawn, nor will members of Congress observe them if they are.

The specific role of the DPS in advising the president changed during the four years because the president himself changed, at least according to some. As the administration moved through the agenda set during the campaign and toward the 1980 election, political considerations became more important. In a sense, the natural rhythm of the four-year term brought the president to the kind of activity he defined as politics: an election campaign. In addition, according to his domestic policy advisers, the president had learned that policy politics was more important than he had previously thought.

MAKING A BUDGET

There is, of course, another agency close to the president that is intimately involved with domestic policy matters. The Office of Management and Budget (OMB) is naturally competitive with the DPS, by virtue of its responsibilities for preparing the budget and clearing all legislative proposals. DPS has the advantage of proximity to the president; OMB has the advantage of expertise and experience. The following description of OMB functions sounds very much like those of the DPS, with its "fingers out there in the government":

> It's the link between the president or the White House and the rest of the government. It's the agency that should translate for the agencies what the president has decided, and then be there on a day to day basis to see that agencies do what the president has decided to do. OMB is not a green-eyeshade agency. It makes policy development in some instances. It is a very professional organization, and I believe it should be. It has the institutional memory to know where the pitfalls are in any kind of policy proposal. It also knows where the roadblocks might be both in the agencies and on the Hill. If properly used, it is an invaluable resource for a president.

The difference between the DPS and OMB is rooted in the longevity of each. One can predict with confidence that OMB will be there president after president, performing similar functions, if not exactly the same in every case. A domestic policy staff will vary more among presidents in organization and function. Still, in order to make OMB work for him, the president must be able to take control of the agency through his appointments. President Carter first appointed one of his closest advisers, Bert Lance, as OMB director. The loss of Lance so early in the administration was a serious blow. Lance's successor, James McIntyre, was also a part of the Georgia group, but his status was considerably below Lance's. He could not expect to override domestic policy advice from other White House sources; instead, he was a contestant in the struggle to gain access to the president.

McIntyre's task was, in many ways, more difficult than that of either his predecessor, Bert Lance, or his White House competitor, Stuart Eizenstat. It is in the nature of the job that the OMB director has a great deal to manage. OMB is a large agency with manifold responsibilities. Lance expected others (principally McIntyre, who served as his deputy) to cope with these problems. He served primarily as a principal aide to the president—one who happened to operate from his position as OMB director. But this arrangement was not particularly beneficial to the agency.

McIntyre did not have Lance's advantage among his peers. His principal base of influence was as the director of an agency whose role had been deemphasized during the Nixon-Ford administrations. He had to restore the credibility of the agency through managing its operations in a way that would impress the president and other White House aides. Accomplishing this task was complicated by the fact that, according to an OMB official, "most of the career staff at OMB were viewed by non-OMB senior people [in the White House] as being holdover Republicans."

The president's people in OMB were suspicious of the role played by the DPS people. They viewed them as having been captured by the agencies ("by various assistant and undersecretaries and deputy assistant secretaries") and therefore as promoting special interests. The OMB staff believed that they more accurately reflected the president's consolidative approach to government. These differences were played out in the budget process, but it was the view of some OMB officials that the DPS people would lobby against OMB's decisions on Capitol Hill if they (the DPS) lost in earlier encounters.

The difference in institutional role between OMB and DPS also led to important differences in the services provided to the president in his dealings with Congress. As with the DPS, OMB provided the type of front-end work that suited the president's style. But the work was associated with the routine and predictable functions of the agency. Despite the alleged deemphasis of OMB during the early months of 1977, certain tasks had to be performed that required OMB assistance. And, in fact, many of the president's priorities—balancing the budget, establishing zero-base budgeting, and reorganizing government—required active OMB cooperation. The summer of 1977 was hectic. An OMB aide explains:

> I have to be quite candid with you. There was a great deal of chaos and confusion in the Office of Management and Budget during that summer. [In addition to preparing the budget and office organization] we were trying to get our ... reorganization plan [of the executive office] finished.... There were tremendous turf battles that took place in that reorganization.... There were questions about the role of the Domestic Policy staff vis-à-vis OMB.... In addition

to that, we had made a pledge to cut down the size of the White House staff, which was an agonizing matter.

In addition to assisting the president and other domestic policy advisers to prepare the budget and other policy recommendations, OMB was expected to have direct relations with Congress. As a part of the internal office reorganization, the OMB's Office of Legislative Affairs was upgraded in status. Hubert L. Harris, another Georgian, was put in charge. Again the institutional role is important in determining how OMB operates. The agency is naturally viewed as centrally involved in budget making and reorganization. Therefore the Congress expects to call on the agency for assistance. But others in the White House are involved in budget decision making too. A budget task force was created in late 1978 to coordinate White House lobbying on the Hill. According to the OMB top staff, this system worked well. There were no "turf problems" with the White House Congressional Relations Office, in part because McIntyre and Moore knew each other well enough to coordinate their efforts.

BUILDING OUTSIDE SUPPORT

The Office of Public Liaison came to perform an absolutely vital function for the Carter approach to congressional relations. If the president was not comfortable in developing personal ties with members of Congress, then the proposals he sent to the Hill had to have sufficient merit to win on their own or had to arrive with strong support from those to be affected, or both. The president sought to ensure that the proposals had merit—working with the units identified above. But merit is typically in the eye of the beholder, and members of Congress keep their eyes on the effects on their constituents. Thus, demonstration of interest-group support was essential if the president's program was to be approved on Capitol Hill.

The public liaison staff was initially under the direction of Midge Costanza, an early supporter of Jimmy Carter. Under her direction the office, according to one aide, "had been defined ... as a much more 'responsive' office than an 'initiative' one. Interest groups based in Washington felt that they could come into the White House with their particular agendas and problems and the door was always open."

In May 1978 Anne Wexler took over as director. She brought a very different perspective to the job. The principal responsibility of the staff became one of building coalitions to support presidential initiatives. The model for this effort was building support for the Panama Canal treaties early in 1978, an operation principally directed by Hamilton Jordan. It was generally conceded that sure defeat for the treaties was transformed into victory by the outreach efforts of this campaign. Wexler tried to do the same for other administration programs, seeking as well to have groups participate in policy development.

To a considerable extent, the Public Liaison staff under Wexler organized itself to accomplish the functions of a legislative body. Coalition building is a common legislative function—indeed, probably the most important such function. In pursuit of coalition building, the public liaison staff organized task forces. These groups were built around major issues or proposals so as to build support and coordinate activities through the process of policy development and approval. A task force included people from the agencies and the White House and had several responsibilities: to identify the full dimensions of an issue (including the effects of proposals), to develop a strategy for building support, to test proposals for their effect on various interests, to keep groups informed of issues and proposals, to maintain good working relationships with the media, and eventually to promote interest-group lobbying for the proposal before Congress.

One might have thought that a Democratic president would seek, in addition, the participation of Democratic members of Congress—to develop a "sense of ownership" among them, as well as among interest groups. That appeared to be the approach relied on by Lyndon B. Johnson. The Democratic Party of 1977 was not that of 1965, however. In addition, the agenda had shifted to less politically attractive issues. During the Johnson administration, the president's proposals were primarily positive ones for the members—distributing benefits to states and districts. President Carter had more consolidative, reorganizational proposals, some of which were designed to reduce benefits. It was unlikely that he would have gone to Congress in the early stages of policy development in any event; but, as it was, his staff was probably correct in believing that the members were not interested in being implicated in programs of such dubious benefit to their constituents.

The Office of Public Liaison thus became vital. After some early defeats, it became apparent that preparing legislative proposals with sincerity and care was not enough to get congressional approval. Support had to be developed and demonstrated. The president's style and, to a certain extent, his program prevented more active cooperation with members of Congress in building support. It therefore fell to the Public Liaison staff to create networks of support in which decision makers would work with those affected by proposals. These networks were very much like the fabled "cozy little triangles" of representatives from executive agencies, congressional subcommittees, and interest groups. The difference? The members of Congress were typically left out of the Wexler networks or triangles, and White House staff were substituted. In fact, the Wexler triangles or networks were designed in part to break the hold of the more traditional groupings.

Moving Inside: Organizing Congressional Liaison

Several factors appear to influence the actual workings of White House congressional liaison efforts under different administrations. What it comes down to is variations resulting from what presidents want from Congress, from their personal approaches (or styles) for getting it, and from the partisan and public support potentially available to them.

Table 8.1 (page 176) provides a profile of recent presidents as tested by these several criteria. The entries suggest several lessons. First, it is clear that landslide elections do not translate into continuing public support. Often they seem to be a consequence of "retrospective voting," (i.e., more "a referendum on the incumbent" than a mandate for the winner). Second, the Johnson experience suggests that it requires a full set of advantages to enact a large-scale program—including a president willing to work closely with his liaison staff. Third, just as President Carter noted in his book, Congress engaged in frequent anti-executive behavior during the 1960s and 1970s. Presidents Nixon and Ford had to deal with Congresses controlled by the Democrats. But by the end of his term, President Johnson, too, faced frequent and strong criticism from Congress (including members of his own party).

The obvious conclusion is that any Democratic president taking office in 1977 was well advised to devote special attention to establishing an effective congressional liaison office. President Carter's profile in table 8.1 suggests that it was especially important for him to do so. He had an ambitious program—not one of the scale of Johnson's Great Society but one designed to make a huge government more effective. His party had large margins in both the House and Senate, but very few were devoted Carter Democrats. His elec-

TABLE 8.1
COMPARING PRESIDENTS

President/ Term	Policy objectives	Approach	Partisan support	Electoral support	Subsequent public support
Eisenhower					
1	Limited	Moderate	Narrow to no majority	Landslide	Steady and high
2	Limited	Moderate	No majority	Landslide	Steady and high
Kennedy					
1	Moderate	Moderate	Large	Narrow	Steady and high
Johnson					
1	Large-scale	Active	Large (moderate in House—1967)	Landslide	Variable—high to low
Nixon					
1	Limited	On call	No majority (but increase in seats)	Narrow	Steady and moderate
2	Limited	On call	No majority	Landslide	Variable—low to lower
Ford					
1	Limited	Active	No majority	None	Variable—high to low
Carter					
1	Moderate to ambitious	On call	Large	Narrow	Variable—high to low

toral margin was extremely narrow. And although his initial public support was quite high, the experiences of Johnson, Nixon, and Ford were informative regarding how quickly that support could disappear.

One other point should be emphasized. It is more or less implicit in the variables listed in table 8.1 that presidents are expected to get Congresses to work for them, not the other way around. Presidents have "policy objectives," and partisan, electoral, and public support is expected to be used by them to achieve these objectives. It is true, of course, that many Congresses are difficult to work with. It is true that congressional structure under the best of circumstances is not well designed for ensuring harmonious and effective relations between the two institutions. Yet even Republican presidents are somehow expected to "lead" Democratic Congresses. Presidents try to shift the burden of responsibility, but they are seldom successful in doing so. The public and the press continue to hold the president accountable. And if that is true for Republican presidents with Democratic Congresses, then Democratic presidents will find it doubly difficult to avoid responsibility for their relations with Democratic Congresses. That condition was to be a source of great frustration for President Carter, since he appeared to favor a separation between how he was evaluated and how Congress was evaluated.

PRESIDENT CARTER'S ROLE IN ORGANIZING
CONGRESSIONAL LIAISON

However politically sensible it may have been for Carter to spend time developing an effective congressional liaison organization, he was unlikely by reason of personal inclination, sense of priorities, or Washington-based experience in fact to spend his time in that way. Yet a liaison system would emerge whether or not the president participated actively in shaping it. This liaison system could be expected to orient itself to Carter's preferences. This is by way of saying that the liaison personnel would try to give the president what they thought he wanted. And there were signals from the president that were bound to have an effect: first and foremost was the choice of Frank Moore as liaison chief; second was the emphasis on cabinet government (and, as a related point, the reduction in White House staff); and third was the president's orientation toward issues over politics. Each of these signals resulted in unfortunate consequences for the liaison operation on Capitol Hill during the early months of 1977.

The selection of Frank Moore embodied the president's preference for managing his program rather than coping with any problems that might develop on Capitol Hill. Moore's appointment appeared to be a consequence of three factors: his experience in Georgia as Carter's liaison with the state legislature, his work in 1976 in coordinating the Carter campaign with various House and Senate campaigns, and, of course, his close association with Jimmy Carter personally. The last appeared to be the most important. In fact, the most relevant experience for future liaison purposes—that of campaign coordination with Democratic House and Senate candidates—had already resulted in considerable criticism of Moore. Dom Bonafede explains:

> Numerous officials come to Washington preceded by their reputations: Moore's arrival, unfortunately, was preceded by criticism 2½ months before he formally became assistant to the president for congressional relations. According to these reports, he was insensitive to the unwritten laws of protocol that help determine the relationship between the executive and legislative branches. It was alleged that he often failed to return phone calls, neglected requests and missed appointments with Members of Congress.[10]

The president himself viewed Moore's task more in managerial than in political terms. As he explains it in his book:

> A *professional management specialist,* Frank had been an associate since 1966 when I hired him as executive director of a multicounty planning and development commission, where he demonstrated an ability to recruit good people and deal effectively with the competing and sometimes suspicious officials of the eight counties and twenty-two towns and cities involved.[11]

This most interesting statement (made after his term in office) is revealing of the president's analysis of the job to be done. The impact of the political realities as described earlier did not appear to play an important role in this appointment. Carter emphasized issues and their management more than politics.

It should be said, of course, that presidents choose whomever they wish for positions of this type, to do the job they judge needs to be done. In the case of Carter, however, members of Congress were concerned that he really intended to carry out his campaign promises—many of which were threatening to programs they supported. Naturally, then, they were anxious to have access to the new president through someone who could act as *their* emissary. Their experience with Frank Moore during the campaign was not reassuring. President Carter explains the problems Moore had during this period as follows:

> Although he worked prodigiously on his infrequent trips to Washington, Frank was unable to return all the telephone calls or answer the great volume of special requests that flooded to me through him. He had to bear the brunt of criticism from all those who were frustrated in their efforts to reach me.[12]

Members would have been more reassured if they had known Carter better—if he had been one of their own. Or they might have been less apprehensive (and critical) if Frank Moore had worked on Capitol Hill or was well known to that population. Failure to return phone calls is not an unknown phenomenon in Washington. But many members of Congress were worried about access to *this* president. Thus the failure to communicate contributed to the doubts they had and therefore defined the special task facing the president in working with the legislature.

The president's initial devotion to cabinet government carried with it organizational implications for liaison operations. For example, the president judged that it was not necessary to have a large congressional liaison staff, since much of the lobbying would be assumed by the departments and agencies. But members of Congress often want direct contact with the president, particularly so if he comes from the outside. One White House aide understood this point and explained it as follows:

> The reason we had such a small staff to begin with is because President Carter originally felt he was dedicated to cabinet government. He asked, "Why have a big White House congressional liaison staff?" HEW had forty people in congressional liaison; the Defense Department had hundreds. Commerce maybe had thirty people. . . . Our idea was to farm out the stuff; let them do it. What we were doing in the White House was to coordinate this. The reason it didn't work was that every Senator and every Congressman first wants to talk to the president. If they can't talk to the president, they want to talk to the next person and during 1977–78 in our administration, they thought it was Hamilton Jordan. They want the closest person to the president who is making decisions.

The president's strong issue orientation was a third unmistakable signal likely to influence the organization and operation of the liaison office. Initially the office assigned House and Senate liaison personnel on the basis of substantive policy areas, rather than assign them a certain number of members for whom they were responsible. One liaison person explained the system:

> There were several organizational options. The Ford and Nixon administrations had divided the Senate up according to members.... We chose instead to divide the workload according to issues, feeling that it would be better for us to have an in-house specialist who understood each particular issue. In addition, it would give each of us the opportunity to get to know all of the senators.

This system was heavily criticized on Capitol Hill and was actually changed on the House side after William Cable joined the liaison staff as chief House lobbyist in May 1977. The issue-based system was retained on the Senate side. Why was it adopted in the first place? One of the liaison personnel emphasized that it was done because of "lack of numbers": "It was our reacting to the lack of numbers. How can we organize this thing so it makes sense?" But, given their magnitude, issues as a basis for organization require as many personnel as organizing to suit the size and complexity of the Congress. When it came time to decide how to "organize this thing so it makes sense," the logical solution adopted was more orientated toward executive management than toward legislative politics. Thus, another opportunity was missed to reassure the Democrats in Congress that the new administration was determined to close the gap between them.

The Congressional Liaison Office

The principal tasks of a liaison office include the following:

1. Leadership of the office and liaison with the president
2. Direct liaison with Congress—House and Senate
3. Liaison with the departments and agencies—and coordination of their efforts with those of the White House
4. Liaison with other White House units with business on Capitol Hill
5. Responding to congressional correspondence

As one can see, a liaison office is constantly in danger of flying apart.

As a communications center, its personnel are pulled in the directions of Capitol Hill, the Oval Office, the departments and agencies, and the other White House operations. And in the middle of all of this "to and fro" is a huge stack of mail and telephone messages. The demand for coordination is constant; the problems of actually coordinating are insurmountable.

Figure 8.1 (page 182) should be viewed more as a locator system than as a standard organization chart. The fact is that Frank Moore's style was not that of a bureau chief but that of team leader. Though devoted to the president, Moore was not in any sense a whip cracker or an enforcer, nor would Carter himself have expected such behavior from his liaison chief.

The liaison office appears to be surrounded in figure 8.1 and, in a very important sense, it was. Its functions complemented or fortified relationships among these several policymaking bodies. It certainly did not control these relationships. Displaying the office in this way graphically illustrates its dependent role and therefore stresses the importance of the office as a communications center.

Each of the liaison organizational units deserves separate treatment. Of course, the units changed over time in function and personnel. The office evolved, not according to some master plan but in response to increased awareness of its political responsibilities as defined by congressional expectations and presidential style.

Chief of Liaison. Frank Moore's role as Carter's chief of liaison has not been well understood. Typically, accounts of his service are highly critical of the job he did on Capitol Hill. Dom Bonafede, a reporter for the *National Journal,* wrote several stories on Carter's relations with Congress and, no doubt, accurately traced the Hill's attitudes toward Frank Moore.[13] A careful reading of Bonafede's reports reveals another important development. Whereas Moore was consistently criticized, he just as consistently received support from the man who made the difference—the president. "Moore is alive and well ... meeting frequently with the president, whose confidence he reportedly retains"[14] (26 March 1977). "Members of Congress who wonder about Moore's closeness and accessibility to the president should have no concern on that score"[15] (12 November 1977). "Carter, meanwhile, continues to express confidence in Moore. He and Zbigniew Brzezinski ... are the only two White House aides listed daily on the president's formal appointments schedule"[16] (13 January 1979). This confidence and daily contact should encourage one to reassess the functions, and therefore the success, of Frank

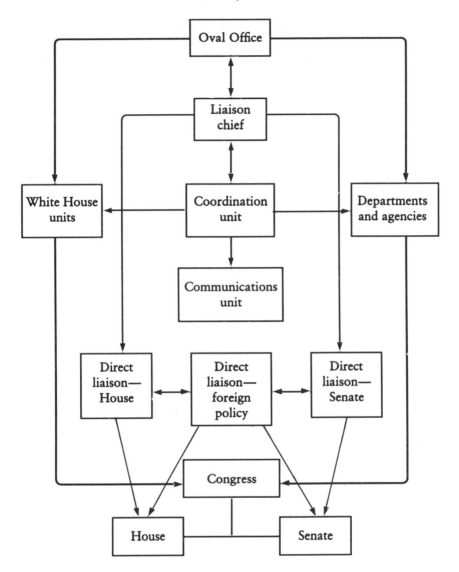

FIGURE 8.1
CONGRESSIONAL LIAISON IN THE CARTER WHITE HOUSE

Moore as a chief of congressional liaison. The members of his own staff relied heavily on Moore's role in maintaining their access to the president—a role absolutely crucial for the nonpolitical president coping with the highly political Congress. Here is how one staff member described it:

> There was no shop in the White House, thanks to Frank, who had better communication and more constant communication with Jimmy Carter on issues and on tactics and on strategy than we did. Bill [Cable] and Dan [Tate] were in to see the president virtually every morning when important issues were on the floor. They went in with Frank, and Frank had access to the president any time of the day or night. From the standpoint of when I first came on board, it was staggering. I would be expected to pick up the phone and call Frank if there was a development on the Panama Canal treaties and other issues on the Hill, and Frank immediately would call the president with it.

It seems apparent that most analysts have evaluated Moore's performance by criteria drawn from a model of presidential-congressional relations that was inapt for the Carter administration. It is perfectly understandable that those testing the Carter liaison operations would do so with reference to the last Democratic president, Lyndon B. Johnson. But criteria drawn from the Johnson administration are unsuitable for measuring Carter. Johnson's style was that of majority leader as president, essentially based on a partnership model of presidential-congressional relationships. Carter's style of outsider as president was based on an independence model of presidential-congressional relations. For the partnership model, it makes very good sense to judge the performance of the chief of congressional liaison by analyzing effectiveness on Capitol Hill. After all, this is the criterion the legislator as president is likely to employ. For the independence model, however, the test is whether the liaison chief is effective in establishing communication between a president with such a style and the Congress. Vital to this linkage is maintaining Oval Office access for liaison personnel. The outsider as president is unlikely himself to reach out, nor is he likely to work easily with insiders unless they (the insiders) are escorted by someone the president trusts. Thus the effective liaison chief for the independent outsider president is one who creates what is unlikely to be there naturally. His attention is drawn as much to his boss as to Capitol

Hill. If he is unsuccessful in keeping the door open to the Oval Office, then whatever goodwill is established among the members of Congress will come to naught. Liaison chiefs act for the president; they have no special policy significance in and of themselves.

Coordination Unit. Leslie C. Francis was the first person "in charge" of this unit. He was added after the initial organizational period. Once the unit was created, certain responsibilities naturally gravitated to it. The coordination unit was "in house," so to speak. Moore was occupied by his continuing relationship with the president and the need for his active presence at meetings and on the Hill. The House and Senate liaison personnel were most effective on site—that is, working the offices, halls, committee rooms, cafeterias, and other hangouts on the Hill. That left certain continuing tasks as local White House business. These were described as follows:

> We had a central coordinating group which worked on several different things.... It really had three elements. Number one, there was a two-person element which wrote the weekly legislative report for the president. We had a second element of agency liaison. These were the people that were responsible for communicating with agency congressional liaison people and for organizing our weekly meetings with the agency congressional liaison people. A third element of this central coordinating unit was the congressional correspondence section, which had some of the hardest working people in the White House.

Of course, "coordination" is a term of convenience for such a unit. In practice, what this function amounted to was an effort to determine who was doing what and where, a large task. The coordination unit could properly be described as too few people trying to learn too much in too short a time. Yet the effort had to be made—someone had to stay behind, so to speak, to mind the shop. Les Francis was that somebody at first; he was followed later by Robert Thomson.

Communications Unit.[17] This hard-working unit dealt with phone calls as well as paper correspondence. The major task of the unit was that of managing letters. Incoming mail from members of Congress to the president or to Frank Moore was handled by the small staff of three persons. Letters were forwarded to the appropriate person or unit for response, or responses were drafted by those in the communications unit. All incoming mail was logged in, and a computer-based tracking system was developed to maintain control.

The unit also initiated mass mailings to Capitol Hill, often to all the members, sometimes to specific members (e.g., just the Democrats or to a state delegation). These letters (from the president or Frank Moore) might be primarily informational, serve to clarify the president's position, or represent an effort to make contact with the members (e.g., congratulating them in regard to some achievement). The volume of work involved can lead to mistakes being made—the wrong letter sent to a member. Incoming mail averaged approximately fifty letters a working day to the president, a hundred letters a working day to Frank Moore. The actual number of mistakes was small, though those made typically received publicity.

Clearly this unit was a major source of information for what was going on between Congress and the president for those who had the time to find out. It was appropriately located as an adjunct to the coordination unit. The correspondence unit had to have accurate knowledge about White House operations so as to draft an intelligent letter. It performed one of those vital functions on which the whole liaison system depended.

Direct Liaison. Those involved in direct liaison work spent most of their time on Capitol Hill, thus requiring good secretarial work in their White House offices. One of the Senate lobbyists explained:

> If Hill lobbyists are doing their job, they are going to be on the Hill most of the day. You simply cannot, if you are a line lobbyist, conduct your business from the White House on the telephone. You've got to have face to face contact and you've got to be up there where the action is. Consequently, you have to have someone down at the White House who is looking out for your interests, someone who can conduct business effectively and efficiently over the telephone when Senators, administrative assistants, personal secretaries, committee chief counsels, and staff directors call.

The Carter lobbyists on Capitol Hill were divided between the House and Senate, as expected. The House lobbyists were initially led by Frederick T. Merrill, Jr., but he left very early in the administration. Merrill had served as legislative coordinator for the Democratic Study Group in the House, 1969–76. William H. Cable joined the liaison staff as chief House lobbyist in May 1977. At the time of his appointment to the White House staff, Cable was staff director of the House Committee on Administration—an excellent post for contact with many members. Earlier he had served on the staff of the House Committee on Education and Labor. Cable brought a political savvy and experience that was badly needed in the Carter White House liaison operation. He had been approached earlier by Frank Moore to join the staff and had said no, partially because he was not pleased with the initial organization of the Hill staff by functional or issue areas. When he agreed to serve on the second request, Cable was given the freedom to organize the lobbyists as he thought best.

At full complement, Cable's staff included twelve persons: five lobbyists, five administrative assistants, and two clerical personnel. The workload was organized by state delegations. Each lobbyist was allowed to pick a group of states so as to manage one-fifth of the total membership (approximately ninety members for each). Cable took the states that were left. Each staff member concentrated on getting to know his or her representatives and their staff. Cable wanted to develop a close, two-way relationship with the members—even soliciting ideas from them as to how the White House might be of assistance to them.

Dan C. Tate led the Senate lobbying team from the start. Tate had served as legislative assistant to Senator Herman E. Talmadge (D-Ga.) for seven years. Robert Thomson joined Tate in April 1977. Thomson had worked with the Senate Democratic Campaign Committee and Senator Lloyd Bentsen's (D-Tex.) unsuccessful presidential campaign (1975–76). Tate and Thomson worked together for over two years and then Thomson became Moore's deputy for coordination (following the Camp David reorganization). Tate favored organizing by issues rather than members. It was his view that it was better to have follow-through on a particular issue. This organization also permitted each Senate lobbyist to get acquainted with every senator. This issue-based organization was unquestionably better adapted to the smaller Senate than to the 435-member House of Representatives.

The liaison team included another lobbyist who was more or less independent, concentrating primarily on foreign policy issues. Robert Beckel had served earlier as executive director of the National Committee for an Effective Congress and thus knew his way around Capitol Hill. He first joined the Carter administration as a deputy assistant secretary of state for congressional relations, working primarily on the Panama Canal treaties. Beckel assisted with the more political aspects of the treaty as they developed domestically. An early memorandum on the political difficulties for the treaty in the Senate eventually found its way to Frank Moore and Moore led Beckel into the Oval Office to brief the president. Following this meeting, Beckel came to work at the White House in congressional relations.

This unusual arrangement was bound to cause some problems between Beckel and the Departments of State and Defense as well as the National Security Adviser and the Central Intelligence Agency (CIA). These units all had their contacts on Capitol Hill. The departments and the CIA had their own liaison staffs and National Security Adviser Brzezinski added a congressional liaison person after Beckel came to the White House. Beckel, however, was given the responsibility of chairing an interagency legislative group so as to effect coordination in foreign and defense policy liaison. The situation for Beckel was difficult, but Carter's interest in foreign and defense policy, plus Moore's close connections with the president, provided support for this ad hoc arrangement.

The Carter liaison team was criticized for its lack of congressional experience. The problem at first was twofold. First and foremost was the appointment of Frank Moore. His unfamiliarity with the workings of Congress was taken as a signal of Carter's lack of interest in building harmonious congressional relations. Second, the office initially was understaffed and poorly organized. By 1978, however, able and experienced Hill lobbyists (e.g., Cable, Thomson, Beckel) had been added and the House liaison unit had been reorganized. The charge of inexperience was no longer appropriate, though it did persist.

MOVING INSIDE: AN ANALYSIS IN SUMMARY

The liaison staff was in a difficult position for moving the Carter administration forward inside the existing national policy process. The lobbyists functioned as a bridge to the type of Washington politics their boss had campaigned against. Yet they faced a strategic problem of some magnitude. It was their responsibility to get members of Congress to cooperate, but the president was not their natural ally in this effort. This is not to say that he could not be used as a resource by liaison personnel. It is rather to stress that they had to manage how he would be used so as to promote cooperation. That was a sensitive and difficult task, since the president was not inclined by his nature or personal preference to respect the work engaged in by his own staff. The lobbyists were in daily contact with those whose business it was to strike bargains and make compromises, rather than, in the president's words, to do "what is right." They were, in effect, white-flag bearers trudging up and down Pennsylvania Avenue. True understanding between the principal leaders of the contending forces was not likely to occur.

Change the metaphor and picture if you will a two-way transmission apparatus—sort of a Rube Goldberg clickety-clack executive-legislative machine. At one end the gears whir away in one direction and do so in the vertical mode. At the other end another set of gears work in the opposite direction and do so in the horizontal mode. Each set must somehow function if the whole machine is to move. Yet each set is independently powered. Now transfer this imagery to the Carter White House and the Democratically controlled Congress. The congressional liaison personnel were located at the center of the transmission, charged with the responsibility of creating a series of wheels and belts so as to achieve forward motion on policy. They had to be political on the Hill and Carter-correct in the White House. The task challenged even the most adept transmitter. And, of course, it was unlikely that all staff members would be equally good at transmission or translation at both ends. What was needed, therefore, was personnel who were effective at each end, plus some in the middle to hold the system together.

Testing for Achievement

This chapter has sought to remain faithful to the proposition that any president will organize his congressional relations to suit his policy goals and personal style. In the case of Jimmy Carter, this fidelity asks for tolerance of an independence model of presidential-congressional relations, one in which the president maintains distance from the bargaining politics so characteristic of Capitol Hill. The tests of achievement are not so different from those applied to other presidents once one accepts that a different model is being employed. They include the following:

1. Did an organization develop that was suited to the goals and style of the president?
2. Did the organization assist the president in achieving his goals?
3. Was there another structure that would have been more accommodating to his goals and style?

The answer to the first question is surely positive in Carter's case. His White House staff was organized to facilitate an outside-in strategy. A structure was established to promote issue identification, program development, and coalition building among interest groups and the public. The congressional liaison staff adjusted its role to presidential preferences. The president was available as a resource, but he was unlikely very often to manage liaison activities. He selected a person to head the liaison unit more on the basis of his needs than on the basis of congressional needs. In so doing, he ensured access for liaison personnel to the Oval Office. A more congressionally oriented, Washington-based liaison chief may not have had the confidence of the president. And the liaison unit organized itself to accommodate the manifold activities of a diverse policymaking apparatus in the White House and the departments and agencies (see fig. 8.1).

My response to the second question is also positive. This president sought to do the right thing. His desire was to focus on substance over process, issues over politics. The DPS, in particular, was designed to assist him in achieving that goal, with OMB contributing where appropriate. The Office of Public Liaison was charged with producing supporting coalitions for major policy proposals. Finally, in what may have been the riskiest (and trickiest) maneuver of all, the president's program, the "right thing," had to be sold on Capitol Hill—and sold with as little political bargaining by the president as possible. It was up to the congressional liaison staff to permit the president to maintain his personal style of independence and distance, *which he interpreted as a strength, not a weakness.* This unusual apparatus did contribute to the realization of the president's substantive and stylistic goals. It produced a number of victories on issues that were unpopular on Capitol Hill: executive reorganization, energy conservation and deregulation, ratification of the Panama Canal treaties, even the elimination of some water projects in congressional districts. It also permitted the president, in his words, to "keep faith" and therefore remain philosophical about specific losses as well as consistently critical of the congressional system.

It is truly difficult to respond to the third question, as it would be for any president. If we do not abandon the initial proposition—that congressional relations will be organized to suit the policy goals and personal style of the president—then a search for a more effective organization in Carter's case concentrates on perfecting a system suited to a president employing an outside-in strategy. Any such search must begin with an evaluation of what went wrong during the first year of the new administration. The record in 1977 was devastating for Carter's image as a competent manager of his own

White House team. The questionable choice, scheduling, and timing of issues, the lack of priority setting, and the seeming determination to establish the correctness of the White House stance on issues—these were among the problems experienced during 1977. These are not insurmountable problems. They may have been partially solved by integrating additional experienced staff into the White House team, revising the sequence and pace of proposals sent to Congress, creating a mechanism for setting priorities, and projecting a less critical posture toward Congress. As the record shows, many of these changes were made in later years, when White House staff judged themselves to have been more effective. Had they come as a part of the Carter approach in 1977, evaluations of the thirty-ninth presidency might read very differently.

Perhaps the most important point to be made in this chapter is that no presidency is predestined to fail, not even one that presumes to ignore Washington political traditions. The evidence suggests that an independence model of presidential-congressional relations invites severe problems for the president. But the problems do appear to be manageable. In that connection, there is much to be learned from the Carter experience for the next outsider who wins the White House.

NOTES

1. Fred I. Greenstein, *The Hidden-Hand Presidency: Eisenhower as Leader* (New York: Basic Books, 1982). The other presidents had many years' experience as elected officials in Washington before serving: Truman, ten years (Senate and vice-president); Kennedy, fourteen years (House and Senate); Johnson, twenty-four years (House, Senate, vice-president); Nixon, fourteen years (House, Senate, vice-president); and Ford, twenty-four years (House and vice-president).

2. Much of the analysis herein is based on oral history sessions with President Carter's senior staff officials and their assistants at the White Burkett Miller Center of Public Affairs, University of Virginia, 1981–84, a project directed by James Sterling Young. All quoted material not otherwise noted is drawn from the transcripts of these sessions.

3. Jimmy Carter, *Keeping Faith: Memoirs of a President* (New York: Bantam, 1982), 88; emphasis added.

4. Ibid., 89.

5. The speech is reprinted in *Congressional Quarterly Weekly Report*, 21 July 1979, 1470–72.

6. The interview is in the *Congressional Quarterly Weekly Report,* 4 September 1976, 2380–83.

7. In her book, Rosalynn Carter confirms her husband's determination to ignore politics and her own effort to get him to consider political effects. See *First Lady From Plains* (Boston: Houghton Mifflin, 1984), 164–65.

8. Eric L. Davis, "Legislative Liaison in the Carter Administration," *Political Science Quarterly* 94 (1979): 301. See also his essay "Congressional Liaison: The People and the Institutions," in *Both Ends of the Avenue,* ed. Anthony King (Washington, D.C.: American Enterprise Institute, 1983), chap. 3.

9. Dom Bonafede, "Stuart Eizenstat—Carter's Right-Hand Man," *National Journal,* 9 June 1979, 944.

10. Dom Bonafede, "Carter's Relationships with Congress—Making a Mountain Out of a 'Moorehill,'" *National Journal,* 26 March 1977, 456.

11. Carter, *Keeping Faith,* 44; emphasis added.

12. Ibid.

13. See Bonafede, "Carter's Relationships," 456; "Carter and Congress—It Seems that 'If Something Can Go Wrong, It Will,'" *National Journal,* 12 November 1977, 1756; and "The Tough Job of Normalizing Relations with Capitol Hill," *National Journal,* 13 January 1978, 54.

14. Bonafede, "Carter's Relationships," 456.

15. Bonafede, "Carter and Congress," 1756.

16. Bonafede, "The Tough Job," 57.

17. This section profits from interviews with personnel from this unit conducted by Stephen J. Wayne. I am much indebted to Professor Wayne for permitting me to listen to his taped conversations.

9

Reagan and Congress

This chapter examines President Reagan's method of, and success in, dealing with Congress. There is perhaps no better indicator of a president's political style than his working relationship with those on Capitol Hill. Ronald Reagan's style contrasts sharply with that of the last president to serve two full terms, Dwight D. Eisenhower. In his account of Eisenhower's leadership, Fred I. Greenstein describes a "hidden-hand" method born of the president's image of himself. "Eisenhower ... concealed his involvement in conventional politicking that would not have been controversial if he had been prepared to be viewed as a political professional."[1]

There was nothing hidden about Reagan's hand in politics, his penchant for relaxation to the contrary notwithstanding. Ronald Reagan's principal legacy in regard to working with Congress was a visibly political, often partisan, one. In fact, if we are to believe currently available accounts for each president, they were opposites. Eisenhower was politically active behind the scenes, but eschewed public display of this involvement. Reagan promoted public perceptions of his political sagacity, but allowed others to orchestrate activity behind the scenes. Maybe it does help in understanding their respective approaches to politics that one was a general, the other an actor.

In developing this chapter on Reagan's legislative record, I turn first to the remarkable 1980 election and the advantages it bestowed on Ronald Reagan for dealing with Congress. Then I discuss how the president organized his congressional relations so as to realize the benefits of his election. The next two sections direct attention first to the astounding success President Reagan had in 1981 and then to how it was that subsequent Congresses coped with what I call the "1981 legacy." A brief analysis of voting scores is followed by final remarks emphasizing a Reagan style that will surely be his legacy in working with Congress.

This actor liked playing the president. He understood the role better than most, possibly because his occupational training prepared him to do so. The distinction between becoming president and playing the president is an interesting and important one. Reagan himself appeared to make it in an interview in 1986: "Some people become president. I've never thought of it that way. I think the presidency is an institution over which you have temporary custody and it has to be treated that way.... I don't think the presidency belongs to the individual."[2] Perhaps one starting point in the exercise of power is knowing who you are and where you are.

The 1980 Election: Advantage Reagan

> Mandates are inherently implausible. For one thing, many people vote for their party's candidate almost reflexively.... Others base their votes on the candidates' apparent personal qualities....
>
> People who believe in mandates usually say that those who voted for a candidate did so because they favored the policies he advocated. The search for the mandate becomes a textual analysis of the winner's campaign utterances. The problem here, of course, is that candidates say a great many things.... Not all these promises can be important. As Chairman Mao might have said, "Many issues, one vote."[3]

Raymond E. Wolfinger is surely correct, and yet as he himself points out in discussing the 1984 election: "'Mandate' was one of the favorite nouns on the election night television coverage."[4] Those who interpret elections search for the message. If a president wins 91 percent of the Electoral College vote, and his party returns with a majority in the Senate for the first time in twenty-six years, it is virtually guaranteed that a "mandate" will be declared to exist. This will occur regardless of the implausibility of the concept in American national elections or solid evidence that, for example, many voters were expressing dissatisfaction with President Carter, not approval of candidate Reagan.[5]

Reading a mandate into the 1980 election outcomes established policy expectations of President Reagan and provided him with significant political advantages in working with Congress. As it happened, Reagan conveyed a rather strong policy message during the campaign—"an unusually coherent social philosophy," as one analyst put it.[6] Thus, those anxious to declare a mandate did not have to search long and hard for a policy message. During the campaign,

Reagan offered a prescription for change and promised to put it into effect once in office. There was none of the ambiguity that came to be identified with the Carter approach. When the pundits declared a mandate to exist, they could then follow that announcement with a clear exposition of what to expect.

Meanwhile, at the other end of Pennsylvania Avenue, House and Senate Republicans returned triumphantly to Washington after the election. In the House, the net increase of thirty-three Republicans was the largest in a presidential election since 1920. But it was the Senate results that stunned observers. No one called that one in advance. Even the respected *Congressional Quarterly* predicted on 1 November that "although the GOP may narrow the 59–41 margin Democrats now enjoy, it is very unlikely Republicans can take control of the Senate in 1981. To do so, they would need to win all of the close races, plus two of the seven that are currently leaning toward the Democratic candidate."[7]

As it happened, Republican candidates won eight of the nine races that were too close to call, five of the seven that were leaning Democratic, and one of eight that were declared safe for the Democrats. The net gain of twelve seats was the second greatest in this century for the Republicans. The fact that the Democratic senatorial candidates as a whole actually outpolled the Republicans was lost, or not discovered, in the short-term rush to declare a Reagan mandate.

Also relevant is the fact that Ronald Reagan ran with his party in 1980, not alongside it. Eisenhower was judged to be above party politics, and publicly he sought to preserve that image. In 1972 Nixon ran more for himself than for his party. Reagan worked at unifying the party at the nominating convention and after. He integrated his campaign effort with that of the national party organization, and he never shied away from appearing with or aiding other candidates. Further, for those who pay attention to such matters (as do most members of Congress), Reagan ran ahead of thirty of thirty-four Senate Republican candidates (counting just the two-party vote). And although he ran behind most successful House Republican candidates in their districts (most presidential candidates do these days), still he did better than President Ford in 1976 in most districts.[8]

The point is that there was more reason than usual in 1980 to interpret the presidential and congressional elections as representing a package deal. The victory for Reagan was decisive, there seemed to be "nontrivial coattail effects,"[9] and the policy message was unambiguous. Even the Democrats and liberals detected a conservative tide in the nation. Defeated incumbent Senator Frank Church of Idaho concluded that "the conservatives are in charge now. This is what they wanted and the people have given it to them."[10] The liberal columnist Anthony Lewis agreed: "What happened in the 1980 election reflected a profound and general turn to conservatism in this country."[11] There was a receptive mood for giving the president a chance, even though to do so was to invite dramatic change.

Remarkably enough, this attitude even carried forward to the partisan Speaker of the House of Representatives, Thomas P. O'Neill, Jr., of Massachusetts. In his book O'Neill discusses the politics of the situation. After the 1980 election, he received "more letters than I had seen in my entire career—asking me to give the president's program a chance." He met with House Republican leaders and agreed to expedite consideration of the program, understanding the advantage he was providing to the administration. As O'Neill explains it:

> Despite my strong opposition to the president's program, I decided to give it a chance to be voted on by the nation's elected representatives.
>
> For one thing, that's how our democracy is supposed to work. For another, I was afraid that the voters would repudiate the Democrats if we didn't give the president a chance to pass his program. After all, the nation was still in an economic crisis and people wanted immediate action....
>
> I was less concerned about losing the legislative battle in the spring and summer of 1981 than I was with losing at the polls in the fall of 1982. I was convinced that if the Democrats were perceived as stalling in the midst of a national economic crisis, there would be hell to pay in the midterm elections.[12]

Specifically in regard to the tax cut, O'Neill was quoted as stating that "we will ultimately send a bill to the president that he will be satisfied with."[13] Speaker O'Neill proved himself correct, and as a consequence unwittingly provided an early announcement of what was to become a major part of the Reagan legacy—unimagined deficits.

Organizing to Take Advantage

President Lyndon B. Johnson observed that "you've got just one year when they [members of Congress] treat you right, and before they start worrying about themselves."[14] He acted on this knowledge and had one of the most productive first years of any president. Ronald Reagan intended to be an activist president too, although in the opposite direction from the one that Johnson took. Therefore, Reagan wanted to act fast, to "hit the ground running," as the phrase has it.

As has been emphasized, the 1980 election and how it was interpreted offered many advantages to the new Reagan administration. As an additional plus, it seemed that members of Congress from both parties were ready for somewhat better treatment by the White House. Presidents Nixon and Carter, in particular, preferred the full length of Pennsylvania Avenue in distancing themselves from Congress. Neither had very flattering views about the institution or its members.

The Reagan style was very different. Although not from Capitol Hill, Ronald Reagan demonstrated respect for the politics practiced there. Whereas he was unlikely to be as close to the members as either Presidents Johnson or Ford, still he would not make the mistake of distancing himself from Congress in either thought or deed. And as the "great communicator," he understood the need to sell his program to those who would vote on it. James P. Pfiffner describes how it went in those months between election and inauguration:

> The president-elect held a series of dinners to which he invited members of Congress. With the realization that Democratic votes would be necessary for his legislative agenda he announced that he would retain ex-Senator Mike Mansfield as ambassador to Japan. He took particular care to court House [Speaker] Tip O'Neill who had chafed at perceived slights from the Carter White House. He and his wife were invited to a private dinner at the White House, and he was also invited to the president's small 70th birthday party. Republican members of Congress were invited to advise the transition teams in the departments. And the president elect sought the advice of Senators Robert Dole, John Tower, and Strom Thurmond in making his cabinet choices.[15]

Members of Congress loved this attention. As Speaker O'Neill explained:

> Reagan had tremendous powers of friendly persuasion.... The president was continually calling members of the House. He didn't always get his way, but his calls were never wasted....

The members adored it when he called, even when they had no intention of changing their vote. The men and women in Congress love nothing better than to hear from the head guy, so they can go back to their districts and say, "I was talking to the president the other day." The constituents love it too.[16]

Senator Paul Laxalt (R-Nev.), one of the president's closest friends and most loyal supporters, advised him in regard to establishing connections with Congress. Laxalt was respected by senior members on both sides of the aisle. Following his advice was bound to help the president. The Laxalt-Reagan association has few parallels in the history of presidential-congressional relations.

The president also acted quickly in establishing a congressional liaison team and in preparing his program for submission to Congress. A veteran Capitol Hill staff person, Tom Korologos, was called on to assist the president-elect in his preinaugural congressional contacts and to build a White House liaison team that would take over after the inauguration.

Korologos himself did not stay on to manage the team. That task fell to another Capitol Hill veteran, Max Friedersdorf. It would be hard to imagine a better choice, given the circumstances. Friedersdorf had served on the liaison team for both the Nixon and Ford administrations, and before that he had worked for a House member from Indiana for ten years. He also had served as chairman of the Federal Election Commission, an agency with many congressional contacts. The executive director of the House Democratic Steering and Policy Committee, S. Ariel Weiss, a seasoned and tough partisan, reacted to Friedersdorf's appointment as follows: "With Max running the show, they are experienced. . . . Initially, their moves have clearly been good."[17] Whether or not they agreed with Reagan's policy preferences, those on Capitol Hill were reassured that they would be dealing with, in Speaker O'Neill's characterization, "an experienced and savvy team." In fact, O'Neill was impressed with the whole White House staff: "All in all, the Reagan team in 1981 was probably the best-run political operating unit I've ever seen."[18] No doubt this was in part because the Speaker himself got quite good service, even as a Democrat: "Reagan's aides were never parochial, and despite our many disagreements, they never showed any animosity toward me. On a few occasions, when lower-echelon people tried to block programs for my district, I would call the White House, where Mike Deaver or Jim Baker or somebody else on the president's team would always straighten things out."[19] Later in the Reagan administration, O'Neill's relationship with Donald Regan was not so amiable.

All presidents must depend heavily on their staffs, but Reagan's style made him more dependent than most. His was a very public presidency, yet, compared to other recent presidents, he had a low tolerance for detail. Further, he proposed a difficult, even contentious, agenda for Congress. Thus he needed an able and experienced liaison staff. Friedersdorf was just the person to provide it. He selected "young-old" people. "I wanted people youthful enough to put up with the long hours and physical demands, yet old enough to be patient and mature."[20] It was an impressive group. The average age was thirty-seven. All the principal lobbyists had experience on Capitol Hill—four in the Senate, four in the House, one in both. In addition, several either had experience as interest-group lobbyists or, like Friedersdorf himself, in executive liaison offices.

Given the credentials of those beneath him, it was possible along the way for Friedersdorf to step down and be replaced by another "pro." In fact, turnover in the liaison office was rather high. Kenneth Duberstein, initially chief House lobbyist, took over the top position in 1982. Then M.B. Oglesby, Duberstein's replacement as head of the House liaison team, took over for Duberstein in managing the whole office in 1982. Following the 1984 election, Friedersdorf returned so as to get the second administration off to a good start. Oglesby stayed on with his close friend, so the liaison office more or less had two chiefs. While a suitable arrangement for Friedersdorf and Oglesby, it did not work well on Capitol Hill, and in the fall of 1985 Friedersdorf left once again. Then Oglesby left in early 1986, and William L. Ball III took over. Ball had been managing congressional relations for the Department of State—again, an experienced hand to guide the White House liaison office. In late February 1988, Ball was chosen secretary of the navy. His replacement was Alan M. Kranowitz, who had been directing White House lobbying efforts in the House.

Dick Kirschten observed that "if the attrition rate of the White House staff is any indicator, proximity to the power of the Oval Office is somewhat akin to the moth's attraction to the flame. There is a high burnout rate."[21] That would seem to be the case with the congressional liaison office. Yet the liaison operation itself appeared to serve well as a feeder system for leadership, and two of the most talented directors were willing to return to the White House staff —Friedersdorf in his old job and Kenneth Duberstein as deputy chief of staff for Howard Baker, then as chief of staff when Baker resigned.

No liaison staff can expect smooth sailing throughout. Staff members act as "point persons" for the president on the Hill, and when it comes to difficult issues, members are unlikely to be cooperative just because the White House lobbyists are experienced and talented. Once the Democrats recaptured control of the Senate and the Iran-*contra* matter broke, the liaison team had its hands full. Fashioning majorities for budgets, domestic priorities, even treaties, and certainly appointments to the Supreme Court would be very difficult. What can be said here is that no more problems were added because of liaison personnel themselves. Apart from the confusion caused by Friedersdorf's returning in 1985, the liaison staff performed ably in coping with deteriorating political conditions.

Finally, the president himself was a tremendous asset for the liaison team. "We had to lasso him to keep him off the Hill" during the first year, according to one close adviser.[22] Members of Congress naturally make comparisons with the immediately preceding occupant of the White House. They found Reagan to be approachable; a willing participant in support of his legislation (if seldom conversant with the details). Relationships with President Carter, even for Democrats, were much more uncertain and distant.

Establishing the Legacy in 1981

Very few presidents can claim legislative triumphs that are truly turning points in domestic policy. In this century, Franklin D. Roosevelt and Lyndon B. Johnson can legitimately make that case. The New Deal and Great Society programs constituted quantum increases in the role of the federal government in social and economic life. In both cases the president and Congress acted quickly to effect a policy shift that was so dramatic as to dominate future agendas. The politics of incrementalism, so characteristic of the American system, was suspended for a short time. We experienced unprecedented policy breakthroughs, unchecked by the normal restraints of separated institutions and intergovernmental divisions.

Ronald Reagan could claim such a breakthrough in 1981. By employing "speed and focus," the White House produced breathtaking legislative successes.[23] Friedersdorf was quoted as saying that "we knew we had to get our bills enacted before the Labor Day recess" and that "the president was determined not to clutter up the landscape with extraneous legislation."[24]

The economy became the first, second, and third objective, and

Reagan staked his reputation on it. By choosing the economy, he added simplicity to both policymaking and the policy process. All social and domestic issues were discussed not in terms of need, equity, or values, but in budget recommendations—how much can be cut back without causing an uproar.[25]

Alongside the maxim "Establish a focus" is the advisory "Don't come up with other mischiefs."[26] For Reagan, certain far-right causes could easily cause mischief. As Chief of Staff James Baker noted: "Abortion cuts both ways hard. If you come down one way or the other, you lose some people. Most of the social issues are polarizing."[27] One learns much about the Reagan legacy from this avoidance of mischiefs. The politician uses ideology, but does not lose because of it. Ideology provides policy direction, but not to the exclusion of political success. Presidents who try to satisfy the fringes of their support, whether it be to the right or left, sacrifice support in the middle, where the majority normally resides. The trick is to press policy preferences to a limit beyond which you would lose support, then compromise and declare victory, saving ideological purity for another day.

What was won in 1981, and with what impact? Allen Schick has pointed out that "Ronald Reagan won the battles but lost the budget."

On four issues he challenged congressional Democrats and obtained the legislation he demanded. The first budget resolution was crafted according to his specifications, as was the reconciliation bill it triggered. The president also emerged victorious in a bidding war over tax legislation. His final triumph came in the closing days of the session when Congress approved a continuing appropriation that satisfied most of his demands.[28]

Schick concedes that winning the battles may have been more important to President Reagan than losing the budget. "Perhaps the budget was only a cover for his real objectives."[29] Whether that was the case or not (and Reagan's then budget director, David Stockman, seems to believe that it was),[30] the effects were clear enough. First, winning most of the battles in 1981 focused attention on the budget and growing deficits. Those favoring additional government welfare programs were literally made speechless. Those supporting current programs were forced to justify them as never before. Many Republicans, including Stockman, wanted to go much further in dismantling the welfare state. Some such advocates felt betrayed by Reagan. Regardless, the 1981 victories produced a significant agenda shift that altered policy politics in Washington.

Second, the effects of 1981 were not limited to one year. Tax cuts went into effect over a three-year period. Defense expenditures were to increase over several years. And although cuts were made in certain domestic programs, Reagan's 1981 plan for social security adjustments was defeated. This combination of less revenue and a significant boost in defense spending, without fully compensatory reductions in entitlement programs, assured mind-boggling deficits through a first and into a second Reagan term. Subsequent policy conversation would be dominated by the legacy of 1981. Democrats too drew from Reagan's thesaurus in preparing for the 1984, even the 1988, election.

A third effect was simply that it was difficult to judge who had won when the president lost, as he did with increasing frequency after 1981. The game was being played on his field, with his ball—that was the effect of 1981. The Democrats prevented him from scoring, but it is hard to win any game by playing defense only. Further, if the Democrats mounted an offensive (typically in cooperation with congressional Republicans), they might find that the president joined them at the goal line to take the ball across (e.g., as with the 1982 tax increase).

The details of the 1981 triumph on Capitol Hill are as follows:

1. Passage of the Economic Recovery Tax Act, a multiyear package that projected a reduction of nearly $750 billion
2. Enactment of a budget reconciliation resolution designed to reduce domestic spending by over $35 billion
3. Approval of a defense plan of nearly $200 billion for 1982, less than the president wanted originally but more than President Carter had proposed
4. Significant reductions in the Aid to Families with Dependent Children (AFDC) benefits, food stamps, certain antipoverty programs, and other minor welfare benefits
5. Savings in Medicaid and Medicare programs, but postponement of an overhauling of the social security retirement system

The first session of the 97th Congress was described as "a great personal triumph for Reagan. Congressional approval of his plan was due largely to his own efforts and strength."[31] Certainly the president played the central role, but his "personal triumph" was accounted for by an extraordinarily effective White House political operation. A strategy was developed and executed for taking advantage of the favorable political conditions.

Since so much of the strategy was centered in the budget, it was understandable that David Stockman, as OMB director, played a key role. A Legislative Strategy Group (LSG), made up of "the inner circle of White House aides," met frequently in Chief of Staff James Baker's corner office in the west wing of the White House. The LSG "wasn't even on the White House organizational chart," but it played a key role in formulating an approach to Congress and, in the process, communicating political signals and policy information among the key players in the White House and on Capitol Hill.[32]

Essentially the strategy was designed to capitalize on advantages and be ever attentive to the political situation. How this was done in the first months of the new administration is itself an important part of the Reagan legacy. No doubt other presidents in similar situations will seek to emulate the Reagan strategy. First and foremost, the LSG sought to concentrate congressional and media attention on the budget. The Reagan White House got high marks for setting priorities and for not dissipating its energies. Yet, making the budget a priority is not exactly an oversimplification of the policy world. The budget is very nearly everything. Therefore, the Reagan strategists had the double advantage of a seemingly simple agenda and yet one that was bound to have a significant and comprehensive policy impact.

Second, Congress itself facilitated this concentration by its budget reform of 1974. It would have been very difficult for the president to keep all eyes fixed on the budget had it not been for the new organization and procedures on Capitol Hill. The Congress provided itself with budget committees, a budget office (as a counterpart to the Office of Management and Budget), and a budget resolution (as a counterpart to the executive budget). The media could now follow the action. Further, a so-called budget reconciliation was tried for the first time by the Carter administration in 1980, thus providing a sort of test run for Reagan. The reconciliation process is designed to enforce the budget resolution within congressional committees. Thus it was a perfect tool for the Reagan strategists in forcing Congress to meet its own budget targets.

Third, the LSG knew by instinct and recent experience that mandates are short lived, particularly those that are illusory to begin with. Thus it was important to act fast. Among other things, members returning to their states and districts after the first six months of a new administration get a decent reading of constituents' attitudes. It was unlikely that the domestic budget-cutting portion of the Reagan mandate would hold up well back home.

Fourth, it was essential that the administration display strong unity behind the president's program. This required White House control throughout the departments and agencies; the appearance of agreement and cooperation within the White House itself; and few, if any, leaks from those unhappy with policy decisions. Such unity is always desirable, but it is essential if the president is to command support on Capitol Hill. Coalition building there naturally started with the Republicans. If Reagan could keep his troops in line, then he needed only a few House Democratic votes to get his program enacted. In this crucial first year, overall congressional Republican support was high, and it was phenomenal in regard to votes on major budgetary and economic proposals. House Republicans averaged nearly 98 percent support on seven key votes; Senate Republicans averaged 97 percent support on nine key votes.[33]

In 1981 the Reagan administration created a legacy for itself. "Politics had triumphed," according to Stockman.[34] "We experienced one of those rare policy breakthroughs, and its effects reverberated throughout the subsequent years of the president's term." Speaker O'Neill conceded that "I ... wasn't prepared for what happened in 1981."[35]

Managing the Legacy — The Subsequent Years

Having directed congressional and media attention to the budget, the White House now had to produce its own plan for reducing the deficit. But the president had conflicting goals. Having just cut taxes, he did not want to turn around and raise them. So that option for deficit reduction was out. He favored further increases in defense expenditures, thus obviating another possible source of deficit reduction. And he was not about to stand alone on social security adjustments, especially with the upcoming 1982 elections. David Stockman even indicates that the president failed to support OMB's effort to make significant cuts in other domestic programs (e.g., farm supports).

As proposed by the administration, the fiscal year (FY) 1983 budget included a deficit reduction plan of $239 billion over three years. The reductions were primarily in what might have been spent if certain cuts were not made. In other words, savings were counted where there was a decrease in the rate of growth. No amount of rhetorical or statistical manipulation could cover up the stark reality of huge imbalances, however. The bottom line was a projected $92 billion deficit for the new fiscal year and abandonment of the plan for a balanced budget in 1984.

For their part, members of Congress were unlikely in an election year to be receptive to President Reagan's proposals. Nor were they anxious to go it alone in cutting domestic programs further or in raising taxes. Yet much of the FY 1983 budget was rewritten on Capitol Hill, and the president was even convinced to approve a tax bill—one primarily designed to close loopholes and prevent tax evasion. Democrats used the deficit to frighten voters about the future of social security, noting that the president's plan for increased defense expenditures and reduced taxes would lead eventually to drastic cuts in retirement and other social welfare programs.

Presidential-congressional politics, as practiced in 1982, essentially became the basic pattern for the remainder of Reagan's term in office. His budget success in 1981 created the conditions for unpleasant confrontations. In the struggle to cope with mounting deficits, the president's personal popularity was his principal resource. Meanwhile, congressional Democrats were emboldened by midterm election successes in 1982 to assert their independence. Unfortunately, they did not have the leadership or the organization to prepare credible alternative proposals. At times, in fact, it seemed that the Senate Republicans were offering the only options to the president's proposals.

Table 9.1 shows how political conditions changed for each of the four Reagan Congresses. Clearly no two were alike, and changes in the 98th, 99th, and 100th naturally contributed to different policy responses to the 1981 legacy. Each deserves brief review.

THE 98TH CONGRESS—THE POLITICS OF AVOIDANCE

Representative Bill Gradison (R-Ohio) was quoted in 1983 as saying: "I don't remember a presidential election starting so early."[36] Political conditions changed rather dramatically following the 1982 congressional elections, for several reasons. First, of course, was the significant increase in the number of House Democrats—from 243 to 269. This change meant that 52 Democrats would now have to defect for the Republicans to win a vote—double the number required in the 97th Congress. Effectively then, the House Democratic leadership was able to resume control over its membership.

TABLE 9.1
POLITICAL CONDITIONS, 97TH–100TH CONGRESSES

	House					Senate				
	Party		Leadership[a]			Party		Leadership[a]		
Congress	D	R	D	R		D	R	D	R	
97th	243	192 (+33)	O'Neill[b] Wright Foley Long	Michel Lott Kemp		47	53 (+12)	Byrd Cranston Byrd	Baker[b] Stevens McClure	
98th	269 (+26)	166	Same[b]	Same		46	54 (+1)	Same	Same[b]	
99th	253	182 (+14)[c]	O'Neill[b] Wright Foley Gephardt	Same		47 (+2)[c]	53	Same	Dole[b] Simpson Chaffee	
100th	258 (+5)	177	Wright[b] Foley Coehlo Gephardt	Same[d]		55 (+8)	45	Same[b]	Same	

a. Includes the Speaker, floor leader, whip, and caucus chairman for the House Democrats; the floor leader, whip, and conference or caucus chairman for the rest.
b. Majority leadership.
c. Republicans won interim elections to increase their numbers to 168 in the House and 55 in the Senate.
d. Jack Kemp resigned as conference chairman in 1987; Dick Cheney was elected in his place.

Actually the Republican losses in 1982 were somewhat smaller than predicted for the average midterm election. But following the 1980 elections, Democrats were fearful that a realignment might be under way—that, as happened in 1934 for Roosevelt's Democrats, Reagan's Republicans might actually increase their numbers. Therefore the twenty-six-seat increase reassured Democratic leaders that the president's popularity was not fully transferable to congressional Republicans. They were bound to be less deferential to Reagan and more optimistic about recapturing the Senate and the White House in 1984.

Second, the president's own popularity was declining. His Gallup poll rating slipped into the 40s during 1982 and declined further to 35 percent in January 1983.[37] Reagan's economic program was not working in the short run. Although inflation had been cut, unemployment and interest rates remained high, and the national debt continued to soar. Doubt was expressed that the president would even seek reelection.

Third was the inevitable media reaction to any exposed failing of the president. Dick Kirschten reflected the views of many commentators when he stated:

> The mood in Washington has changed vastly since the heady first months of the Reagan administration, when the president adroitly pulled off a series of startling coups. One no longer hears of a Reagan Revolution or of an emerging Republican majority. Democratic gains in the 1982 elections, while not shattering, nonetheless indicated disenchantment with Reagan's leadership.[38]

The one encouraging result from the 1982 election was that the Republicans retained their Senate majority status for the first time since 1930. Thus the Reagan White House continued to enjoy the advantage of sequence—gaining Senate approval first, then pressuring the House for action.

With one major exception, these political conditions led to a politics of avoidance throughout the 98th Congress. The exception was passage of social security reform. Acting on a bipartisan basis, Congress accepted the recommendations of a National Commission on Social Security Reform. Referred to as "artful work" by Representative Barber B. Conable, Jr. (R-N.Y. and a member of the National Commission), passage of this legislation removed a major negative issue for Reagan in 1984.[39] Democrats pounded away on Republican candidates in 1982 on social security. They would not be able to do so again.

Otherwise, major issues were postponed. Neither Congress nor the White House had the solution to the budget impasse. Deficits continued to mount. The end-of-session reviews in 1983 and 1984 highlighted the separation between the two branches and its consequences.

> 1983: Congress and President Reagan generally kept to their own turf in 1983—each branch going about its business with little involvement from the other side.[40]
>
> 1984: A year of politics and procrastination on Capitol Hill left many members of the 98th Congress disappointed with their track record and a long list of unsolved problems for the new Congress to address.[41]

Whether resolved or not, however, the 1981 legacy dominated presidential-congressional policy politics in the 98th Congress. The hard facts were that the Reagan agenda would carry through into the 1984 election, forcing Democrats to discuss budget deficits and taxes. Meanwhile, the economy improved steadily during the 98th Congress, and with it the chances that Ronald Reagan would seek a second term.

THE 99TH CONGRESS: THE POLITICS OF ASSERTIVENESS

Elsewhere I have labeled the 1984 contest an approval election, that is, one in which the voters said yes to an existing government of split-party control (Republicans controlling the White House and Senate, Democrats the House of Representatives).[42] Ronald Reagan won a huge landslide, winning the electoral count of every state but Minnesota (and the District of Columbia). Meanwhile, a large proportion of incumbent representatives and senators were also reelected —95 and 90 percent respectively. Obviously a high return rate of congressional incumbents means relatively little shift in the partisan balance there. In 1984 the Republicans had a net gain of fourteen House seats and a net loss of two Senate seats. In this respect, the 1984 election was not very different from two previous landslide reelections by Republicans in recent decades—those by Eisenhower in 1956 and Nixon in 1972. In neither case was there a major change in the partisan balance within Congress.

Nevertheless, if "mandates are inherently implausible" under circumstances where it is logical to assume that the voters were sending a policy message (as in 1980), they are doubly so where voters are affirming a split-party Congress and reelecting a minority-party president by one of the greatest landslides in history. How is one to interpret such behavior in policy terms? One common explanation was simply that Ronald Reagan's popularity exceeded that of his political party, that the voters approved of him more than they approved of his policies. Yet no president is a personality only. He holds the most important policy and partisan position in Washington. Thus, who he is mixes with what he favors. And he may be expected to interpret reelection as approval of his behavior in office.

Given the mixed signals of an approval election of this type, it is not surprising that the 99th Congress was more assertive. House Democratic leaders acknowledged the president's popularity but were bound to take more initiative than before. The Republicans were still in the majority in the Senate, but Howard Baker (R-Tenn.) did not seek reelection and the new majority leader, Robert Dole (R-Kans.), was selected in part because of his greater independence from the administration. Then, of course, however popular the president might be, he could not run again.

It was also the case that the second term brought changes in the management of the White House. Donald Regan took over as chief of staff, with James Baker assuming Regan's previous position as secretary of the treasury. Regan's style was better suited to the board room than the White House. He had limited tolerance for members of Congress, and would have less with each passing month.[43] Having an antipolitical chief of staff was strangely inapt for a political president. It raised questions about how attentive he was in regard to his own staff operations, questions that resurfaced during the Iran-*contra* hearings.

Finally, the agenda itself encouraged a more assertive posture for Congress. The 1981 legacy continued. There was no escaping the heavy burden of the deficits. Congressional anxiety increased during the 98th Congress and was bound to result in greater initiative in the 99th. The president's budgets were deemed "dead on arrival" by congressional Democrats—a declaration suggesting that they were prepared to provide an alternative. Then foreign and defense policy issues became more and more contentious—for example, sanctions on South Africa, aid to the *contras,* the strategic defense initiative, arms control, the MX missile.

To declare that Congress was more assertive is not to say that Reagan was helpless or that the legislative branch somehow took charge of the government. One of the most sweeping tax-reform bills in history was passed. Other presidents—most recently Carter

—campaigned for changes in the tax laws, but Reagan made it a priority for his second term, and presidential-congressional cooperation was achieved beyond the expectation of the most seasoned political observers. Congress publicly announced its limitations in coping with the budget by enacting the Gramm-Rudman-Hollings measure, a procedure for establishing automatic budget cuts should Congress fail to meet designated targets. The procedure did have the effect of focusing even greater attention on deficits, but it turned out not to be a substitute for the hard choices that had to be made.

The 99th Congress closed to very mixed reviews. Yet, under the circumstances, it is hard to imagine what more one could have expected from either end of Pennsylvania Avenue. For his part, despite his overwhelming victory, Reagan was unable to match the accomplishments of his first two years. But he was far from being an incapacitated lame duck. For its part, Congress demonstrated a capacity to produce major legislation despite split-party control between the two chambers. Leadership in both chambers received high marks for their efforts. "The record of the 99th Congress belies early predictions that it would dissolve in partisan rancor."[44] Yet no one believed that we could govern only with Congress. In other words, it all went about as well as could be expected, given what the voters had done in 1984.

The 100th Congress: The Politics of Survival

Presidents who serve two terms are understandably anxious about the second midterm election. There is talk about the "six-year itch," that is, voter dissatisfaction with the president and his party in the sixth year. And there is talk about lame-duck status as a president enters the final two years. Neither phenomenon is an immutable law, but talk is reality too, and it can be unsettling to the president and his advisers.

In 1986 Ronald Reagan accepted the electoral challenge of his status and campaigned heavily for Republican Senate incumbents and challengers. He did so in spite of the conventional wisdom that presidential coattails are threadbare in midterm elections. The results were close to being a disaster. The Democrats recaptured their majority status in the Senate with a net gain of eight seats. Seven Republican incumbents were defeated, and Democrats won two seats held by retiring Senate Republicans. One Republican won a seat previously held by a Democrat.

There was no discernible six-year itch in voting for the House of

Representatives. Incumbents were returned at an exceptionally high rate—98.5 percent. The net loss of five House Republicans was the second smallest loss for the president's party in a midterm election in this century and the smallest by far for a minority-party president.

Loss of the Senate forced a change in White House strategy. Appointments requiring confirmation were in jeopardy, majority building for treaties was altered, and the advantage of playing one chamber off against the other was lessened, if not lost altogether. There was also a change in House leadership. Speaker O'Neill retired, and a more aggressive Jim Wright of Texas assumed the chair. Determined to establish his own leadership style, as distinct from that of O'Neill, Wright was unlikely to cooperate very often with the administration.

These political developments encouraged a more defensive posture by the White House regardless of what else might occur. In other words, managing the government as a lame-duck minority-party president while working with a Congress controlled by the other party is something less than an ideal formula for success. But there was more. Analysts barely had time to ponder the 1986 election results when it was revealed that the administration had been dealing with Iran in a complicated maneuver involving the release of hostages, arms shipments, and the diversion of profits to the *contras* in Nicaragua. The following summary judgment reflected the dominant perception of the president's condition as he entered the last two years of his administration.

> Ronald Reagan is heading into the final two years of his Presidency with his credibility damaged, the competency of his administration questioned and investigations under way into the conduct of his foreign policy. . . .
>
> Although supporters rallied to him, and critics said they did not want to see a crippled Presidency, many in Washington agreed that Reagan's ability to govern has been severely damaged and that the next few months will test his mettle more than anything in his tenure so far.[45]

No doubt having the Watergate debacle in mind, the president acted quickly to manage the Iran-*contra* affair. National Security Council personnel were fired, an independent counsel was requested, an investigating commission was appointed, and a Department of Justice probe was launched. Later Donald Regan, White House chief of staff, was replaced by Howard W. Baker, the former Senate majority leader.

No amount of initiative from the White House was likely to interfere with congressional investigations. Several were announced, and eventually a committee from each house was appointed. These committees agreed on joint hearings to be conducted during the summer. The president was determined to prevent the Iran-*contra* affair from interfering with his agenda. Although he made several moves to control matters, he could not manage it all. It was not an auspicious start for the last two years of his presidency.

In looking ahead to the 100th Congress the forecasters predicted distractions due to the Iran-*contra* imbroglio and confrontations over the budget. In his response to the State of the Union Message, the new Speaker of the House, Jim Wright, stressed an equal partnership between the president and Congress. He then proceeded to outline important areas of disagreement:

> The basic disagreement is not over how much we spend. It's where we spend it—what we get for it—and who pays the bill, ourselves or our children.
>
> The president's newest budget would cut $5.5 billion from the education of our young—and spend that same amount on research just for one new weapon.
>
> It asks more for the Pentagon, more for foreign aid, more for space, more for "star wars," more for the war in Latin America.
>
> But it would cut education, cut the clean water program, cut Medicare and Medicaid, cut what we do for the disadvantaged, and—are your ready for this?—the president's budget would make deep cuts in our commitment to drug enforcement.[46]

The direct confrontations were not long in coming. The president had pocket-vetoed a water-pollution-control bill at the end of the 99th Congress. The bill was quickly passed again by large margins in the House and Senate at the start of the 100th Congress. Reagan vetoed it directly this time, and his action was overridden in both chambers (401–26 in the House, 86–14 in the Senate). In late March, Congress presented him with a highway bill that he opposed. Again he accepted the challenge and vetoed it. And again the veto was overridden—this time by the very narrowest of margins in the Senate (67–33), following active lobbying by the president to sustain his veto.

Although he lost both battles, the president established his own combative posture in the face of the Iran-*contra* distraction. This aggressiveness probably benefited him later in the year when the impact of the hearings had abated. Even at the time, Senator George Mitchell (D-Me.) observed in regard to the highway bill's defeat: "I don't think it's a total loss for the president. This was an opportunity for the president to demonstrate aggressive, personal involvement in government."[47] His action certainty suited Reagan's determination not to suspend politics as a result of the Iran-*contra* affair or become too protective or defensive.

The events of 1987 consistently threatened presidential leadership. A brief review of some of the more dramatic presidential-congressional conflicts illustrates what a remarkable year it was.

□ The joint hearings of the House and Senate Select Committees to investigate the Iran-*contra* affair took place throughout the summer, from 5 May to 6 August. There were forty days of public hearings, four days of closed meetings, thirty-two witnesses, and nearly 10,000 pages of transcripts. Lt. Col. Oliver North was the star witness; his testimony and questioning took up approximately 14 percent of the transcript pages. A highly critical report was issued on 18 November, signed by all fifteen Democrats and three Republicans. Six Republicans issued a minority report.

□ Supreme Court Justice Lewis F. Powell retired on 26 June, providing President Reagan with an opportunity to appoint a conservative who would then tip the political balance on certain crucial cases. The president nominated Robert H. Bork on 1 July. Confirmation hearings before the Senate Committee on the Judiciary did not begin until 15 September, thus allowing ample time for those for and against Bork to mount their campaigns. The two weeks of hearings were very nearly as riveting as those of the Iran-*contra* committees. The Bork nomination was then rejected by the Senate. The president's next nominee, Douglas Ginsburg, withdrew following revelations regarding his personal life.

□ The stock market took a record tumble on 19 October, followed by demands for presidential-congressional cooperation to reduce the deficits. This major event drew the attention of everyone in official Washington, but revealed again the differences between the president and congressional Democrats for resolving the budget issue. A White House–congressional summit was begun on 27 October, and an accord was finally reached on 10 November. The president was forced by circumstances to accept tax increases.

◻ Mikhail S. Gorbachev visited the United States 8–10 December to sign a treaty banning intermediate-range nuclear-force missiles (INF) and to discuss outstanding issues between the two nations. Senate approval of the INF treaty was an issue where the president could expect cooperation from the Democrats and criticism from the far-right wing of his own party.

There were many other extraordinary developments that led to conflict between the branches—for example, the involvement of Speaker Wright in seeking to bring peace to Central America, passage of a revised Gramm-Rudman-Hollings procedure, a reinterpretation by the Reagan administration of an agreement with the Soviet Union regarding the testing of antiballistic missile (ABM) weapons, the reflagging and protection of Kuwaiti ships in the Persian Gulf (without the invocation of the War Powers Act). And through it all was the continuing battle over the budget.

By late summer, it was generally conceded that Ronald Reagan was weaker even than previous lame-duck presidents. "Out of steam," "paralyzed," "impotent," "aging" were a few of the judgments made in newspaper headlines. "The Reagan Presidency Fades into Its Twilight: Congress Becomes the Dominant Force" expressed a common sentiment by the fall.[48] The argument was made that Reagan had lost control of the agenda, in part because he had not sufficiently reset the issues in the 1984 campaign. "In 1984 he ran on fluff and feel-good advertising" is the way one Democratic political consultant put it.[49]

Regarding domestic affairs, Democratic leaders were still struggling with the 1981 legacy. They found it very difficult to form a new program in the traditional Democratic cast. And where they did take initiatives, as with trade legislation and welfare reform, there was the threat of presidential veto. In foreign policy, it is inherently difficult for Congress to assume leadership if the president fails. Thus, the president was crippled by the Iran-*contra* affair more than congressional Democrats were advantaged. And, in the end, the president recouped much of his status through the summit meeting with Gorbachev and his leadership in arms control.

The end-of-the-year evaluations of Reagan were much more positive. He actually won more *contra* aid and forced Democrats to withdraw certain broadcast regulations in the final appropriations measure.

On the heels of his December arms-control summit with Soviet leader Mikhail S. Gorbachev, some Democrats grudgingly conceded that Reagan ended 1987 on a roll.

"The president did come on strong in the last month of the year," said Rep. Dennis E. Eckart (D-Ohio). "It was like old times."[50]

Prospects for the second session of the 100th Congress were for continued conflict between the two branches. Many of the divisive issues carried over into the election year. Helen Dewar's description of the end of the first session is a decent portrait for 1988: "Like two muscle-bound wrestlers, Reagan and the Democrats held each other in a clumsy hammerlock to the end."[51]

Scoring the Reagan Administration

It is common to review how the president scored on Capitol Hill and compare his record with that of other presidents. Figure 9.1 shows the percentage of votes won by the president—that is, votes on which he took a position. The scores are calculated by *Congressional Quarterly*. Note that President Reagan's scores decline steadily after 1981. President Eisenhower, the only other president to serve two full terms during the period, did better in two ways: He had a more successful first term (79 percent compared to 72 percent), and he scored high in the second year of his second term (76 percent compared to 57 percent for Reagan).

I have combined two other administrations so as to make comparisons—Kennedy with Johnson, Nixon with Ford. The first of these shows a very high average score (84 percent) and defies the third-, fourth- , and fifth-year losses exhibited by the other three (Eisenhower, Nixon-Ford, and Reagan). Johnson had phenomenal success in getting his way with Congress in the final month of 1963 and in 1964 and 1965. The average score during this period was nearly 90 percent. And Johnson asked for a lot compared to Eisenhower, who in 1953 had a high score but few legislative requests.

Nixon and Ford, like Eisenhower, had a decent increase in the sixth year, despite the fact that Nixon was forced to resign the presidency. Their overall average for the second term, however, was low: 56 percent.

Jimmy Carter had an average but steady record in support scores. Remarkably, however, it is closest to that of Nixon in his first term (76 percent average compared to 73 percent) in spite of the fact that Carter had strong Democratic majorities in both the House and Senate and Nixon's party was a minority in both chambers.

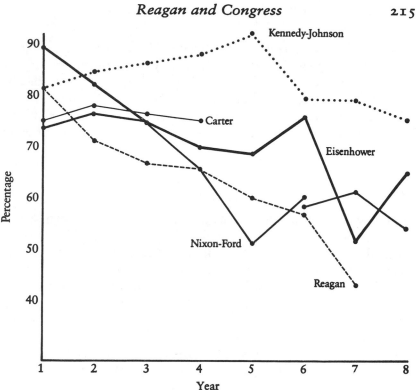

FIGURE 9.1
PRESIDENTIAL SUPPORT SCORES, EISENHOWER TO REAGAN

AVERAGES: Eisenhower = 72%; Kennedy-Johnson = 84%; Nixon-Ford = 65%; Carter (4 years) = 76%; Reagan = 62%.

SOURCES: Various volumes of *Congressional Quarterly Almananc* and issues of *Congressional Quarterly Weekly Report*.

The steady decline in Reagan's support scores fits the basic pattern of his association with Congress. That is, he had phenomenal success in his first year with a set of proposals bound to dominate the subsequent agenda. He indeed "struck while the iron was hot," so to speak. What he won in 1981 was likely to increase Democratic opposition to his subsequent requests as they struggled to regain an identifiable program of their own. Republicans too were left to struggle with the unpopular choices of cutting popular programs or raising taxes.

Reagan's support score for 1987 (43 percent) was the lowest

recorded for a president by *Congressional Quarterly*. His average for the first seven years was the lowest of any president in this set, even Nixon-Ford. Yet it is uncertain whether these scores are the best measure of the success or failure of the Reagan presidency. In an era of budget-deficit politics, Congress is unlikely to prefer presidential solutions to their own; nor, perhaps, would Reagan expect them to do so.

Conclusions

In the words of the British scholar Nigel Bowles, "Reagan successfully fused policy prescription with politics."[52] He took advantage of favorable conditions in 1981 to produce "quick and profound policy change." It was the nature of this initial success, however, that he could not expect to realize anything like it again. That is not to say he lacked other triumphs. Enactment of a tax-reform program was a significant and unexpected achievement. Instead, it directs attention to the scope and effects of what occurred in 1981, which were akin to the policy breakthroughs of the Great Society. Ronald Reagan did not reduce government to nearly the same extent as Lyndon Johnson expanded it. But he created the policy conditions for a contractive politics that had never been played before.

Thus President Reagan left a policy and political legacy for Congress and the next president. His 1984 opponent, Walter Mondale, described the policy legacy for the Democrats this way:

> Democrats are in a real box. Reagan has practiced the politics of subtraction. He knows the public wants to spend money on the old folks, protecting the environment and aiding education. And he's figured out the only way to stop it is to deny the revenues. No matter how powerful the arguments the Democrats make for the use of government to serve some purpose, the answer must be no.[53]

Of course, the "politics of subtraction" can produce discomfort for legislators of both parties. No elected representative is anxious to cut back programs affecting constituents. Democrats, then, were denied their traditional platform, even as voters appear to support more spending. Republicans were pressured to support their president even when it hurt. Meanwhile, the president's popularity remained relatively high, declining only as an effect of an affair of his own making—Iran-*contra*—and not of the economic and budgetary legacy left for Congress and the nation.

Presidents who achieve policy breakthroughs may not be the best ones to control the subsequent effects. There seems to be a policy trap for successful presidents. Being identified with, and committed to, programs for which they receive political credit, they are then ill prepared to propose solutions to the problems these programs create. Perhaps presidents of achievement should be limited to one term!

NOTES

1. Fred I. Greenstein, *The Hidden-Hand Presidency: Eisenhower as Leader* (New York: Basic Books, 1982), 60, 61.
2. *Time,* 7 April 1986, 27.
3. Raymond E. Wolfinger, "Dealignment, Realignment, and Mandates in the 1984 Election, in *The American Elections of 1984,* ed. Austin Ranney (Durham, N.C.: Duke University Press, 1985), 293.
4. Ibid., 292.
5. See, for example, Gregory B. Markus, "Political Attitudes during an Election Year: A Report on the 1980 NES Panel Study," *American Political Science Review* 76 (September 1982): 560.
6. A. James Reichley, "A Change in Direction," in *Setting National Priorities: The 1982 Budget,* ed. J.A. Pechman (Washington, D.C.: Brookings Institution, 1981), 229.
7. Christopher Buchanan, "Modest GOP Congressional Gains Expected," *Congressional Quarterly Weekly Report,* 1 November 1980, 3242.
8. Charles O. Jones, "A New President, a Different Congress, a Maturing Agenda," in *The Reagan Presidency and the Governing of America,* ed. Lester M. Salamon and Michael S. Lund (Washington, D.C.: Urban Institute, 1985), 266–69.
9. Gary Jacobson, *The Politics of Congressional Elections* (Boston: Little, Brown 1983), 136.
10. *New York Times,* 6 November 1980, A29.
11. Ibid., A35.
12. Thomas P. O'Neill, Jr. (with William Novak), *Man of the House: The Life and Political Memoirs of Speaker Tip O'Neill* (New York: Random House, 1987), 344.
13. Quoted in Gail Gregg, "Reagan Proposes Dramatic Reduction in Federal Role," *Congressional Quarterly Weekly Report,* 14 March 1981, 445.
14. Quoted in Harry McPherson, *A Political Education* (Boston: Little, Brown, 1972), 268.
15. James Pfiffner, "The Carter-Reagan Transition: Hitting the Ground Running," *Presidential Studies Quarterly* 13 (Fall 1983): 627.

16. O'Neill, *Man of the House,* 341–42.
17. Quoted in Dick Kirschten, "The Pennsylvania Avenue Connection—Making Peace on Capitol Hill," *National Journal,* 7 March 1981, 384.
18. O'Neill, *Man of the House,* 345.
19. Ibid., 342.
20. Kirschten, "The Pennsylvania Avenue Connection," 385.
21. Dick Kirschten, "Governors Get the Red Carpet ... the Message Is Pure Reagan," *National Journal,* 1 March 1986, 519.
22. Stephen J. Wayne, "Congressional Liaison in the Reagan White House: A Preliminary Assessment of the First Year," in *President and Congress: Assessing Reagan's First Year,* ed. Norman J. Ornstein (Washington, D.C.: American Enterprise Institute, 1982), 50.
23. Pfiffner, "The Carter-Reagan Transition," 627.
24. Wayne, "Congressional Liaison," 56–57.
25. Wallace Earl Walker and Michael R. Reopel, "Strategies for Governance: Transitions and Domestic Policymaking," *Presidential Studies Quarterly* 16 (Fall 1986): 747.
26. Ibid., 746.
27. Quoted in ibid., 747.
28. Allen Schick, "How the Budget Was Won and Lost," in Ornstein, *President and Congress,* 14.
29. Ibid., 43.
30. David Stockman, *The Triumph of Politics: Why the Reagan Revolution Failed* (New York: Harper & Row, 1986), 376.
31. Irwin Arieff et al., "The Year in Congress," *Congressional Quarterly Weekly Report,* 19 December 1981, 2505.
32. Stockman, *Triumph of Politics,* 4 and passim.
33. See Jones, "A New President," 276–77.
34. Stockman, *Triumph of Politics,* 376.
35. O'Neill, *Man of the House,* 345.
36. Quoted in Diane Granat et al., "Partisanship Dominated Congressional Year," *Congressional Quarterly Weekly Report,* 26 November 1983.
37. "Opinion Roundup," *Public Opinion* 7 (February-March 1984): 34.
38. Dick Kirschten, "President Reagan After Two Years—Bold Action but Uncertain Results," *National Journal,* 1 January 1983, 4.
39. Quoted in Paul Light, *Artful Work: The Politics of Social Security Reform* (New York: Random House, 1985), vii.
40. Granat et al., "Partisanship Dominated Congressional Year," 2467.
41. Diane Granat et al., "98th Congress Leaves Thorny Legacy for 99th," *Congressional Quarterly Weekly Report,* 20 October 1984, 2699.

42. Charles O. Jones, "The Voters Say Yes: The 1984 Congressional Elections," in *Election 84: Landslide Without a Mandate?* ed. Ellis Sandoz and Cecil V. Crabb, Jr. (New York: New American Library, 1985), chap. 4.

43. Diane Granat et al., "On Balance, a Year of Taking the Initiative," *Congressional Quarterly Weekly Report,* 28 December 1985, 2727.

44. Jacqueline Calmes, "The 99th Congress: A Mixed Record of Success," *Congressional Quarterly Weekly Report,* 25 October 1986, 2648.

45. John Felton, "Iran Arms and 'Contras': A Reagan Bombshell," *Congressional Quarterly Weekly Report,* 29 November 1986, 2971.

46. The speech is reprinted in *Congressional Quarterly Weekly Report,* 31 January 1987, 203–5.

47. Quoted in Paul Starobin, "Highway Bill Overridden After Close Call in the Senate," *Congressional Quarterly Weekly Report,* 4 April 1987, 604.

48. Article by Ronald D. Elving and Janet Hook, *Congressional Quarterly Weekly Report,* 17 October 1987, 2499–2503.

49. Quoted in ibid., 2501.

50. Janet Hook, "Budget Deal Enacted at Last, Congress Adjourns," *Congressional Quarterly Weekly Report,* 26 December 1987, 3183.

51. Helen Dewar, "Full Plate of Leftovers Awaits Hill, Reagan in 1988," *Washington Post,* 23 December 1987, A6.

52. Nigel Bowles, *The White House and Capitol Hill: The Politics of Presidential Persuasion* (Oxford: Clarendon Press, 1987), 217.

53. James M. Perry and David Shribman, "Reagan Era Restored Faith in Government until Recent Slippage," *Wall Street Journal,* 30 November 1987, 1.

10

Bush and Congress

It's easy to underestimate George Bush because he's so damn genteel and nice. — *Thomas Ashley*

Bush is a genuine conservative, an American Tory. There are known characteristics of that breed: they care about the society and the government that is handed to them; they want to make small adjustments; they want to keep the boat afloat. Bush is a professional in public service, which means that he has respect for other professionals. — *Nelson W. Polsby*

In a postelection article entitled "Low Expectations," Burt Solomon of the *National Journal* explained that Bush entered the White House "with no obvious mandate and with a residue of bad feeling left from the unsavory campaign." Therefore, Solomon reasoned, "there's little expectation that Bush's first 100 days as President will rival Reagan's or Franklin D. Roosevelt's in 1933. Nor should they."[1] Solomon quotes Richard E. Neustadt as saying that he would not be surprised if Bush "tried to lower expectations."

This kind of analysis was typical in the aftermath of the 1988 election. No one concluded that Bush's forty-state win carried with it a mandate for specific action on the nation's agenda. George Bush had not spoken to the issues in the campaign, and the Democrats had retained virtually their same healthy margins in the House and Senate. It was not an inspiring election for those who believe in party government and who test the political system by its principles.

By the end of its first year, the lowered expectations of the administration had the approval of a near-record number of Americans. George Bush's popular approval far exceeded that of Ronald Reagan at the end of his historic first year in office. It was also markedly higher than that of any other post–World War II president except John F. Kennedy. And this record was achieved in spite of low support in Congress by the standard measures. In fact, Bush's presidential support score in Congress in 1989 was the lowest by far for the first year of any postwar president—11 points below Richard Nixon in 1969!

During the budget impasse in September and October 1990, President Bush's popular approval ratings dropped significantly, the result both of bad economic news and the prospect of a prolonged military presence in the Persian Gulf. Yet his rating remained substantially above that of Ronald Reagan at the same point in his presidency, in spite of the fact that Bush's legislative support scores in Congress dropped to new lows. And his popularity soared to record heights following the successful conclusion of the war with Iraq.

Why should the popularity of a no-mandate, limited-action president exceed that of a Ronald Reagan, whose political circumstances were better suited to party government? This is one of the questions of central concern in this chapter. I argue that the outcome in Bush's case fits the politics of our time, a politics that meets none of the party government standards by which it is typically tested. Put otherwise, the perplexity for analysts is reduced when they shift their evaluative criteria from that of a party government perspective to that of a mixed representational perspective of diffused responsibility.

What the Voters Did and Whether They Liked It

A closer look at the post–World War II national election results shows even greater confusion than is indicated by the split-party results. Consider the following patterns:

For the Democrats

- President wins narrowly, House and Senate Democrats realize substantial gains (1948).
- President wins narrowly, House and Senate Democrats retain majorities but either lose seats (1960) or stay the same (1976).
- President wins in a landslide, House and Senate Democrats realize significant gains (1964).

In each of the four elections, the Democrats won control of both ends of Pennsylvania Avenue. But there were ample reasons in three elections (1948, 1960, and 1976) to question the extent to which the voters were endorsing a "party in power" concept. There were reasons in each case for congressional Democrats to act independently of the president. Only in 1964 might one be justified at the superficial level of congruous election results to declare a mandate for the "party in power." That is, in 1964 Lyndon Johnson and congressional Democrats won overwhelmingly in an election with strong ideological overtones, thus seemingly meeting primary conditions for responsible party government. Parenthetically, it might be observed that even in that situation one must question whether all criteria of the party responsibility model were met, since the Republicans were spoken of as a dispirited and ineffective opposition.

For the Republicans

- ☐ President wins in a landslide, House and Senate Republicans win bare majorities (1952).
- ☐ President wins in a landslide, House and Senate Republicans realize substantial gains, achieving majority status in the Senate (1980).
- ☐ President wins in a landslide, House and Senate Republicans (as the minority) stay the same (1956, 1988) or House Republicans realize small gains and Senate Republicans realize slight losses (1972, 1984).
- ☐ President wins narrowly, House and Senate Republicans (as a minority) realize small gains (1968).

These variations, too, fail to satisfy the conditions for responsible party government. The Eisenhower and Reagan victories came close. In the Eisenhower case, however, the Republicans went outside the party in order to nominate a winner (Taft being the "responsible party" choice). In the Reagan case (1980), the Senate win was stunning, but a Democratic House majority allowed for a special kind of divided-government politics that does not well suit responsible party criteria.

Are voters pleased with these results? The fact that they continue to produce split-party control is at least partial evidence that they are not consciously moved to make the corrections desired by the party responsibility advocates. But there is more direct evidence. In a *Wall Street Journal*/NBC poll taken in January 1990, voters expressed a preference for divided government by a margin of 63 to 29 percent, better than two to one.[2]

Clearly, such results are deeply disturbing to advocates of unified and responsible party government. In reflecting on recent developments in Eastern Europe and the Soviet Union, James MacGregor Burns concluded that these nations have little to learn from us beyond our Bill of Rights and an opposition party. In fact, "we can, paradoxically, learn from them."[3] Burns then listed a standard set of party responsibility reforms. Here is an excellent example of the dissatisfaction among the party responsibility advocates with the American people and their political system. What the voters want, apparently, is not good for them. It is hard to know exactly what part of democratic theory one turns to for support of that proposition.

What the Voters Thought They Were Getting in 1988

Whether it is legitimate to interpret an election as having conveyed a mandate, we now have ample evidence on what voters thought about the choice facing them in 1988. These thoughts have relevance in regard to viewing the president as a representative. How did voters perceive Candidate Bush? Who did they think he was? What did they think he favored? Which groups liked which candidates? The answers to these questions should help us understand whether President Bush met their expectations. They may even explain subsequent public approval ratings.

Consider, first, that Americans do not like being placed on an ideological scale. Therefore it is not surprising that, when asked, large numbers place themselves in the middle. Among those who are willing to identify themselves, conservatives consistently outnumber liberals in recent years. At no time during the 1980s did the number of liberals come close to matching the number of conservatives, as measured in three major polls. The averages through 1988 were as follows:[4]

	Liberals	Conservatives
National Opinion Research Center	24.5%	33.4%
CBS News/*New York Times*	19.1	34.0
Roper Organization	20.4	43.4

This conservative advantage may be said to be amplified in politics by the interesting disjuncture between how the public views societal and personal ideological trends. According to one 1988 survey, 52 percent of respondents judge that American society is more *liberal* now than twenty years ago, while only 17 percent of the respondents considered themselves to be more liberal than in the past (29 percent judged themselves more conservative).[5] That the country has moved left while voters are moving right is a familiar Republican campaign theme.

Asked by a Harris poll in August 1988 whether they "prefer a president who is a conservative, a moderate, or a liberal," respondents split as follows:[6]

A conservative	40%
A moderate	41
A liberal	13

Taken together, these data clearly suggest a campaign strategy in an open race, one requiring that each candidate's image must be fixed in the voters' minds. Barbara Farah and Ethel Klein point out that

> Michael Dukakis declared that he did not like labels and that his campaign would focus on competence, not ideology; the Republicans put ideology squarely on the campaign agenda.... By early September the "L word" had become a major theme of the Bush campaign, and the role that ideology was to play in the campaign was evident.[7]

As Farah and Klein show, the strategy worked. In May, 27 percent of the electorate considered Dukakis a liberal; by election day, 56 percent rated him that way. Of those who so categorized Dukakis, over 60 percent then voted for Bush.[8]

Next, consider the groups that supported George Bush and those that supported Michael Dukakis. Table 10.1 provides an overview. It holds few surprises, to be sure. But it confirms the moderate-to-conservative basis of Bush's support. Among the social, economic, and religious groupings, Bush scored best with married men, the middle-aged, the college educated, white-collar workers, homemakers, high-income voters, whites, and Protestants. His average support among these groups was 59 percent. He also did extremely well in the South and had impressive showings in the Midwest and West. Though retaining 56 percent of the rural and small-town vote, his

TABLE 10.1
SOURCE OF SUPPORT, BUSH AND DUKAKIS, 1988

	Bush supporters		Dukakis supporters	
	50–55%	56%+	50–55%	56%+
Party				
Republicans		☒		
Democrats				☒
Independents	☒			
Sex and marital status				
Married men		☒		
Married women	☒			
Unmarried men	☒			
Unmarried women				☒
Age				
18–29	☒			
30–44	☒			
45–59		☒		
60+	☒			
Education				
Not HS graduate				☒
HS graduate	☒			
Some college		☒		
College graduate		☒		
Postgraduate	☒			
Occupation				
Professional/manager		☒		
White collar		☒		
Blue collar			☒	
Teacher/student			☒	
Unemployed				☒
Homemaker		☒		
Retired	☒			
Union household				☒
Income				
Under $ 10,000				☒
$10,001–19,999			☒	
$20,000–29,999	☒			
$30,000–39,999		☒		
$40,000+		☒		
Race and region				
White		☒		
East	☒			
Midwest		☒		
South		☒		
West		☒		

TABLE 10.1 — *Continued*

	Bush supporters		Dukakis supporters	
	50–55%	56%+	50–55%	56%+
Black				☒
Hispanic				☒
Religion				
White Protestant		☒		
Catholic	☒			
Jewish				☒
Fundamentalist or				
White Evangelical		☒		
Community size				
Large cities				☒
Suburbs/small cities	☒			
Rural/small towns		☒		

SOURCES: Compiled from data in Gerald M. Pomper, *Election of 1988: Reports and Interpretations* (Chatham, N.J.: Chatham House, 1989), 133–34.

majority was substantially below that of Reagan in 1984 among these voters. The composite profile of the Bush voter is that of an individual who is privileged in American society, probably anxious to preserve present advantages, and unlikely to support new welfare programs.

In contrast, the groups heavily supporting Dukakis had ample reasons to ask more of government. They included unmarried women, the less educated, the unemployed, union households, low-income voters, blacks, Hispanics, and those living in large cities. The average support for Dukakis among these voters was over 60 percent.

The logical next questions to consider in evaluating what happened in 1988 between the voters and George Bush are these: What did voters like about Bush? What did they not like about Dukakis? What issues were important in voting for each candidate? Table 10.2 provides the answers, based on data in the Cable News Network/*Los Angeles Times* poll.[9] Bush voters primarily liked his experience, competence, and vision. Among the positive characteristics, these three contributed 73.6 percent to his vote (39.7 percent of the 53.9 percent received by Bush). They did not like Dukakis's liberalism, his personality, the risk of making a change, and the possibility that he would not stand up for America. Among the negative characteristics, these four contributed 64.9 percent to Bush's vote (35 percent of 53.9 percent).[10]

What of the issues? Bush scored particularly well among voters for whom defense, abortion, crime, taxes, and trade were important issues; he scored less well among those for whom the deficit, ethics, drugs, unemployment, and the environment were important issues. Consider these results in terms of how active Bush was likely to be once in office. He was expected to support a strong defense, "stand up for America." The president has limited responsibilities in regard to abortion or crime policy, Bush's tax statement was to hold the line, and a comprehensive trade bill had just recently passed the Congress. Those who wanted a more activist government in regard to drugs, environmental protection, and unemployment voted in greater numbers for Dukakis.

There appear to be several consistent messages from the preceding review:

1. In recent years, more Americans have moved right than left in the political spectrum, yet conclude that the society may have moved left.
2. An overwhelming majority of Americans favored a moderate or conservative in the White House, presumably one who is less active in expanding government.
3. Those groups supporting George Bush favored the status quo, thus maintaining present advantages.
4. Issue voting in 1988 did not support an activist program for President Bush. He was expected to maintain a strong defense, low taxes, and a strong economy.

The Postelection Charge to George Bush

The 1988 results were probably as predictable during the last month of the campaign as in any recent election. Close observers pretty much knew what was going to happen in both the presidential and aggregate congressional returns. As a consequence, it was a dull election night for the analysts, one with few of the surprises that television, in particular, likes to cover.

Postelection interpretations were uniformly pessimistic about what to expect from a Republican president and Democratic Congress. Editorial writers at the *Economist* were quite blunt:

After eight years in the shadows, he has his own presidency. But George Bush will never enjoy the popularity of Ronald Reagan ...

TABLE 10.2
WHY VOTERS VOTED AS THEY DID IN 1988

	Percentage mentioning	Percentage voting for	
		Bush	Dukakis
Most positive Bush characteristics			
More experience	34	97	3
More competent	27	73	26
Vision of future	17	52	46
Impressive in debates	7	54	46
Avoid a recession	4	80	19
More likable	3	52	42
Most negative Dukakis characteristics			
Too liberal	28	94	6
Personality	19	55	43
Too risky a choice	15	76	24
Won't stand up for America	8	65	33
Won't be elected	4	63	34
Issues important to Bush voters			
National defense	23	84	15
Abortion	20	63	36
Crime	18	67	31
Taxes	15	70	29
Trade	5	57	42
Issues important to Dukakis voters			
Budget deficit	25	39	60
Governmental ethics	17	31	67
Drugs	14	41	58
Unemployment	10	35	64
Environment	11	28	70

SOURCES: Compiled from data in Gerald M. Pomper, *The Election of 1988: Reports and Interpretations* (Chatham, N.J.: Chatham House, 1989), 143; and *National Journal,* 12 November 1988, 2854.

nor will he have the same opportunities to shine. This new president ... will find that ruling is often a mocking word whose substance will elude him for much of the next four years.[11]

Most commentary was a variation on a doubting theme. Looking back on what had happened, all agreed that there was no mandate. Looking ahead to the new administration, most expressed apprehension. The result was a rather gloomy forecast: an untested president, lacking the popular image of his predecessor, faced having to cope with a demanding agenda without a mandate and sharing power with a Democratic Congress.

Columnists and editorial writers produced slight variations in what were otherwise virtually interchangeable reviews. For Richard Cohen of the *Washington Post,* George Bush now had "to prove that his character is a match for his ambition," a matter not resolved by a "dirty campaign" and no "clear mandate."[12] Albert C. Hunt concluded that had Bush "tried to lay out an agenda, it would have made his task over the next four years considerably easier." Now he had to campaign further just to have a mandate.[13] Lou Cannon judged that there were "obstacles left and right," but "Bush's best insurance against a successful challenge from his right is to have Reagan in his corner."[14] Haynes Johnson described the 1988 election as "issueless, avoid-pain, postpone-decisions, float-along-America." "With Democrats more strongly in control of Congress, Bush faces potentially greater opposition on Capitol Hill than has the more popular Ronald Reagan."[15] "George Bush is no Ronald Reagan," Fred Barnes discovered. Reagan set an ideological tone, Bush's campaign issues "are irrelevant to the way he intends to govern as president."[16]

One of the most balanced efforts to look back in order to see ahead was an editorial in the *Washington Post*. It is worth quoting at length.

> The truth of the matter is that the whole argument over the nature of Mr. Bush's mandate is in a sense merely incidental to a much larger and more immediate issue: How, on the basis of his campaign rhetoric and whatever the voters consider his mandate to be, a newly installed President Bush will handle the challenge of creeping Gramm-Rudman deadlines, burgeoning federal government costs and a Democratic Congress not exactly bursting with enthusiasm to help him out of the fiscal and financial pressures that are intensifying. His mandate in this poorly focused election may not have been to fix the budget deficit, but until he does, he can do little else. Given all this, we expect Mr. Bush's plans cannot be grandiose; his claims and demands will not be dramatic. He will reveal himself as a man whose hope is to make the so-called Reagan revolution work, to somewhat extend its social sympathies and to vindicate the past eight years in the next four. He will also be doing

a lot of bailing out. If you will pardon the expression, in this context we think the Bush presidency is more likely to be about competence than ideology.[17]

However realistic this analysis, and its implicit advice, may be, following it carried substantial risks in a political world dominated by a party responsibility or unified-government perspective. That is, the president is expected to lead, no excuses accepted. Thus, moving from postelection to preinauguration analysis was likely to be based on the president-as-activist-leader set of expectations. By mid December, the columnist Tom Wicker judged that "President-elect Bush has hit the ground limping." He found that Bush was "hedging on major program decisions, still damaging by delay his supposed choice to head the Pentagon, and still assembling an administration dominated by familiar faces."[18] And by his inauguration, the new president was advised to become a symphony conductor.

> He must find a way to persuade, cajole and stimulate the mighty institutions of government, the vast electorate and, perhaps most important, the rest of the world, to follow his lead, to respond to his cue, to make a thundering symphony out of disharmony at the flick of his conductor's wand.[19]

The president with no mandate was soon to be criticized for moving too cautiously; indeed, for permitting the world symphony to play without him. However rational it might have been in the postelection period to exercise prudence, doing so invited failure by the tests of the responsible party model president.

The First Year: Doing Well by Doing Poorly

The new Bush Administration was marked by a preference for competence, not ideology. The President's style was one of reactive problem solving, not strategic vision. His approach to Congress ... was one of compromise, not confrontation. His approach to policy disagreements was personal communication and diplomacy rather than "going public" to bring pressure to bear.... The Bush presidency in its first year might be characterized as one of consolidation, seeking a "new balance," not confrontation and change.[20]

This positive evaluation is of particular interest because it comes from the author of *The Strategic Presidency: Hitting the Ground Running*. In that book, James P. Pfiffner points out that a new administration has to move quickly.

> They must shift gears from campaigning to governing, and they are faced with the gigantic task of taking over the U.S. government. They want to take advantage of the "mandate" from the voters and create a "honeymoon" with Congress.... Early victories may provide the "momentum" for further gains. The desire to move fast is driven by the awareness that power is fleeting.... The need to "hit the ground running" is also important because of what scholar Paul Light calls the cycle of decreasing influence.[21]

So how is it that the Bush presidency can get a high first-year rating while seemingly violating the strategy recommended by Pfiffner and many others? The answer appears to lie in the fact that the requisite conditions for "hitting the ground running" were not met. Bush did not have a mandate; lacking a marriage, there was no honeymoon; power had already fled; therefore, influence was unlikely to cycle down, as predicted by Paul C. Light.[22] In other words, Pfiffner discovered in the Bush presidency a different kind of White House, one that required new criteria for measuring success.

Much of the difference in 1989 is captured in the concept of *copartisanship*. A unified government is properly tested by the criteria of partisanship, that is, whether those who claim affiliation with the majority party support their leaders in the White House and Congress. The important test is this: can a president realize the potential of his party's congressional majorities? Presidents can be expected to vary in their personal and political capacities to do so; for example, compare Lyndon Johnson with John Kennedy or Jimmy Carter. But the test itself is reasonable enough. And the argument stands that the president should move quickly, since the midterm elections are less than two years away.

As explained, the 1988 election did not produce a majority government. Both parties won. One interpretation even had it that "Democrats in Congress are approaching their relationship with President-elect Bush not so much with rancor as with confidence that they share his mandate to govern."[23] Several leaders were quoted as saying that they expected many areas of cooperation. But they also made it clear that cooperation would be based on negotiation among equals. "The people who will be sitting down with George Bush were also winners in the election" is the way House Democratic

Whip Tony Coelho of California put it. Speaker Jim Wright of Texas understandably agreed: "If there is a mandate, it clearly is for Bush as president and a Democratic Congress to build upon the constructive program we embarked on last year."[24] Winning, under the circumstances, clearly required a carefully developed strategy, one suited to the conditions of co-partisanship.

As used here, co-partisanship refers to a situation in which each political party has independent sources of power to the extent that (1) the power will be used to participate broadly in the policy process (including initiating proposals), and (2) negotiation carries rewards for both sides (see chapter 2). Co-partisanship is naturally associated with divided government—a president of one party, a Congress of the other (one house or both). Depending on advantages, however, one branch may be more powerful, thus reducing the need to negotiate, or one branch may be uncertain as to who benefits, possibly inducing a stalemate. Therefore, if the congressional Democrats have a veto-proof majority, they may prefer to ignore the president's preferences; or if no one knows for certain what are the political and economic effects of a budget solution, each side may thwart the other. As suggested, then, co-partisan agreements may be the outcome for some issues, stalemate the outcome for others.

A critical precondition to co-partisan politics is the independent but variable power base for each of the contending forces. There has to be a reason for one side to negotiate with the other. Each institution begins with impressive constitutional status. Seldom can one act independently of the other, though the president's authority as commander-in-chief gives him a significant edge in foreign and defense issues. The more intangible sources of power can vary dramatically, as has been outlined by many presidential and congressional scholars.

As to George Bush, the postelection analysis of his weaknesses was reviewed earlier—dirty campaign tactics, no program, no mandate, no honeymoon, untested as the "top banana." And so there was work to be done if the Democratic Congress was not to run roughshod over him. Far from being in a position to dominate Washington politics, George Bush had to prove himself worthy of co-partisan negotiation. He had to create and maintain an independent power base that was not conferred by his forty-state win. Thus were the strategic imperatives of his first year identified. He could do well in interbranch, co-partisan politics by doing poorly in meeting the standard party responsibility criteria.

In the previews of his assuming office, three issues in particular were listed as absolutely requiring attention, and each would result in high conflict between Bush and Congress: the budget, aid to the *contras,* and the savings-and-loan disaster. Bush sought to defuse these conflicts by reaching agreements with congressional Democrats, taking a conciliatory initiative that was hard for the Democrats to counter. Bush began with this tactic in his Inaugural Address:

> To my friends—and yes, I do mean friends—in the loyal opposition—and yes, I mean loyal: I put out my hand.
> I am putting out my hand to you, Mr. Speaker.
> I am putting out my hand to you, Mr. Majority Leader.
> For this is the thing: This is the age of the offered hand.
> And we can't turn back clocks, and I don't want to. But when our fathers were young, Mr. Speaker, our differences ended at the water's edge. And we don't wish to turn back time, but when our mothers were young, Mr. Majority Leader, the Congress and the Executive were capable of working together to produce a budget on which this nation could live. Let us negotiate soon—and hard. But in the end, let us produce.[25]

What President Bush failed to add was that, rhetorically, he had taken his listeners back to an era when divided government was the exception, not the rule. Never mind. He wanted to establish a conciliatory, cooperative posture toward those who, by some interpretations, shared his mandate.

The record shows that a significant measure of cooperation was achieved in the early months of the administration for each of the three contentious issues. Following an initial, bruising fight over the nomination of former Senator John Tower to be secretary of defense, budget makers at both ends of Pennsylvania Avenue reached an agreement that then passed both houses in the form of a budget resolution. A bipartisan accord was reached on Central American policy that "drained most of the political poison for the year out of debates."[26] And Bush offered a recovery plan for the savings-and-loan association that formed the basis of a bill passed in Congress by late summer. Thus the legislative, if not the appointive, record of the early period seemingly accomplished the strategic goal of avoiding debilitating political and policy struggles. The Bush administration hit the ground conciliating.

Contributing to the success of this strategy was a crisis of leadership among congressional Democrats that surely reduced their confidence and effectiveness, providing the cautious president with the latitude to frame his strategy. First, and with the least significant effect, was the election of a new Senate majority leader. Having served since 1977, Senator Robert C. Byrd (D-W.Va.) decided not to seek another term as leader. In a somewhat surprising result, George J. Mitchell (D-Me.) defeated two opponents for the position. The president's advantage was that of working with a new leader, one striving to develop a style that would gain him support. The president could help or hinder that process.

A second early advantage for Bush was created by a pay bill. A public furor developed over the size of the increase and the manner by which it was to go into effect. Traditionally skittish about voting themselves pay hikes, members of Congress created a blue-ribbon commission to make recommendations for all three branches. The commission proposed sizable increases, which were endorsed by both Presidents Reagan and Bush. Beyond the amount, a 51 percent hike, was the procedure that authorized the increase unless Congress voted to kill it within thirty days. After a great deal of wrangling and devastating media and public reaction, both the House and Senate voted against the increases. Newt Gingrich (R-Ga.) concluded that "this [pay hike controversy] has sparked a level of anti-Congress feeling that is more intense than any political feeling since Watergate."[27] Staggering from self-inflicted wounds, Democrats in Congress were in no position to take advantage of Bush's weakness and lay claim to national policy leadership.

The controversy over the pay raise had several unfortunate effects for congressional Democrats: it drew attention to honoraria received by members speaking to outside groups, set the House against the Senate, and questioned the leadership capability of Speaker Jim Wright of Texas. Wright was heavily criticized for his handling of the issue at the very time that he was under investigation by the Committee on Standards of Official Conduct (the ethics committee). And the matter of pay focused attention on exactly the charges being leveled against the Speaker—that he had sought to circumvent House rules on honoraria limits through the sale of books to groups to which he spoke.

Meanwhile, the House Democratic whip, Tony Coehlo of California, was under investigation for questionable investments. Thus, two of the top three House Democratic leaders were hampered by serious charges of ethical lapses. Coehlo was the first to resign, avoiding a full investigation. Five days later, on 31 May, in a dramatic resignation before a packed House, Speaker Wright spoke to his colleagues:

Let me give you back this job you gave me as a propitiation for all of this season of bad will that has grown up among us. . . . I will resign as Speaker of the House effective upon the election of my successor and I'll ask that we call a caucus on the Democratic side for next Tuesday to choose a successor. I don't want to be a party to tearing up the institution. I love it.

To tell the truth, this year, it has been very difficult for me to offer the kind of moral leadership that the organization needs because every time I have tried to talk about the needs of the country . . . the media have not been interested in that. They wanted to ask me about petty personal finances. You need somebody else. So I want to give you that back.[28]

On 6 June, Thomas S. Foley of Washington was elected Speaker, and over the next two weeks a completely new House Democratic leadership team was put in place: Richard A. Gephardt of Missouri, majority leader; William H. Gray of Pennsylvania, whip; Steny H. Hoyer of Maryland, caucus chairman; and Vic Fazio of California, caucus vice-chairman. All these members had had leadership experience *but not in these positions and not as a team.*

Thus the House Democrats began the summer having to accommodate new faces in new places. The effect was positive for President Bush's cautious and consolidative strategy for building support and creating his own presidency. He did not have to be concerned that congressional Democrats would fill the vacuum by assuming control of the agenda and of policy development. The outcome might have been very different had Speaker Wright not been crippled by ethics investigations, since Wright was a policy-oriented, New Deal Democrat anxious to participate actively in agenda setting and policy development.

The advantage for President Bush in congressional Democratic preoccupation with leadership problems should not be overstated. It bought him time by directing attention to the disarray among the opposition party on Capitol Hill. It did not place him in command of policy politics in Washington. This point is illustrated by the president's effort to cut the capital gains tax, thus fulfilling a campaign promise. The president succeeded in the House with help from Democrats in the Committee on Ways and Means. But it was a costly win. Senate Democrats pressed for compensatory tax hikes on the affluent, eventually preventing the capital gains cut from being voted on and succeeding in having it removed from the reconciliation bill in conference with the House.

The presidential support score for Bush at the end of his first year was the lowest of any first-year president since the *Congressional Quarterly* has been producing that measure (i.e., since World War II). Bush's score was 63 percent—11 points below Nixon's first year in 1969 and nearly 20 points below Reagan's.[29] But it was difficult to interpret exactly what that score meant. Probably it suggested the need for analysts to consider the political and policy conditions of the time, as well as the variation in what it is presidents want Congresses to do. President Bush was clearly interested more in foreign and defense than domestic policy. And his action in Panama seemed to enhance his public status.

Then there is the matter of how well a president does otherwise by getting high support scores on Capitol Hill in his first year. Bush needed to establish an independent advantage so as to participate actively in co-partisan politics. He was unlikely to gain that advantage merely by doing what was necessary to get an impressive support score, since to do so would require acquiescence to Democratic initiatives *if they were, in fact, forthcoming from the new leadership team*. This point is different from that made earlier about a conciliatory posture so as to avoid early confrontations with Congress. In those cases, the administration took the initiative with proposals designed to get Democratic support.

More promising for creating advantages was the consolidation of the administration's team (separating itself from the Reagan presidency) and seeking a broader base of public approval than was forthcoming in the 1988 election. If successful in these moves, then the White House would have positioned itself strategically to bargain more effectively in subsequent cross-partisan policymaking.

The record shows that both these goals were achieved during 1989. The administration was criticized for moving too slowly in filling important subcabinet positions (and the rejection of John Tower to be secretary of defense was not the recommended way to begin forming a team). But the criticism was typically based on the accepted theme of "hitting the ground running." In fact, as noted earlier, there were good reasons not to adopt that pace. Further, the Bush administration was the first elected since 1928 to follow one of the same political party and the first since 1836 to have a vice-president succeed through election. The importance of these facts is simply that George Bush had to move carefully to create his own presidency. He had to do so without damaging the party or the presidency of his predecessor. By historical record, there were not readily available precedents for accomplishing these goals. And surely the concept of "hitting the ground running" was less applicable.

There is further evidence in public opinion polls that an activist president who scores well with Congress may not be viewed as doing that well otherwise. Consider the following poll results, as reported in the *Washington Post* in January 1990:

1. The president's approval rating reached nearly 80 percent.
2. The Congress's approval rating was half of that, just under 40 percent.
3. Many more respondents judged that Congress "has the most power in Washington" (53 percent compared to 15 percent identifying the president as having the most power).[30]

Thus the president ended his first year in office having improved his approval rating while receiving a poor support score from a Congress with a low public approval rating (while seemingly being held responsible as the most powerful branch of government). One lesson would seem to be that doing well with Congress was not required for President Bush to do well with the public. A second lesson may have been that Congress would be held responsible for national policymaking, not a pleasing prospect for Democrats during a period of budget containment.

To summarize, co-partisanship in 1989 resulted in postponement of many issues because of a lack of clear direction. In fact, the results were not wholly unlike those of the 1988 election. Senate Minority Leader Robert Dole of Kansas put it this way: "There hasn't been any demand, any mandate in the Congress and executive branch for major changes. We've done some sort of nibbling around the edges." House Democratic leaders essentially agreed. Majority Leader Gephardt stated that "we're usually a reactive institution. It's very hard for Congress to lead."[31]

The year ended with international events taking center stage. U.S. forces invaded Panama on 20 December and Eastern European regimes fell like dominoes as the new year began. Though the president did not escape criticism inside Washington—it was said that he was too aggressive in Panama and insufficiently involved in Eastern Europe—presumably an international agenda provides many more advantages for him than a domestic one.

The Second Year: Waiting for Saddam

It seems to me that Bush is two personalities. There is the personal presidency and there is the policy presidency. The personal presidency is remarkably proactive, almost over active. This guy gets up at five in the morning, goes out and he jogs five miles and then he comes back and has four meetings and then he writes 50 personal notes to people and then he goes out and runs around town, prepares for another trip.... It is almost impossible to imagine George Bush taking a nap in the afternoon, waking up at nine A.M., falling asleep in an audience with the Pope.

The policy presidency of George Bush is reactive, not quite passive, anything but proactive. His instinct when it comes to issues is to say: "Let's let things germinate." Not, there's a problem, we better solve it; or, there might be a problem, let's do something before it becomes a problem.... Maybe the problem will go away. Maybe it will turn out to be less severe than we thought. If it does turn out to be worse and the time has come to act, then I'm perfectly comfortable looking at the alternatives and making a decision. It is not that I'm reactive because I don't want to deal with this [problem].[32]

These comments by a seasoned Washington political analyst suggest a virtual war between proactive personal behavior and reactive policy behavior. The evidence seemingly supports this analysis. Can the two behaviors be reconciled in a way to assist in understanding the president's strategy of decision making? I think they can, and the second year shows how. The second-year strategy was no more satisfying to the advocates of an activist presidency. Whereas the first year could be explained by political and policy conditions, the second year was more revealing of the melding of these conditions with personal style for explaining White House strategy.

The proactive personal behavior does carry over to politics and policymaking, but not necessarily to problem solving. It shows up in a remarkably energetic effort to stay in contact with those with whom the president must negotiate should problems develop. Thus there is almost a boy-scoutish "Be Prepared" approach that, as suggested above, awaits events and then acts to resolve a sure thing. By this approach, the president's strategy is, if you will, to be actively, not passively, reactive. That may even be what the analyst quoted above means by his modification "and not quite passive."

This style as strategy can be illustrated in both domestic and foreign policy in 1990. On the domestic front, the analysts were not encouraging: "Vulnerable to Events," "Stalemates of Last Decade Haunt Agenda for 1990," "[State of the Union] Address Reflects Modest Bush Agenda," "With the Issues Emotional and Elections

Near, Bush-Congress Budget Fight Is Likely to Be Nasty."[33] There were few optimists and little reason for optimism.

As they had for nearly a decade, virtually all the domestic issues were dealt with in the context of the budget deficit. Basically, short of an economic crisis, the budget process worked to the president's political advantage, particularly a cautious president with a limited "proactive" social agenda. The advantage works like this. Under the Gramm-Rudman-Hollings procedure, the president is told what his budget must be. For fiscal year 1991, the budget could be unbalanced by $64 billion (plus a fudge factor of $10 billion). The Bush administration proposed a budget with a $64.7 billion deficit, well within the prescribed limits. The president acts first in the process and therefore can manage economic indicators, revenue estimates, and savings on expenditures to his advantage. Put otherwise, he can produce what he is told to produce by managing the numbers.

In co-partisan politics, it is then predictable that congressional Democrats will declare the president's budget to be unrealistic, often "dead on arrival." In making that declaration, Democratic leaders are essentially stating that they are then prepared to offer an alternative that is realistic. And in 1974 members of Congress put in place a budget process at their end of the avenue. So, as the clock moves inexorably toward the end of the fiscal year, attention naturally shifts to Capitol Hill, where partisan wrangling dominates the debate. The president can deal himself in or out of this battle. But the setting is there—in Congress—not in the White House. And the president can assume the posture of cooperating, cajoling, or condemning—all the while reminding the public that it is Congress, not the president, that must ultimately approve the budget.

This script was followed in 1990 with variations to suit the changing circumstances.

> President Bush's $1.2 trillion budget for fiscal 1991 got predictably bad reviews when it reached Congress Jan. 29: It can't be taken seriously, snapped the Democratic majority....
>
> Democratic leaders dismissed the budget with familiar complaints that it would spend too much on defense and too little on domestic programs, do little to combat chronic deficits without new taxes, and meet the $64 billion deficit limit for 1991 mainly by relying on overly favorable economic forecasts.[34]

It is not necessary to review the very long story of budget making in 1990. Suffice it to say that the protracted struggle resulted in severe criticism of both White House and congressional leaders. The president did deal himself back into the process when new forecasts projected an economic downturn. A budget summit was convened once the Democrats had passed a budget resolution, and President Bush even went so far as to rescind his campaign pledge not to raise taxes. Still, a budget agreement proved elusive over the summer. Negotiations resumed after the August recess, finally producing a package on the last day of the fiscal year.

Unfortunately, the initial agreement reached between the White House and the leaders of Congress was not acceptable either to the left among the House Democrats or the right among House Republicans. The co-partisan goal was to have at least half of each party vote for the package—130 Democrats and 89 Republicans for a 219-vote majority. Early on the morning of 5 October, neither party achieved the 50 percent goal. The package was defeated, 179–254, with 40 percent of Republicans and 42 percent of Democrats in favor.

Neither Bush nor congressional leaders were seemingly prepared for this outcome, in spite of signals that it might occur. Nor was it likely that either was capable of a preparedness sufficient to the task of preventing intense partisan clashes. The impasse reflected the intractability of the deficit issue and illustrated the potential for stalemate in co-partisan politics. To propose increasing taxes and cutting programs is to touch the nerve ends of party differences. The achievement of getting a plan at all was overshadowed by its defeat on the House floor.

The president's veto power is clearly an important resource in co-partisan politics. By summer 1990, President Bush had established this authority as an important weapon in checking the initiatives of congressional Democrats. He had vetoed thirteen bills by that time, and Congress was unable to override any one of them. The further threat of vetoes for legislation carried over to the final weeks of the second session (one list cited eighteen bills for which a veto was recommended) added weight to the president's influence. Robert A. Roe (D-N.J.) observed that "every time we go to the bathroom around here somebody says, 'Check on the White House. They are going to veto.' "[35]

Practically the whole government appeared to be in suspended animation prior to the August recess. Few major bills had passed, the only appropriations measure to pass was a supplemental bill for fiscal year 1990, and a budget agreement seemed as illusive as ever. And with an election pending, Congress returned in September to an extraordinary workload to be handled in a brief time.

September and October 1990 were among the more remarkable months in contemporary national policymaking. As one might expect, the White House and Congress were consistently criticized as being ineffective. Yet the record shows the passage of the largest deficit-reduction package in history (including election-year tax increases), consequential reform of the budget process, and enactment of several significant measures (e.g., reauthorizations for farm, housing, and Head Start programs; a tough clean-air plan, immigration reform, a crime bill, and a new child-care program). The concentration of effort in round-the-clock sessions was bound to invite criticism, even ridicule, of the system. There was virtually no positive commentary on either the process or its product once Congress adjourned.

In foreign policy, events early in 1990 moved so swiftly that the president could hardly do anything but "Be Prepared." Developments in Eastern Europe and the Soviet Union dominated the news. The president was criticized for not playing a more active role in responding to or even managing these events. Senate Majority Leader George Mitchell advised President Bush to go to the Berlin Wall, many members of Congress and media analysts proposed more tangible support for Lithuania in its struggle for independence, others were critical of the president for not offering more economic aid to Eastern Europe. The president's strategy throughout was one of "watch and wait," while maintaining the closest ties to the relevant foreign leaders. Since the developments themselves were overwhelmingly favored by most Americans, including most members of Congress on both sides of the aisle, there were few political costs to the president's strategy.

The situation in the Middle East was quite different. The growing tension between Iraq and its neighbors, Kuwait in particular, certainly required careful monitoring. But, as it happened, "waiting for Saddam" turned out to be considerably more engaging for the United States. When the wait was over, and Iraq invaded Kuwait, the president moved swiftly to activate the communication network he had built up during the period of his presidency and before. Whether he should have waited is a debatable issue that I will not review here, except to take note of the criticism in Congress and elsewhere by those who believed that the administration sent misleading signals to Saddam Hussein before the invasion. The point I wish to make is that President Bush's actively reactive strategy was well illustrated by the Iraqi invasion and his subsequent efforts to mobilize a worldwide response.

The Iraq-Kuwait situation significantly altered domestic politics once Congress reconvened in September. In particular, the budget summiteers had to reconsider proposed cuts in defense as well as aid to Arab nations that supported the UN sanctions. Broad support for American actions in the Persian Gulf translated into short-term support for President Bush as well. His public approval ratings increased once again, in spite of a limited record in working with Congress, then declined with the threat of recession and the prospect of an extended stay in the Middle East, then recovered somewhat during the final months of 1990, and skyrocketed with the national euphoria that accompanied the war with Iraq.

The Bush strategy in the Persian Gulf was to mobilize a broadly based international coalition against Iraq. This approach included a series of resolutions in the United Nations, leading to one authorizing "all necessary means" if Iraq failed to withdraw from Kuwait by 15 January 1991. This international effort proceeded without a parallel action on Capitol Hill. President Bush consulted with congressional leaders, but he did not seek, nor did he believe he required, a resolution to take the actions he believed necessary. Some members of Congress proposed that it be called back into session to debate such an action. No such session was held. Congressional leaders were perplexed as they sought to define the legislative role in authorizing the use of military force, particularly, as in the Persian Gulf, where war seemed inevitably to follow. Meanwhile, the White House was anxious to preserve the flexibility judged necessary for world leadership in contemporary times. A resolution authorizing presidential use of force was a first order of business for the 102d Congress. Following a vigorous debate, the resolution passed both houses despite the opposition of Democratic congressional leaders.

Conclusions

Study of the Bush presidency is fruitful for revealing the dynamics and strategies of co-partisan government. It provides a better case even than the Reagan administration as a result of the need for Bush to improve his political position following the 1988 election. He entered office with limited "political capital," relatively few "political advantages," and therefore a weak "strategic position."[36] The prospects were for a possible loss of control to congressional Democrats. Bush's potential advantage was that of low expectations—not a very impressive "chip" in the politics of high stakes.

The argument here is that the president's strategy has been one of trying to compete for and maintain his share of authority. To accomplish this goal, he has had to seek the public support that was not evident in the election. He had to press his outside advantage, primarily in foreign and defense policy, while initially benefiting from a failure of the congressional Democrats to capitalize on their inside advantage of greater numbers and leadership of both houses. Public support is not typically a reliable advantage for presidents. It is subject to many interpretations, and it can change quickly. But everything is relative. Lacking other resources, public approval will be viewed as a significant source of support. In co-partisan politics, a president will turn to whatever advantage is available.

Comprehending co-partisan government begins with accepting its legitimacy and understanding its dynamics. To do otherwise typically encourages the analyst to propose recommendations for institutional reform. The Bush White House and the Democratic Congress competed for shares of power in the national policy process. The capacity of each to compete effectively varied with the advantages they had available (e.g., Bush's public support, his status as a world leader; Congress's constitutional role in declaring war, the 1990 election results as slightly favoring the Democrats). The resulting conflict produced considerable anxiety as the contending forces pressed their advantages and played for time. The lengthy budget summit in 1990 was a particularly dramatic example of co-partisanship at work; its failure shows the intensity of interbranch competition on fiscal issues. The carryover of many major bills to the final weeks of the second session was also illustrative, as was the passage of several of these bills.

Focusing only on the delay involved, or the compromises made, or the stalemate that results, fails to acknowledge the change in politics that occurred. Thus, for example, an executive-congressional budget-making process was at work in 1990. It was not a pretty sight, especially for the advocates of partisan or responsible party government. But one should not miss the historic nature of the event. In fact, a cross-institutional budget process has been developing for some time—a forest that many bark and leaf fanciers have simply missed.

Postscript

As originally written, this chapter focused on the first two years of the Bush administration. During the last two years co-partisanship broke down in the face of the declining status of both the president and Congress. The president's failure to be sufficiently proactive in regard to the economy resulted in a steady decline in his approval rating, the one slim advantage he had earlier. Meanwhile, a series of scandals involving the bank, post office, and restaurant of the House of Representatives plagued Congress, fueling a strong term-limitation movement. The result was the type of stalemate that James L. Sundquist had predicted for split-party government.[37] But the conditions were very special—a consequence of weakness at both ends of Pennsylvania Avenue. David R. Mayhew had shown in a influential book, *Divided We Govern,* that divided government could be just as productive as unified government under most circumstances.[38] What the last two years of the Bush administration demonstrated was that gridlock could occur when neither the Republican president nor the Democratic Congress was moved to negotiate with the other because of perceived weakness of the other institution. Thus, congressional Democrats passed legislation that they were certain would be vetoed by the president, and he obliged, just as certain that his action would be upheld (as it was in all but one instance).

Gridlock came to be a major issue in the 1992 campaign. President Bush was unable to restore his high public approval ratings, and record numbers of congressional incumbents retired or were defeated in the primaries. Change was a theme in both the presidential and congressional campaigns. Voters continued to split their tickets, though the patterns were quite different. Voters had a three-way choice for president, with many 1988 Bush voters choosing Ross Perot, thus permitting Bill Clinton to win the presidency. Meanwhile, Republicans realized a small net gain in House seats and later gained a Senate seat in Texas in a special election following the appointment of Lloyd Bentsen to the cabinet. Unified government technically had returned to Washington, but the victory was more like that of Carter in 1976 than that of Johnson in 1964.

NOTES

1. Burt Solomon, "Low Expectations," *National Journal,* 12 November 1988, 2838.
2. Reported in "Washington Wire," *Wall Street Journal,* 19 January 1990, 1.
3. James MacGregor Burns, "U.S. Model for Eastern Europe?" *New York Times,* 8 February 1990, A21.
4. "Opinion Roundup," *Public Opinion,* November/December 1988, 30.

5. Ibid., 31.

6. Ibid., 34.

7. Barbara G. Farah and Ethel Klein, "Public Opinion Trends," in *The Election of 1988: Reports and Interpretations,* ed. Gerald M. Pomper (Chatham, N.J.: Chatham House, 1989), 110–11.

8. Ibid., 111.

9. Cable News Network/*Los Angeles Times* exit polls reported in William Schneider, "Solidarity's Not Enough," *National Journal,* 12 November 1988, 2855.

10. Gerald M. Pomper, "The Presidential Election," in Pomper, *The Election of 1988,* 143. Also reported in Schneider, "Solidarity's Not Enough," 2854.

11. *Economist,* 12 November 1988, 9.

12. *Washington Post,* 10 November 1988, A23.

13. *Wall Street Journal,* 11 November 1988, A10. The *Journal*'s panel of political experts agreed with the dire forecasts. " 'George Bush's lack of a mandate is an enormous problem,' says Kevin Phillips.... Worse, he figures Mr. Bush will be in the White House 'when the chickens finally come home to roost.' " 11 November 1988, A12.

14. *Washington Post,* 14 November 1988, A2.

15. *Washington Post,* 18 November 1988, A2.

16. *New Republic,* 28 November 1988, 8.

17. *Washington Post,* 14 November 1988, A10.

18. *New York Times,* 16 December 1988, 39.

19. David Hoffman, "George Bush Takes Up the Baton," *Washington Post National Weekly Edition,* 16–22 January 1989, 6ff .

20. James P. Pfiffner, "Establishing the Bush Presidency," *Public Administration Review,* January/February 1990, 70.

21. James P. Pfiffner, *The Strategic Presidency: Hitting the Ground Running* (Chicago: Dorsey Press, 1988), 7.

22. Paul C. Light, *The President's Agenda* (Baltimore: Johns Hopkins University Press, 1982), chap. 2.

23. Susan F. Rasky, "Democrats See Reason to Work with President," *New York Times,* 13 November 1988, 1.

24. Quoted in Tom Kenworthy, "Wright Vows 'Cooperation' with Bush," *Washington Post,* 11 November 1988, A8.

25. Text of address in *Congressional Quarterly Weekly Report,* 22 January 1989, 143.

26. Janet Hook, "New Leaders Felt Their Way Gingerly through Session," *Congressional Quarterly Weekly Report,* 12 December 1989, 3299.

27. Quoted in Janet Hook, "Pay Raise Is Killed, but the Headaches Persist," *Congressional Quarterly Weekly Report,* 11 February 1989, 263.

28. Text of address in *Congressional Quarterly Weekly Report,* 3 June 1989, 1347.
29. Janet Hook, "Bush Inspired Frail Support for First Year President," *Congressional Quarterly Weekly Report,* 30 December 1989, 3540.
30. As reported in the *Washington Post,* 21 January 1990, A1.
31. Quoted in Hook, "New Leaders Felt Their Way Gingerly through Session," 3284.
32. Personal interview, 21 July 1989.
33. Headlines, in sequence, from *National Journal,* 6 January 1990, 6; *Congressional Quarterly Weekly Report,* 6 January 1990, 9; *Washington Post,* 1 February 1990, A1; *Wall Street Journal,* 29 January 1990, A20.
34. Jackie Calmes, "Bush Dealing from Strength as Budget Season Opens," *Congressional Quarterly Weekly Report,* 3 February 1990, 299.
35. As quoted in Janet Hook, "Avalanche of Veto Threats Divides Bush, Congress," *Congressional Quarterly Weekly Report,* 22 September 1990, 2991.
36. Terms used respectively by Light, *President's Agenda;* Richard Neustadt, *Presidential Power and the Modern Presidents* (New York: Free Press, 1990); and George C. Edwards III, *At the Margins: Presidential Leadership of Congress* (New Haven: Yale University Press, 1989).
37. James L. Sundquist, "The New Era of Coalition Government in the United States," *Political Science Quarterly,* Winter 1989–90, 629–30.
38. David R. Mayhew, *Divided We Govern: Party Control, Lawmaking, and Investigations, 1946–1990* (New Haven: Yale University Press, 1991).

II

Clinton and Congress

In a news conference after winning the heavyweight championship, Cassius Clay, as he was then known, responded sharply to reporters' badgering with this comment: "I don't have to be who you want me to be. I am free to be who I am." It was Muhammad Ali's declaration of independence from the archetype sports hero created by those who earn their living tracking and testing the winners. If you are the greatest, then you are free to be who you are—even, perhaps, to establish that persona as a gauge by which others will be measured.

Is Bill Clinton free to be who he is? Or does he have to be what others want him to be? These questions direct attention to the essence of our national political system. They invite consideration of how the president's role is defined. The very exercise of stipulating conditions under which presidents serve specifies constraints on the freedom of any one incumbent to interpret his status while clarifying the need to do so. By the way, the answer to both questions is "not exactly."

Like Ali, Clinton is a winner; unlike him, he is not the champion. And, in fact, by constitutional design there is no champion in the national government. The most outstanding feature of the American system is the separation of powers. Presidents are temporarily in charge of one institution of this interdependent, competing government. They play a vital role, but ours is not a presidential system, as many contend. It is a separated system. Therefore others with authority to act will express themselves meaningfully on the limits of presidential power.

The separationist feature of the government is ignored or misunderstood by some and deplored by others. Scholars of democratic systems typically categorize the American system as presidential, even while acknowledging the separation of powers as its principal characteristic (see chapter 2). How the least stable branch in longevity wins the label over a high-return-rate Congress, a merit-based bureaucracy, or a life-term Supreme Court is not explained or even much engaged as an issue by these scholars. Equally odd is the tendency to criticize the mislabeled American system as resulting in stalemate, especially if the voters have exercised their right in constitutionally separated elections to return split-party government, as they have a majority of the time since 1945.

Many journalists and political reformers contribute to presidency-centered expectations of the workings of the national government. Often these expectations derive from the classic party responsibility model in which a winning political party, led by its president, is expected to carry out a governing mandate. As it happens, there is much for these analysts to criticize, since the demanding conditions for party government are seldom met, perhaps twice since 1945—64 and 1980. Not to be deterred, however, these commentators press on, testing each president and Congress by criteria drawn from a model rejected at the Constitutional Convention. Meanwhile, the most common form of government in the post–World War II period—a president of one party, a majority of the other party in one or both houses of Congress—is viewed as a mistake to be corrected. Virtually all reforms are directed toward ensuring single-party government, few if any are designed to make split-party government work better. Yet the voters persist in sending two-way governments to Washington.

So, like other presidents, Bill Clinton is free to shape his presidency, understanding that others will define it too. He is well advised in this exercise to resist the temptation to meet presidency-centered expectations. Those who favor this perspective seek the champion that few, if any, presidents can be. All presidents are winners, however, and their victories carry very different entitlements. A presidential win in the separated system confers the right to make the most of these allowances in finding one's place in the continuous government. In other words, presidents are authorized to use their political, personal, and policy advantages for persuading others to accept their leadership. Not surprisingly to those who follow the election returns and monitor public approval ratings, presidents vary dramatically in the scope and depth of their benefits for competing in the separated system.

Presidents Are Not Created Equal

Presidents enter the White House under very different circumstances. First are the elected first-termers. Some, such as Eisenhower (1952) and Reagan (1980), have impressive wins; other first-time winners, such as Kennedy (1960), Nixon (1968), and Carter (1976), are elected by the narrowest of margins. Second are the reelected presidents, all three of whom have been Republicans since World War II. Eisenhower (1956), Nixon (1972), and Reagan (1984) won in landslides, and yet Democratic majorities were returned in Congress (one house or two). Third are the takeover presidents: Truman (1945), Johnson (1963), and Ford (1974). These vice-presidents serving as president are very special in that they assume someone else's organization and priorities and must determine how to cope. Two takeover presidents, Truman (1948) and Johnson (1964), were themselves elected—a fourth variation in White House occupancy. Finally, there is one elected heir-apparent in the postwar period, Bush (1988)—a situation that poses problems not unlike those of the takeover presidents, as is well described and analyzed in Walter Dean Burnham's excellent essay on Bush as an understudy.[1]

Variation in how presidents came to be there suggests differences in strategies for getting the job done. If all goes well in the election for the president and his party in Congress, he is able to pursue an *assertive* policy strategy, at least until the midterm elections. A mandate is declared by those who conclude that congruous presidential and congressional election returns contain a policy message. There are two clear-cut cases since 1945—Johnson (1964) and Reagan (1980)—going in opposite policy directions. More often the policy message from these elections is difficult to read. In some instances the president wins narrowly, as with Truman (1948), Kennedy (1960), Nixon (1968), and Carter (1976), and congressional results are mixed. The president is well advised to adopt a *compensatory* strategy under these circumstances—seeking to bolster his position organizationally or substantively in working with Congress. Reelected presidents return to office with mixed messages also, but their personal performance has received a strong endorsement. Since in each instance the voters returned a split-party government, a *guardian* strategy, one designed to protect earlier achievements, appears to be appropriate. And the strategies for the nonelected, takeover presidents depend heavily on the legacy of their predecessor—*custodial* for Truman and Johnson, more *restorative* for Ford.

These variations—assertive, compensatory, guardian, custodial, and restorative—make it unlikely that a standard set of expectations will apply to the status and performance of all presidents. Not even the same president reenters office duplicating his previous resources. Yet, as suggested, there are patterns that assist in placing a new president and appraising his performance. It is also true that presidents sometimes ignore the limiting conditions of their service. For example, Carter appeared to pursue a more aggressive policy strategy than his narrow win would suggest was possible.

The Clinton Case

How does President Bill Clinton fit into the separated system? With whom should he be compared? What strategy should he pursue? How should he organize and develop his presidency? What can we expect by way of legislative production during his term in office?

"Change" was clearly the dominant theme of the 1992 election; less certain was the direction or the object of change. It is appropriate, then, to identify what would stay the same following the election. Electing a single-party, Democratic government for the first time in twelve years, the second time in twenty-four years, did not alter the fundamental separationist feature of American national government. The Democrats were back in charge of the elected branches of government. But the return of unified government did not make Congress subservient to the executive or the House of Representatives subservient to the Senate. If anything, the interim period of split-party government had accentuated and strengthened the separation of the institutions. The two houses of Congress, in particular, substantially improved their capacity and strengthened their resolve to participate and compete more actively in phases of the policy process (e.g., agenda setting, problem definition, program development and implementation), phases traditionally thought to be the province of the executive. Members of Congress also redefined the separation of powers in regard to international security issues, justified in part by the rise of economic issues with the end of the Cold War. If, for example, trade issues were to be central to foreign policymaking, then most members judged that they had a legitimate right to weigh in because of constituency interests. No longer could a president expect to gain bipartisan acquiescence on such issues (a practice often overstated in the past anyway). Cross-partisan support could be expected, however, since international economic issues cut across party lines (as with the North American Free Trade Agreement—NAFTA).

Thus, one legacy of the period of split-party government was a substantially more policy-aggressive Congress, one that was unlikely to forgo this new institutional positioning with the election of a Democratic president. However "change" was to be interpreted as resulting from the 1992 elections, therefore, it was reasonable to expect members of Congress, including Democrats, to participate actively in fashioning policy responses to Clinton initiatives.

For his part, Bill Clinton won the presidency in a three-way race with one of the smallest percentages of the popular vote of any president in this century. If "change" voters are defined as those not voting for Bush, then Clinton shared them with Perot, roughly on a 2-to-1 basis. "Change" was a theme too in the congressional elections, where the mood was likewise anti-incumbent. It was not possible, however, to offer a uniform interpretation for presidential and congressional results. Huge numbers of endangered incumbents retired, others lost in primaries. In the general election, many voters continued to split their tickets, voting against the incumbent Republican president and against their incumbent Democratic member of Congress. The Democrats retained their majorities in Congress but by a reduced margin in the House and by the same margin in the Senate (actually a net loss of one seat with the victory of Republican Kay Bailey Hutchison in the Texas special election for Lloyd Bentsen's seat). Most incumbents experienced a reduced margin of victory in 1992.[2]

Clinton's win fits into the category of such elected first-termers as Truman, Kennedy, Nixon, and Carter, who won narrowly and whose logical governing strategy was *compensatory* in nature. Such presidents often strive to strengthen their strategic position because the election has conveyed a mixed, even ambiguous, message. Thus, for example, it was unlikely that Democrats in Congress would fall easily into line solely based on their reading of the 1992 election returns, since all exceeded Clinton's vote in their states and districts. Still, Democrats were back in charge of the government after twelve years and shared a common fate regardless of the disconnection between the change-oriented themes of the presidential and congressional elections. To this point at least, most congressional Democrats want this new-generation president to succeed.

What exactly is involved in a compensatory strategy? It derives from acknowledging that the president's major postelection assignment is to determine how to fit himself into an ongoing government. Critical to achieving that task is the identification of policy and political goals and an understanding of strengths and weaknesses for accomplishing those goals. Recall what it is that the president wins in an election: the opportunity and forum to convince others with authority in the permanent government that he is right, bearing in mind than many, if not most, of these others were there when he arrived and will still be there when he leaves. The difference in status between campaigning and governing was illustrated by a young staff person who recently left his post in the administration. In the campaign he observed that "I felt I was indispensable." In his post as senior adviser to an assistant secretary of health and human services, however, most of his hours were consumed running a series of meetings to keep the ball rolling. "I quickly became aware that working in government is a hard slog."[3]

For his part, President Clinton has impressive personal skills associated with his policy interests and knowledge and his ability to communicate with the public. He relies on these skills as the principal compensation for a mixed electoral record and an unformed organizational faculty. In fact, he depends heavily on this campaign-oriented tactic in garnering support for his proposals, especially after the failure of an inside strategy for passing his economic stimulus package. A recent count shows that he had 145 official appearances outside Washington in the first thirteen months of his administration, only eight of which were outside the country.[4] George Bush was thought to be the champion of travel. Clinton has so far outdone him, dramatically so in domestic travel.

An alternative compensatory strategy to Clinton's campaign style is less personal and more organizational and institutional. By this alternative technique, the president creates a structure designed to facilitate goal achievement. In an important sense, he becomes larger than himself through an organization articulated to realizing his policy goals in the permanent government. Delegation is important for creating such a structure. But delegation comes at a cost of sacrificing personal discretion. If, like Clinton, the president's strength in style is more freewheeling or if his confidence in himself exceeds that which he has in his subordinates, then delegation will be difficult to achieve.

Presidents who view themselves as large already will find it hard to conceive of themselves as becoming larger still by delegating to smaller people. Yet not even the most brilliant mind and energetic body can expect to fulfill all the expectations of a president in a separated system. Further, others in government will demand to see the president, not trusting that his minions represent his authority extended. By his own rationale, the president will have to give them an audience.

Another challenging feature of the Clinton presidency for Washingtonians is the role of the first lady, Hillary Rodham Clinton. Her position is innovative and therefore must be absorbed into the system. Not only is she a force to be reckoned with in weighing the power and strategic positioning of the Clinton White House, but she has responsibility for health-care reform, the number-one policy priority of the president. Having a major player in the White House who is not clearly stationed within the organization (e.g., Harry Hopkins for Roosevelt) has always been somewhat unsettling to others with authority to act. When that person is a family member, such as Robert Kennedy for his brother or Nancy Reagan for her husband, apprehension is greater still. Kennedy, however, won Senate confirmation and had clearly designated duties as attorney general. Mrs. Reagan seemingly was interested primarily in protecting her husband, exercising influence mostly on personnel matters. Mrs. Clinton, in contrast, has responsibility for a major policy area, as well as strong and active interests in other issues of central importance to her husband's presidency.

Then there is the active policy role for the vice-president. Clearly the president does have confidence in Al Gore, entrusting him with responsibility for major policy issues, thus creating another power center in the White House. There is precedent for an active vice-president, as Walter Mondale was for Jimmy Carter, but Gore's status is extraordinary.

In the separated system, presidential power is defined as much outside among those others with authority to act as inside among those designated to serve temporarily in the White House. How, then, are those outside to orient themselves to an essentially nonhierarchical and poorly articulated organization that attempts to re-create the campaign for each issue and within which the president, the first lady, and sometimes the vice-president have primary influence and control? Members of Congress and their staffs, cabinet officials, and senior executives may initially orient themselves to the president as leader but then proceed on their own, essentially redefining the role of the White House to suit changing conditions and perceptions of who is in charge of what. It is useful to be reminded that the president either finds his place in the separated system or it will be found for him.

The Clinton presidency surely challenges the separated system. In spite of a limited electoral mandate, the president has pursued an ambitious program with an unconventional organization and strategy. His approach to Congress has been campaign style—from the outside in, seeking to translate his personal enthusiasm into public support. His organizational concept, to the extent that he has one, is also personal in nature, with the president at the center in constant motion, often circling outside Washington among his publics, and a staff, all with equal access, striving to keep up—a sort of "spokes of the amoeba" notion. And his partner in life, politics, and government occupies a critical yet historically and structurally unspecified position of influence.

The Record So Far

One common mistake in evaluating the separated system is to measure achievement entirely by presidential success. Analysts appear to require markers in judging progress in governing, and presidential terms serve that purpose. A president receives credit or blame for what happens during his period of service, and we affix presidents' names to political time (the Eisenhower years, the Johnson years, etc.). In fact, one outstanding feature of the separated system is the continuity of government and its work. The system is not held in place, to be shaped and reformed by a new president, though he is given an opportunity upon entry to establish his influence.

One consequence of overstating the role of the president is to misjudge the capacity of the rest of the system to act under varying political conditions. Thus, for example, it is believed by some that split-party governments result in stalemate, or that a bicameral Congress cannot compensate for presidential inattention to issues, or that so-called lame-duck periods are unproductive, or that scandal in the White House paralyzes the whole government. David R. Mayhew's book *Divided We Govern* offers convincing evidence that these judgments are wrong. In identifying 267 major pieces of legislation in the post–World War II period, Mayhew shows no difference in production between single- and split-party governments and high productivity during the Watergate scandal, when one might have gotten the impression that the government was frozen in place.[5] In my own detailed analysis of lawmaking, for a sample of Mayhew's list I found an increasingly active role for Congress, including taking initiative when the president is less active.[6]

In the Clinton administration, it is useful to step back from the breathless coverage that a personalized and innovative presidency invites to consider its contribution to the workings of the contemporary separated system. It is early for a definitive exercise of this type, yet not too soon to begin thinking about the matter. My present reading in regard to domestic policymaking is that the Clinton style basically facilitates the workings of a post–split-party government. As noted, both houses of Congress have, in recent decades, developed a capacity and taste for being actively involved in many phases of the policy process. This president has shown an extraordinary penchant and talent for identifying major issues and maintaining their priority status on the agenda. In a style reminiscent of his media-oriented campaign, President Clinton builds public interest in and support of policy action in a number of problems that have been on the agenda for some time. Though he typically offers a plan, he also conveys the message that he is willing to bargain—quite unlike the uncompromising stances of Jimmy Carter. Thus, those members of Congress who have grown accustomed to active policy roles can be satisfied that they retain influence in the new government.

Can this version of the single-party, separated system produce? The record suggests that it can. A number of legislative initiatives that were in the pipeline were enacted into law during the first session of the 103d Congress. Other significant proposals on major issues, most notably health care, were making their way through the Congress. In fact, the bulk of the agenda for the 103d Congress had a lineage traceable to previous administrations and congresses. Health care, education, welfare, trade, crime control, family leave, campaign finance, retraining—these are not new issues. A review of twenty-one major legislative issues treated by the first session of the 103d Congress reveals no more than four or five new initiatives. The legislative production is attributed in part to the eagerness of Democrats in Congress to demonstrate that they can produce in spite of the president's problems. That a separated government is fully capable of compensating for the deficiency or preoccupation of one part is seldom acknowledged. Often, in fact, such situations are used to illustrate presidential weakness rather than system strength.

What is the effect of scandals such as the Whitewater incident, which so preoccupies the media? The effect is primarily on White House staff operations because of the personal nature of the Clinton presidency. The perpetual campaign as compensatory strategy features continual attention to press coverage. Staff members are likely to measure success or failure primarily by how positive or negative is the treatment of their candidate or president, rather than how productive the government is during his tenure. Therefore, an incident such as Whitewater commands a great deal of staff time and energy even while the rest of the government proceeds apace. During early March 1994, the White House staff had to cope with the resignation of the president's chief counsel, Bernard Nussbaum; the issuance of a

number of subpoenas by Special Counsel Robert Fiske; further revelations regarding the Clintons' financial affairs; and demands for
congressional hearings. Meanwhile, members of Congress were bus-
ily engaged on several legislative fronts—the president's budget, an
education bill, lobbying disclosure, an anticrime measure, health-care
reform, communications regulation, and federal worker buyouts
were among the more important subjects being considered.

Congressional committees were predictably active for the time
of year. Thus, for example, on 16 and 17 March, when an evening
news viewer in Keokuk, Iowa, might have thought that the Washington workday was devoted exclusively to Whitewater, there were
twenty-seven Senate and sixty-one House committee meetings sched-
uled (hearings and markups). Not one of these meetings dealt directly with Whitewater.

A presidency-centered perspective focuses on White House
events, often to the exclusion of the actual workings of the separated
system. A personalized, campaign-oriented presidency such as that of
Clinton amplifies this tendency even more, thus making it difficult
for White House staff to devise an exit strategy in the face of an epi-
sode like Whitewater. Since the Clinton presidency is so very public,
much like an election campaign, staff members are oriented to, even
preoccupied with, press coverage. They naturally seek to protect
what the president judges to be his strength—public contact and
support. Given the press role as translators of public opinion, however, the relationship between the White House and the media will
assuredly be competitive and tense. Depersonalizing the presidency
requires a greater dependency on organization through delegation,
and President Clinton has not demonstrated either a preference or a
facility for this approach.[7]

A President, Not a Presidency?

Bill Clinton is authorized to shape his presidency as he sees fit. He
has chosen a highly personalized, campaign-oriented, and innovative
form that has positive features for our present version of separated
government in that it accommodates the greater policy role of Congress developed during periods of split-party government. The fact is
that an active and relevant agenda is being exposed and that the
work of government in most departments and on Capitol Hill is being done. Far from gridlock, the separated government is doing its
job.

The Clinton style is, however, risky for him and demanding on his staff. By drawing attention to himself, he feeds the popular misconception that the president is the presidency, the presidency is the government, and that ours is a presidential system. There is, then, no relief for him because his performance invites exactly the unrealistic expectations accompanying a presidency-centered, party government perspective.

But, of course, Bill Clinton is not the sole judge of what his presidency will be. Observers are therefore encouraged to employ a more realistic test that concentrates less on the president as person and more on the presidency as an institution, defined not only by who the president thinks he is but also by how others define his role in the separated system.

NOTES

1. In *The Election of 1992: Reports and Interpretations,* ed. Gerald M. Pomper (Chatham, N.J.: Chatham House, 1993), chap. 1.
2. For details, see ibid., esp. chap. 5.
3. Quoted in the *Washington Post,* 25 April 1994, C4.
4. As derived from the *Weekly Compilation of Presidential Documents,* Office of the Federal Register, vols. 29, 30 (Washington, D.C.: Government Printing Office, 1993, 1994).
5. David R. Mayhew, *Divided We Govern: Party Control, Lawmaking, and Investigations, 1946–1990* (New Haven: Yale University Press, 1991), chap. 4.
6. See Charles O. Jones *The Presidency in a Separated System* (Washington: Brookings Institution, 1994), chap. 7.
7. Seemingly this has been the case even in foreign policy, where the president is generally acknowledged to be weak. A *Washington Post* columnist asked "What surprised you most?" to "someone who has attended many of [the Clinton] administration's most important meetings about foreign policy and national security." The answer: "How much of the meeting was not about the meeting.... And how much Bill Clinton hates making decisions on foreign policy. The only thing he would hate more would be letting someone else make the decisions. That he won't do." Jim Hoagland, *Washington Post,* 31 May 1994, A17.

Index